Acknowledgements

This book would not have been possible without the efforts and contributions of many. Russ Eanes graciously tested a pre-print copy of the guide and offered invaluable feedback. Alessandro Mambelli was instrumental in editing the Italian phrasebook. Of course, no guidebook would be possible without a trail. The tireless efforts of Via di Francesco organizations in Tuscany, Umbria, and Lazio ensure that a route exists to walk. A special thanks to Piccola Accoglienza in Gubbio for sending credenziale to pilgrims across the world and to Luca and Elena of the Via di Francesco in Toscana for welcoming the author into their home at the beginning of his journey.

A Note on Terminology

To indicate dates, we use the commonly accepted academic terms of BCE (Before the Common Era) and CE (Common Era). For dates when the era is not specified, assume Common Era.

A Note on Text Type

Words in languages other than English are italicized, with the exception of common words after they are introduced (see Italian phrasebook).

A Note on Guidebooks

Each traveler has a different style of traveling. Some prefer light, minimalist guidebooks while other choose more thorough guides. This guide is intended to be comprehensive and thorough but concise. We also offer a Kindle e-book of this guide. We encourage those with a paper copy to remove any pages that are no longer necessary for their journey.

Visit us online for extended planning info, accommodation booking and gear advice at **caminoguidebook.com**.

Contents

■ Elevation Profile   1

■ The Way of St. Francis: Pilgrimage to Assisi & Rome   6

The Way of St. Francis..................6
St. Francis....................................7
The Many Ways of St. Francis...................12
Routes and Waymarking.........................12
The Camino de Santiago &
  Way of St. Francis...................17

■ Travel along the Way of St. Francis   18

Pilgrim Practicalities, Passports................18
Visas & Entry...18
When to Go & Time Necessary...............19
Sleeping...20
Meals, Restaurants, & Supermarkets........24
Vegetarian, Vegan & Celiac Options........25
Transportation..26
Business Hours & the Riposo..................27
Money, Costs & Budgeting....................28
Laundry..29
Phones & Internet...................................29
Post Offices...30
Bathrooms..30
Luggage Transfer & Tours........................30
Medical Care...31
Safety Issues..31
Pilgrim Associations................................31
Mountain Biking the Way........................32

■ Preparing to Walk the Way of St. Francis   34

Packing for the Trail................................34
  Backpacks...34
  Footwear...34
  Clothing..34
  Sleeping Bags..34
Water and Refills.....................................35
Dehydration and Heat-related Illness.......35
Fitness & Training...................................35
Blister Prevention & Foot Care................35
Route Finding, Trail Markings, Maps
  & GPS..36
Daily Stages & Regional Sections.............37
Packing List & Sample First Aid Kit........38

Peace Prayer of St. Francis

Lord, make me an instrument of your peace:
where there is hatred, let me sow love;
where there is injury, pardon; where there is doubt, faith;
where there is despair, hope; where there is darkness, light;
where there is sadness, joy.
O divine Master, grant that I may not so much seek
to be consoled as to console, to be understood as to understand,
to be loved as to love.
For it is in giving that we receive,
it is in pardoning that we are pardoned,
and it is in dying that we are born to eternal life.
Amen.

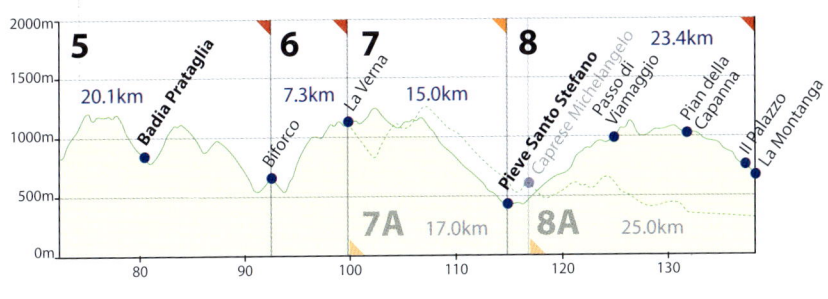

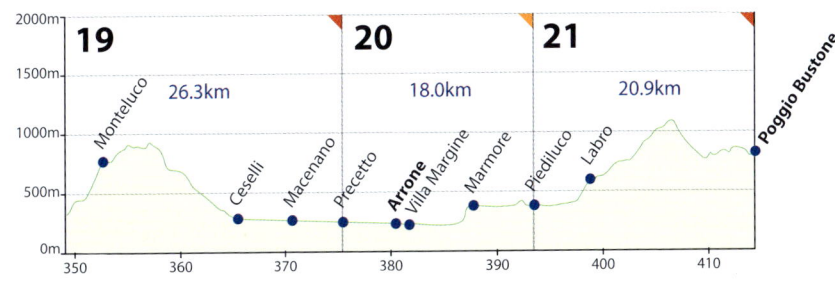
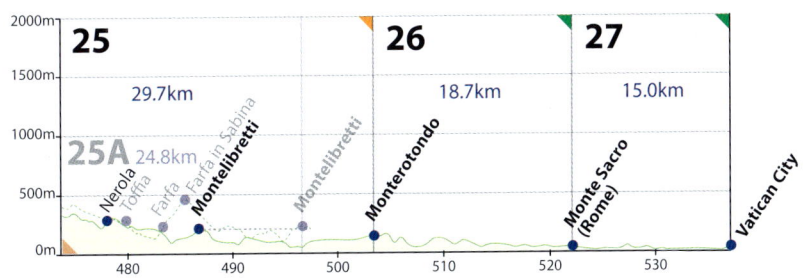

WAY OF ST. FRANCIS

The Way of St. Francis: Florence - Assisi - Rome
Written by Matthew Harms
Edited by Anna Dintaman and David Landis

First edition, 2023
Copyright © 2023 Village to Village Press, LLC

Village to Village Press, LLC, Harrisonburg, VA, USA
www.villagetovillagepress.com

ISBN: 978-1-947474-22-2

Cover Photographs by Matthew Harms
Front: Basilica di San Francesco (Assisi)
Back (left to right): Final cobblestone climb to the La Verna Sanctuary,
   Views of Assisi from the Rocca Maggiore (Assisi), Arriving to St. Peter's Square (Rome)

Text, photographs, images and diagrams © Village to Village Press, LLC, 2023
Photos by Matthew Harms except p. 11-12, 19-30, 33, 35, 211 by Russ Eanes
Cover and book design by David Landis

Village to Village® is a registered trademark of Village to Village Press, LLC.
Map data based on openstreetmap.org, © OpenStreetMap contributors

All rights reserved. No part of this publication may be reproduced, stored in a retrieval system or transmitted in any form or any means, digital, electronic, mechanical, photocopying, recording or otherwise, except brief extracts for the purpose of review, without the written permission of the authors.

Disclaimer: *Every reasonable effort has been made to ensure that the information contained in this book is accurate. However, no guarantee is made regarding its accuracy or completeness. Reader assumes responsibility and liability for all actions in relation to using the provided information, including if actions result in injury, death, loss or damage of personal property or other complications.*

The Way of St. Francis — 40

Florence to La Verna, 100km 40
- 1: Florence to Pontassieve, 18.9km 46
- 2: Pontassieve to Consuma, 17.3km 50
- 3: Consuma to Stia, 17.2km 54
- 4: Stia to Camaldoli, 16.1km 60
- 5: Camaldoli to Biforco, 20.1km 66
- 6: Biforco to La Verna, 7.3km 72

La Verna to Assisi, 190km 78
- 7: La Verna to Pieve Santo Stefano, 15.0km 82
- 8: Pieve Santo Stefano to La Montagna, 23.4km 86
- 9: La Montagna to Citerna, 23.8km 92
- 10: Citerna to Città di Castello, 20.1km 100
  - 7A: La Verna to Caprese Michelangelo, 17.0km 104
  - 8A: Caprese Michelangelo to Sansepolcro, 25.0km 108
  - 9A: Sansepolcro to Città di Castello, 29.0km 112
- 11: Città di Castello to Pietralunga, 30.3km 116
- 12: Pietralunga to Gubbio, 26.1km 122
- 13: Gubbio to San Pietro in Vigneto, 16.3km 128
- 14: San Pietro in Vigneto to Valfabbrica, 21.6km 132
- 15: Valfabbrica to Assisi, 13.3km 136

Assisi to Rieti, 142km 146
- 16: Assisi to Foligno, 19.4km 148
- 17: Foligno to Poreta, 24.6km 156
- 18: Poreta to Spoleto, 15.4km 160
- 19: Spoleto to Precetto/Ferentillo, 26.3km 166
- 20: Precetto/Ferentillo to Piediluco, 17.9km 170
- 21: Piediluco to Poggio Bustone, 20.9km 174
- 22: Poggio Bustone to Rieti, 17.7km 178
  - 22+: Rieti to Greccio, 23.8km 182

Rieti to Rome, 105km 186
- 23: Rieti to Poggio San Lorenzo, 21.4km 188
- 24: Poggio San Lorenzo to Ponticelli, 20.2km 192
- 25: Ponticelli to Monterotondo, 29.7km 198
  - 25A: Osteria Nuova to Montelibretti, 24.8km 202
- 26: Monterotondo to Monte Sacro, 18.7km 206
- 27: Monte Sacro to Rome, 15.2km 210

Italian Phrasebook — 220

Recommended Reading — 222

About Us — 224

Legend — 225

WAY OF ST. FRANCIS

The Way of St. Francis

The Way of St. Francis is a roughly 550km pilgrimage route across central Italy that connects many of the major sites from the life of St. Francis. St. Francis, a beloved figure both in life and after death, sought to live as closely as possible to his understanding of Jesus' example. Francis walked widely throughout central Italy, joyfully preaching and inspiring others to live a simple life of poverty and care for the poor and sick.

Famous for his love of nature, he considered all of the natural world his family. Stories recount St. Francis blessing trees, preaching to birds, and making peace with a wolf. In 1979, Pope John Paul II named St. Francis as the Patron Saint of Ecology. Following the Way of St. Francis through the beautiful Italian countryside today, it's easy to see why the saint held his natural surroundings so dear.

Waymarks along the Way of St. Francis

Starting in Florence, the birthplace of the Renaissance, the Way of St. Francis climbs through the rugged Tuscan mountains to the Franciscan Sanctuary at La Verna, where St. Francis received the stigmata. From La Verna, the route continues to Assisi, St. Francis' birthplace and the locus of his ministry. Further south, the route traverses the Rieti Valley, known as the "Holy" or "Sacred Valley" (Italian: *Valle Santa*) for its four major Franciscan sanctuaries. Finally, the route culminates at St. Peter's Basilica in Rome, where St. Francis traveled as a pilgrim, beggar, and supplicant of the Pope.

The Way of St. Francis allows modern pilgrims to journey in St. Francis' footsteps, traveling on footpaths that he may have walked in life. As a walking pilgrimage route, the Way of St. Francis is a modern creation and does not follow a single historical pilgrimage route, though there is a long history of pilgrimage to both Assisi and Rome. As the Way of St. Francis grows in popularity, pilgrim services continue to increase, though they are fewer and farther between than on popular Camino de Santiago pilgrimage routes in Spain and Portugal. Traversing the Apennine Mountains of central Italy, the path's frequent ascents and descents are not for the faint of heart! Still, its countless stunning vistas are well worth the effort.

St. Francis

St. Francis was born in Assisi sometime in late 1181 or early 1182 to Pica de Bourlemont, a French noblewoman from Provence, and Pietro di Bernardone dei Moriconi, a prosperous textile merchant. Francis' mother had him baptized Giovanni, but when Pietro returned from business in France, he informally named his son Francesco ("Frenchman"). The name stuck.

Though he was not a noble, his family's wealth meant that Francis' youthful years were indulgent ones. He admired troubadours and their songs of love and chivalry, and he had dreams of knighthood. His biographers remark that he enjoyed revelry and spent lavishly on parties with his noble contemporaries in Assisi. By all accounts, he was a popular, witty, and charismatic young man, but not particularly religious.

In 1202, his fortunes changed when Assisi went to war with neighboring city-state Perugia. Assisi's forces were routed and Francis was taken prisoner. He spent a year in prison before being ransomed by his family. In captivity, he contracted an illness that contributed to his frailty later in life. During this time, he began to reconsider his life; but after his return to Assisi and a long period of recovery, he still had grand visions of knighthood. In 1205, he decided to travel to Apulia with another knight from Assisi to join forces with Walter of Brienne on behalf of Pope Innocent III.

It was at this point that his religious conversion began in earnest. Before leaving Assisi, Francis had a vision: in a hall containing armor decorated with the cross, he heard a voice telling him that the weapons were for him and his soldiers. As he left for Apulia, Francis was convinced that he would become a great knight; but immediately after setting out, Francis became ill in Spoleto, and his companions left him behind. Here, Francis heard another voice. In *The Legend of the Three Companions*, three of Francis' followers, Brothers Leo, Rufino, and Angelo, recount the vision:

> *"'Who can do more good, the master or the servant?' The master, [Francis] answered. 'Then why are you looking for the servant, rather than the master?' Ah. Lord, what would you have me do? 'Return home; and there you learn what is right for you to do. The vision you had in a dream, you must interpret in a completely new way.'"*

English translation from *Francis of Assisi: Early Documents*,
  ed. Regis Armstrong, J.A. Wayne Hellmann, and William Short.

Francis returned to Assisi, embracing prayer and solitude as a period of transformation took hold in his life. His friends noticed his changed demeanor and asked if he intended to marry. Francis responded that he planned to marry a woman of "surpassing fairness," referring to "Lady Poverty." One day, crossing the Spoleto Valley on horse, Francis came upon a leper. Francis initially retreated in repulsion, but gained control of his aversion and embraced the man and gave him all the money he had. Later, Francis made a pilgrimage to Rome. Embarrassed at the small offerings at St. Peter's tomb, Francis gave away all the money on his person, exchanged his clothes with the tattered ones of a beggar, and spent the rest of the day begging alms outside of the doors of the basilica.

Back in Assisi, praying in the dilapidated San Damiano Chapel, Francis heard another voice saying, "Go, Francis, and repair my house, which you see is falling into ruin." (From *"St. Francis of Assisi," Catholic Encyclopedia*, Charles Herbermann, 1913). Taking the instructions literally, Francis took a load of his father's cloth to the market in Foligno, where he sold it. Francis then returned to Assisi and attempted to give the money to the priest at San Damiano for repairing the chapel. The priest, knowing the source of the money, refused the gift, and Francis, fleeing his father's wrath, hid in a cave near the chapel. Leaving the cave after a month, Francis was locked up in the basement of his home by his father, though his mother later released him. Francis' father, not content with having his money returned to him, appealed to civil authorities to have Francis' inheritance renounced. Francis, claiming to be in God's service, was taken before the Bishop Guido of Assisi. There Francis disavowed his inheritance, stripped himself naked, and threw his clothes at his father's feet, claiming God as his father. At this point, the Bishop took pity on Francis, covering him in his own cloak.

Now estranged from his family, Francis walked the hills north of Assisi, singing. Coming upon robbers, Francis announced that he was the messenger of the "great king." Unimpressed, the robbers promptly beat him, robbed him, and left him in a snowbank. Destitute, Francis made his way to Gubbio, where he worked for a time in a monastery kitchen in return for meager food. After receiving a cloak and pilgrim staff from a friend in Gubbio, Francis returned to Assisi where, by begging for stones in town, he restored San Damiano and several other churches in the area.

In 1208, at the site of the present day Chapel of Santa Maria degli Angeli, Francis heard a mass recounting the commissioning of Jesus' twelve disciples, in which they were told to go with nothing to proclaim the Kingdom of God. Inspired to follow these words literally, Francis gave away all his remaining possessions, obtained a coarse wool cloak (as were worn by the poorest Umbrian peasants) and tied it with a knotted rope, which became the Franciscan habit.

PILGRIMAGE

Francis built a small chapel—the *porziuncola* (literally, "small portion" [of land])—in Assisi for his home base and continued wandered in the area repairing churches and serving in lazar houses (homes used to quarantine patients with leprosy). He gathered a group of followers, which soon numbered 11.

In 1209 or 1210, Francis and his followers traveled south to Rome to seek official sanction of their order from the Catholic Church. Though initially welcomed skeptically, they received approval from Pope Innocent III, who was influenced by a dream of Francis holding up the Basilica of St. John Lateran in Rome.

After returning from Rome, the Franciscan order grew rapidly as Francis and his followers, the Friars Minor, traveled throughout central Italy, preaching, praying, and caring for the sick and poor. Women soon joined the Franciscan movement, led by Sister Clare, forming a second Franciscan order. Later a third order of laity was formed for people who followed the Franciscan way of life but took no religious vows (now known as the Secular Franciscan Order).

As his movement grew, Francis traveled widely. He made several attempts to travel to the Middle East and win a peaceful end to the Crusades. Though his first two journeys failed (leaving him shipwrecked on the Dalmatian Coast and bedridden in Spain with illness), he traveled to Egypt with the Fifth Crusade and crossed battle lines to meet with Malek al-Kamil, the sultan of Egypt. Though unable to broker peace, Francis was received kindly and was granted permission to travel to visit sacred sites in the Holy Land.

Statue of St. Francis at the Montecasale Hermitage (p. 94)

WAY OF ST. FRANCIS

His efforts at dialogue had long-reaching consequences: after the fall of the Crusader Kingdom, only the Franciscans, of all Catholics, were allowed to stay in the Holy Land as custodians of Christian sacred spaces. When he returned to Italy, Francis sought time for prayer and meditation as he worked on drafting a set of rules that would provide structure for the now large Franciscan order, traveling between mountain hermitages to avoid the large crowds that followed him.

As he traveled, stories of his works and miracles followed. In Greccio, inspired by his time in Bethlehem, Francis organized what is considered the first live nativity scene. At La Verna in 1224, Francis is said to have received the stigmata—miraculous marks corresponding to the wounds left on Jesus' body by crucifixion. As his health deteriorated, Francis traveled to Rieti in 1225 for medical treatment on his eyes. While Francis stayed at La Foresta, eager crowds trampled the vineyard of the poor priest who resided there, but Francis' prayers miraculously restored the crops. Around this time, Francis began writing his *Canticle of the Sun* (or "Praise of the Creatures"), a song praising God for all of creation. He later finished the work—one of the first pieces of literature written in Italian—in a hut that St. Clare built for him outside of the San Damian's Chapel in Assisi.

In 1226, in poor health and extremely weak, Francis returned to the Porziuncola chapel in Assisi, where he died on October 3, 1226. Less than two years later, Pope Gregory IX declared Francis a saint and began the construction of the Basilica of St. Francis in Assisi, where St. Francis was buried in 1230.

St. Francis is one of the most beloved of all saints. As the Irish Franciscan Paschal Robinson noted, "Francis entered into glory in his lifetime, and he is the one saint whom all succeeding generations have agreed in canonizing." His attempts to literally follow Jesus' call to poverty, care for the poor, and love for the enemy endeared him to all who met him and are an inspiration to many today.

PILGRIMAGE

Known as *Il Poverello* ("The Little Poor One"), he humbly embraced poverty and menial labor, and welcomed all—friends, sinners, and adversaries—alike, with courtesy and respect. In 2013, the new pope, Cardinal Jorge Bergoglio, took Francis as his papal name, inspired by St. Francis, "the man of the poor [and of] peace," to advocate for a "poor church, for the poor."

The richness of St. Francis' personality means that the story of his life has had far-reaching influence. In the book, *Francis of Assisi: The Life and Afterlife of a Medieval Saint*, historian Andre Vauchez describes many historical readings of St. Francis' life. To some, Francis was a paragon of Catholic orthodoxy, able to work within the strictures of the Catholic Church at a time when many of his reforming peers were pronounced heretics. To others, his charisma and mysticism recall a spiritual form of Christianity muted by the institutional church. Today Catholics, Protestants, and even non-Christians can relate to Francis as a caretaker of the poor, promoter of peace, and protector of nature.

Still, despite his global reach, few religious figures are as geographically rooted as St. Francis. He was born and died in Assisi; and though Francis wandered widely as an adult, he traveled mostly throughout central Italy (particularly Umbria), returning regularly to his home base at the Porziuncola in Assisi.

As you walk from Florence to Rome, countless streets, churches, and places named after St. Francis are a constant reminder of his legacy in the region.

St. Francis taming the wolf of Gubbio (right)

Inside Eremo della Casella (left)

WAY OF ST. FRANCIS

The Many Ways of St. Francis

Pilgrims have traveled to Assisi for hundreds of years, but the Way of St. Francis from Florence to Assisi to Rome, unlike the Camino de Santiago, does not follow one cohesive, historical pilgrimage route. Rather, the modern Way of St. Francis is an assortment of many "Ways of St. Francis," the result of the efforts of numerous enthusiasts, authors, organizations, and government bodies, who have developed a variety of walking routes that follow in St. Francis' footsteps.

These various routes often overlap, connecting to many of the same Franciscan sites, but they also diverge between major sites and sometimes start and finish at different locations. The routes feature a range of different waymarking styles (though blue/yellow blazes and the yellow tau are common across many routes), and some itineraries choose not to follow marked routes at all.

Routes and Waymarkings

The **Tau** is inseparable from St. Francis. The tav (**ת**) is the last letter of the Hebrew alphabet and within some Christian traditions has been transliterated to the Greek tau (**τ**) and seen to symbolize, variously, the end times, God's chosen people, and the cross. In St. Francis' day, Pope Innocent III used the tau as a spiritual symbol, noting that the prophet Ezekiel used it to mark those chosen by God (Ez 9:4). St. Francis regularly used the symbol as his signature, and his contemporaries saw Franciscan friars—in simple habits with outstretched arms—as living representations of the tau. Today the tau is ubiquitous along the Way of St. Francis, much as the scallop shell is a constant companion on the Camino de Santiago.

Via di Francesco and Via di Roma
(La Verna/Rome to Assisi)

Likely the best established route, the **Via di Francesco** (aka the Via Francigena di Francesco) is comprised of two routes (a "northern" and a "southern" option) that converge in Assisi. The northern route starts in La Verna (La Verna-Assisi), and the southern route starts in Rome (Rome-Assisi). The **Via di Roma** follows the same route as the Via di Francesco, but always in a southward direction toward Rome (La Verna-Rome).

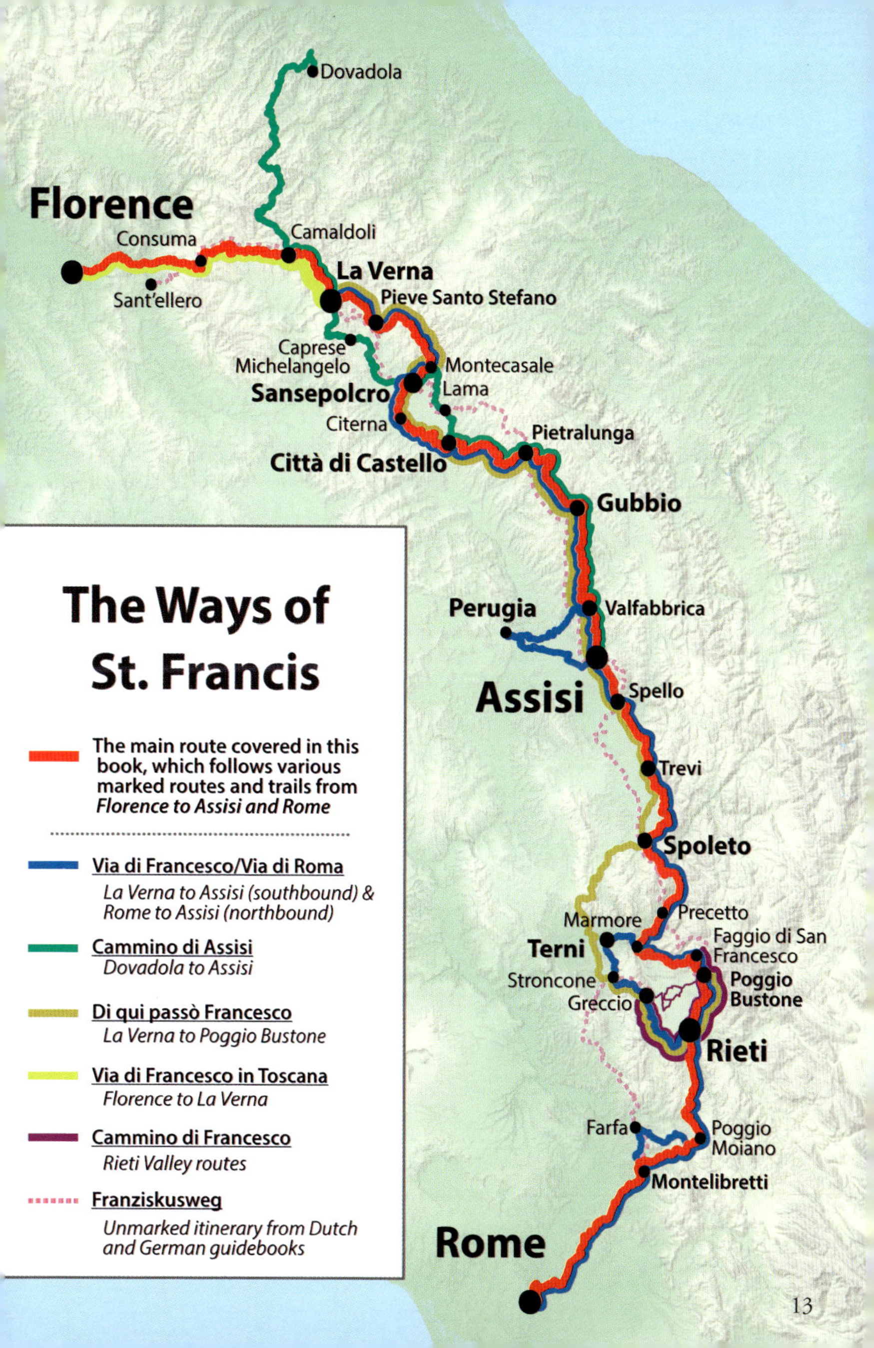
Dovadola
Florence
Consuma
Camaldoli
Sant'ellero
La Verna
Pieve Santo Stefano
Caprese Michelangelo
Montecasale
Sansepolcro
Lama
Citerna
Pietralunga
Città di Castello
Gubbio
Perugia
Valfabbrica
Assisi
Spello
Trevi
Spoleto
Precetto
Marmore
Terni
Faggio di San Francesco
Poggio Bustone
Stroncone
Greccio
Rieti
Farfa
Poggio Moiano
Montelibretti
Rome
The Ways of St. Francis
The main route covered in this book, which follows various marked routes and trails from *Florence to Assisi and Rome*
Via di Francesco/Via di Roma
La Verna to Assisi (southbound) & Rome to Assisi (northbound)
Cammino di Assisi
Dovadola to Assisi
Di qui passò Francesco
La Verna to Poggio Bustone
Via di Francesco in Toscana
Florence to La Verna
Cammino di Francesco
Rieti Valley routes
Franziskusweg
Unmarked itinerary from Dutch and German guidebooks

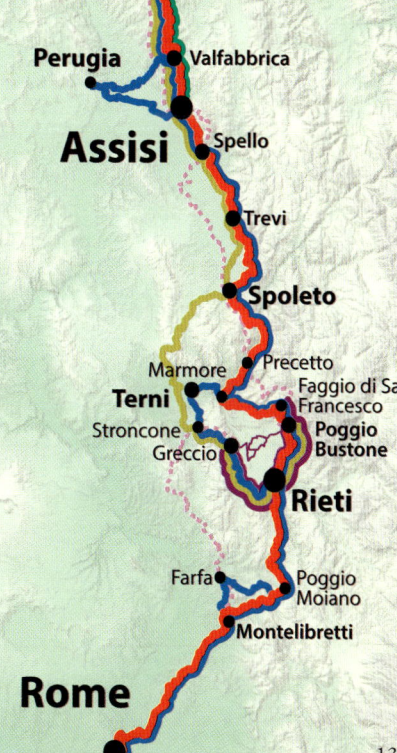

WAY OF ST. FRANCIS

Both route directions are marked with blue and yellow painted stripes (similar in style to GR trail markings), as well as large blue and yellow metal signs. The blue and yellow metal signs appear only after crossing into the Region of Umbria, south of Sansepolcro. An Italian guide covers this route, and an online resource (viadifrancesco.it) provides GPS tracks (mostly representative of waymarking on the ground) and basic information on services along the route.

Cammino di Assisi
(Dovadola to Assisi)

This way is another well-established route, which starts in Dovadola in the Italian Region of Emilia-Romagna and continues to Assisi, visiting sites associated with St. Anthony and St. Francis. From Camaldoli to La Verna, the Cammino di Assisi overlaps with other Ways of St. Francis. From La Verna, the Cammino di Assisi and the Via di Francesco crisscross one another until Città di Castello. From Città di Castello, the Cammino di Assisi largely follows the same route as other Ways of St. Francis all the way to Assisi. The Cammino di Assisi is marked with painted green arrows; stickers of St. Francis happily walking and/or dancing; and red, green, and white wooden arrows.

Di Qui Passò Francesco
(La Verna to Poggio Bustone)

Di Qui Passò Francesco (loosely translated in English as "On the Road with St. Francis") is the project of Angela Maria Seracchioli. This route starts in La Verna and mostly overlaps with the Via di Francesco until Spoleto, where it diverges toward Terni, approaches Rieti from Greccio, circumnavigates the Rieti Valley, and finishes in Poggio Bustone. A print guide, originally in Italian with an English translation, exists for the route, and an online resource (diquipassofrancesco.it) includes lists of accommodations. Along this route, some accommodations have joined an association of service providers who happily host pilgrims and who are identified by a tile plaque. Di Qui Passò Francesco is marked with a painted yellow T, or Greek tau. Due to its association with St. Francis and Franciscans, the tau is also used liberally on other routes.

PILGRIMAGE

Via di Francesco in Toscana
(Florence to La Verna)

In Tuscany, two routes start from Florence and culminate in La Verna. Since 2019, a local organization has greatly improved waymarking along these route, and the trail is marked with five-sided plaque with red arrows and circular and rectangular stickers. You'll also see yellow taus and blue/yellow marks.

Cammino di Francesco
(Rieti Valley routes)

This way is a series of routes that connect various Franciscan sites and sanctuaries in and around the sacred Rieti Valley. These routes are marked with intermittent carved wooden signs with a picture of St. Francis, the sky, and a dove.

Sentiero Francescano della Pace
(Assisi to Gubbio)

This route follows the journey that St. Francis took from Assisi to Gubbio after giving up his inheritance. Between Assisi and Gubbio the route is the same as other Ways of St. Francis—only in reverse—and is marked with large information panels.

Franziskusweg:
A Dutch guide (Roodenberg) and two German guides (Ochsenkühn; Elsner) outline overlapping *Franziskusweg* (St. Francis Way) itineraries between Florence and Rome. The main difference between the Franziskusweg and other Way of St. Francis routes comes after Rieti, where Franziskusweg routes turn northwest, winding through Greccio and Farfa before reconnecting with the Via di Francesco/Via di Roma in Montelibretti. There is no official Franziskusweg waymarking, and the itinerary follows a variety of different marked and unmarked paths and roads.

WAY OF ST. FRANCIS

Other Routes and Waymarking:

While many Way of St. Francis routes have specific waymarking, those styles are sometimes used in other places. Before La Verna, blue and yellow stripes and yellow taus are used liberally to indicate the Way of St. Francis. In other places, you'll find additional Way of St. Francis waymarking that is not associated with one particular route—namely sign boards with broad tau symbols pointing you in the direction of particular sites or towns.

The ***Club Alpino Italiano (CAI)*** marks and maintains a robust network of hiking paths throughout Italy (beyond the various pilgrimage routes). These hiking paths are numbered and marked with GR footpath-style red and white painted stripes (and noted with red numbers on our stage and city maps).

CAI signboards

In addition to the routes already mentioned, other waymarked routes intersect for shorter distance: Cammino di San Benedetto, Chemein de Velezay-Assisi, Via Romeo, and Via dei Monasteri, to name a few. To limit confusion, notes are included on relevant waymarking on day stage sidebars.

Route Covered in this Guide

Narrowing down these many options proved a challenge, but the routes selected for this book follow specific goals. First, the route includes as many Franciscan sites as possible while seeking to avoid urban, paved roads when possible. Due to the huge variety in waymarking and signs, this book prioritizes sections with better marking and includes descriptions of specific waymarking for each day stage.

Though services can be sparse in places, each stage end has lodging and food, and nearly all have access to public transport. For stages that can be dangerous in bad weather, alternative stage options are provided when available. To avoid an overly circuitous route, the itinerary covers 537km in 27 stages, that can be completed in 4.5-5 weeks, including rest days. In the end, the main trunk of the route generally follows the Via di Francesco in Toscana from Florence to La Verna and the Via di Francesco from La Verna to Rome.

For maximum flexibility, this book includes maps and information for an additional 200km of alternative day stages and side routes, noting the pros and cons of each, so you can customize the walk to cater to your particular interests and abilities.

PILGRIMAGE

The Camino de Santiago & Way of St. Francis

If you, like many pilgrims who walk the Way of St. Francis, have previously walked a Camino de Santiago route in Spain or Portugal, you may wonder how the Way of St. Francis compares to the Camino. At its core, the Way of St. Francis is quite similar to the Camino de Santiago. Both are long-distance pilgrimage routes; both have regular services and amenities that enable hiking with a relatively light pack (though you will need to be prepared to carry more food and water on the Way of St. Francis); and both encourage travelers to walk with a pilgrim credential in order to receive recognition for a completed pilgrimage.

Key differences exist between the two experiences. The Way of St. Francis follows **differently-marked trails with more variable waymarking styles and quality** than the Camino. You'll have to pay closer attention to maps and trail markings on the Way of St. Francis, particularly at intersections. To assist with navigation, we highly recommend walking with GPS tracks for the route either on a dedicated GPS device or smart phone (free at caminoguidebook.com, see p. 36).

There are **fewer walkers** than on popular Camino routes. This means more solitude and less overcrowding, but you'll find fewer pilgrim dorms and pilgrim-specific amenities. Services are more than sufficient, but you will **need to carry more food and water** than on the Camino de Santiago—potentially 1.5 days' worth of food and several liters of water—and you'll have less flexibility in selecting where to end your day. **Parts of the route are quite remote**, without cell service, and potentially dangerous in inclement weather. Challenges are described on a stage-by-stage basis, but be prepared to navigate in remote environments and carry the appropriate gear to stay warm and dry in cold, rainy weather. If hiking alone, consider carrying a satellite communication device like Garmin InReach or SPOT tracker.

⚠ **The Way of St. Francis is a tough route!** The average day stage in our guide has 750m of **climbing**, and several stages surpass 1,000m of elevation gain. For reference, a large portion of the stages on the Way of St. Francis are at least as physically demanding as the Camino Primitivo, the hardest days on the Camino del Norte, or the Napoleon Route on the first day from St-Jean-Pied-de-Port on the Camino Francés. What's more, the Way of St. Francis often follows **rough hiking trails**, particularly in Tuscany. These trails sometimes have loose, rocky surfaces and can be muddy and slick in wet weather. Walkers would benefit from trekking poles. Reasonably fit walkers can manage this route, but you should be comfortable hiking with a full backpack on sometimes rocky surfaces with significant ascents and descents.

Signage along the way

WAY OF ST. FRANCIS

Pilgrim Practicalities

This information will get you started, and more extensive details are online.

Credenziale (Pilgrim Passport)
The *credenziale* (or *credential*) is a document that identifies the bearer as a pilgrim, with space for stamps from accommodations and sites. The credential serves as proof of completing the pilgrimage as you collect at least one stamp per day along the journey. Some pilgrim-only accommodations (see Sleeping p. 20) require that pilgrims present a valid credential in order to stay there.

The **best way to obtain a credential** is to apply ahead of time through the Credential Office at the Diocese of Gubbio's Piccola Accoglienza (pilgrim support association). Follow directions at viadifrancesco.it/en and fill out an online form at piccolaccoglienzagubbio.it/credenziale/en. The credential is free, but donations are suggested to cover the cost of shipping. Allow two months for delivery to locations outside of Italy.

Credentials are also available in Florence at the St. James Episcopal Church (B. Rucellai 9, info@stjames.it, ☏055294417) ⏰Mon-Fri from 9am-12pm. Staff at the church are wonderfully helpful, but providing pilgrim credentials does take time away from other important work, so apply for the credential in advance if able. You can also obtain a credential in person at the Assisi Pilgrim Office (*Statio Peregrinorum*, see Stage 15, p. 138, for information on the Assisi Pilgrim Office.)

Testimonium (Certificate of Completion)
The *Testimonium* is a document of completion awarded to those who walk the last 100km or bicycle the last 200km to Assisi and/or Rome. The testimonium in Assisi is called the **Testimonium Peregrinationis Peractae ad Sanctorum Francisci et Clarae Civitatem** and is offered at the Pilgrim Office in Assisi. A separate one is provided at the Pilgrim Office at St. Peter's Square in Rome. (See Stages 15 and 27, p. 138, 216, for more information on the respective pilgrim offices).

Visas and Entry

Italy is among the 26 Schengen states of the European Union (EU) that have no internal borders. Citizens of the USA, Canada, Australia, New Zealand, and some South American countries are issued a free visa upon arrival with valid passport, limited to 90 days within a 180-day period. Most African, Asian, Middle Eastern, and some South American nationalities must apply for an advance visa. Check EU regulations to see if your nationality requires an advance visa. ⚠ Check for relevant travel updates at caminoguidebook.com.

TRAVEL ON THE WAY

When to Go and Time Necessary ☺
Seasons & Climate
While the Way of St. Francis can be walked in any season, **spring and fall** are generally considered the best time to walk, offering cooler temperatures than the summer months with accommodations and other services generally open. Both seasons have a large percentage of sunny days, though occasional rain is still likely. Flowers are in bloom in the spring. On the edges of spring and fall, it's possible to encounter snow at higher elevations.

Summer is the driest and hottest time of year. Temperatures can soar above 40°C/104°F at lower elevations. At higher elevations, temperatures are more moderate. Accommodations and other services are open. ⚠ We do not advise walking in the **winter**. In the mountains, the route will be covered in snow and dangerous to navigate. Many accommodations are closed for the winter months, severely limiting overnight options.

Monthly temperature and rainfall charts are included for Florence (p. 41), Assisi (p. 147), and Rome (p. 187).

Trip Length
The full itinerary from Florence to Rome requires a bare minimum of 4 weeks, though we recommend taking 4.5-5 weeks to allow for rest days and extra time to explore the wealth of fascinating sites and cities. Assisi warrants an extra day, and Florence and Rome each deserve several days to visit. Detours to Greccio and/or Farfa add 1-3 extra days.

We've split up the 537km journey to Rome into 27 daily stages, with an average of 20km (12.4mi) per day. Feel free to deviate from this pace, staying at intermediary accommodations, which are noted on maps and in the text. For especially challenging sections, we've included specific recommendations on how to further shorten daily stages. The majority of stage start/end points are accessible by public transportation, making it easy to skip a stage here or there if necessary.

If you prefer to walk only part of the Way of St. Francis, consider some of these 1-2 week itineraries:
- Florence-La Verna (100km, 6+ days)
- Florence-Assisi (290km, 15+ days)
- La Verna-Assisi (190km, 9+ days)
- Assisi-Rome or Rome-Assisi (250km, 12+ days)
- Assisi-Rieti or Rieti-Assisi (145km, 7+ days)
- Rieti-Rome (105km, 5+ days)

WAY OF ST. FRANCIS

Be aware that the Florence to Assisi section is more difficult than the Assisi to Rome section, though both have challenging areas. Waymarking on the Via di Francesco/Via di Roma is designed for both northbound and southbound travel between Assisi and Rome. Whichever direction you choose to walk on the Way of St. Francis, we'd recommend finishing in either Assisi or Rome (not in Rieti, for example), in order to be able to receive a Testimonium.

Sleeping

Accommodation types on the Way of St. Francis vary widely, ranging from budget pilgrim-oriented lodging to high-end boutique hotels. It's best to reserve a bed or room at least 1-2 days in advance, since the way has fewer walkers than more popular pilgrimage routes, so smaller accommodations are not prepared without notice. Family-run lodging is a part-time side occupation for some. Phone or email are the best ways to make contact; email or WhatsApp can be preferable because of the language barrier, where both parties can utilize Google Translate or similar to get their message across. Accommodations with online booking or a website have a symbol (links at caminoguidebook.com). Note that many lodging owners do not speak English (see phrasebook p. 220).

TRAVEL ON THE WAY

The vast majority of stage endpoints in this guide have multiple accommodations, generally with at least one budget-friendly option. Where a stage end has only one accommodation, we note where other lodging options are available in the close vicinity. Often there are intermediate accommodations between stage endpoints. In these locations, town services are usually more limited. Pilgrim infrastructure is more robust from La Verna southward, where pilgrim traffic is higher.

☺ Most accommodations are open from the beginning of April to the end of October, though open dates vary. Some accommodations are open year round, and others operate with more abbreviated schedules.

Dormitories and Shared Rooms D

Unlike popular Camino routes in Spain and Portugal, the Way of St. Francis does not have a highly-developed system of standardized, low-cost dormitory accommodations (albergues) intended for walking or biking pilgrims. Instead a variety of private businesses, religious institutions, and municipal governments offer shared-room accommodation on a more informal, ad hoc basis.

Dorm types

Private: In major cities like Florence and Rome, youth hostels offer dormitory beds, though these are not geared specifically toward pilgrims. In other cities and towns, private accommodations, like hotels and bed and breakfasts, offer special pilgrim rates, sometimes in shared rooms. Where shared rooms are a possibility, we use the dorm symbol D; where pilgrim rates are for private rooms, we use the hotel symbol H.

Parrocchiale (par): Church organizations—parishes, convents, and monasteries—are the most common type of pilgrim-specific accommodation. This type of lodging might be an official pilgrim dormitory or simply space in a spare room. A few of these accommodations require a pilgrim credential for entry. Many run on a donation basis and offer Mass or other religious services. They tend to have a simple, quiet, and prayerful atmosphere, usually staffed by nuns, priests, or volunteers.

Bed Bugs, or *Cimex lectularius,* blood-sucking parasitic insects, are on the rise around the world and are a risk in lodgings with high rates of traveler turnover. While bed bugs do not carry any known diseases, bites can be very uncomfortable and cause painful rashes for some people, and the insects are very difficult to get rid of once infested. Some ways to avoid bed bugs include pretreating your sleeping bag and backpack with permethrin or other insect repellent. Bed bugs travel in luggage and backpacks, so be sure never to place your pack on your bed.

WAY OF ST. FRANCIS

Rifugios (rif): In the mountains, the path occasionally passes a mountain hut, or *rifugio*. At their most basic, rifugios are rustic buildings that provide only a dry, enclosed space with a floor, fireplace, and (possibly) benches and a table. These basic rigufios are not ideal pilgrim accommodations, since they lack amenities like showers or beds; but they do offer shelter from the elements in emergency situations, so we note them in this guide, labeling them with the rifugio symbol. Rifugio can also describe a more developed mountain hut, run by a private owner or mountaineering society, with dorm-style beds, showers, and even meals. To indicate that these rifugios are suitable pilgrim accommodations, we use the dorm symbol, as well as relevant amenity symbols in the accommodation listing. Occasionally, private room accommodations use the term "rifugio" in their name but are not actual mountain huts.

Municipal (muni): In some towns, the local government offers space in municipal buildings. These tend to be very simple and are rare along the Way of St. Francis.

Prices in "dormitory" pilgrim accommodations range from €10-30 per person. Accommodations that run on donations (don, *offerta libera* in Italian) do not have a fixed price, but they rely on donations to continue to provide services. Donation does not mean free, so give as you are able. Some pilgrim lodging does not supply sheets or pillow cases, so carry at least a sleeping bag liner and pillow case (some can supply linens for an additional fee). Amenities range from very basic to all the "bells and whistles" like Wi-Fi, washer, dryer, guest kitchen, etc.

Casale Il Viandante in Ponticelli

TRAVEL ON THE WAY

In this book, dorm prices refer to a bed in a shared room. If an accommodation also offers private rooms, the prices indicate dorm bed/single room/double room prices (for example, €10/30/50). For private accommodations, we list the single/double prices per room. Prices indicate approximate high season rates and are subject to change.

Hotels and Private Rooms
In addition to dorm accommodations, there are many private room options.

Hotels are the most common type of private accommodation. Room prices usually range from €30-70, though they can be more expensive. For the most part, breakfast is included in the price. If you're walking with a partner or friend, you can lower your individual costs by sharing double rooms. Sometimes hotels offer meals.

Bed and Breakfasts (BB) are usually rooms in private homes and include, as the name indicates, a bed and breakfast. Rooms may have private or shared bathroom facilities. Some offer a guest kitchen. Bed and breakfasts, by law, do not provide meals other than breakfast. Priced like budget hotels, they are usually affordable.

A **Foresteria** is a hotel run by a convent or monastery. They usually offer meals in addition to breakfast. Prices are similar to hotel prices.

Agriturismi (singular: Agriturismo) are rural homes, hotels, or apartments. Usually, an agriturismo will provide meals (often including agricultural products from the property), and sometimes they have kitchens. Since they're located in more remote settings, it's advisable to check in advance about meal or kitchen availability. Sometimes owners can provide groceries with advanced notice. Agriturismi are usually priced higher than hotels, though not always.

Apartments/Vacation Homes often have a wider range of amenities than hotels (usually with equipped kitchens, washer/dryer, etc.). Prices vary.

Camping is possible in a few formal campgrounds, but carrying a tent is uncommon because "wild camping" is not generally permitted in Italy. Reasonably priced lodging is available each night, and camping generally doesn't represent significant cost saving.

WAY OF ST. FRANCIS

Food and Meals

Italy is synonymous with delicious food, and the fare along the Way is no exception. The typical Italian **breakfast** consists of an espresso and a pastry. A larger continental breakfast might include meat, cheese, yogurt, and juice. You're unlikely to find a full English breakfast or greasy diner, so if you're accustomed to a more filling meal to start your day, consider buying extra food from a grocery store. Italians typically eat **lunch** during the afternoon break (or *riposo*) and **dinner** later in the evening between 8-10pm. Restaurants generally don't open for the evening meal before 7:30pm.

Italian **bars/cafés** are open all day, offering drinks, sandwiches (often a small bun with meat and cheese), pastries, and other light, pre-prepared foods. Most open early enough (generally no later than 8am) for a quick breakfast on the way out of town, and they are good options for an afternoon snack before restaurants open or when grocery stores are closed.

Pizza is ubiquitous in Italy. In larger towns, you can often find pizzerias open all day that sell pizza by the slice or by weight, while restaurants often sell whole pizzas. In the evening, the typical **restaurant dinner** features an appetizer (thinly sliced meats, bread, olive oil, cheese), first course (usually a pasta dish), main course (usually a meat dish—chicken, beef, pork, veal, etc.), vegetable sides (salad, grilled or sautéed vegetables), bread, wine, and a dessert followed by coffee or a *digestivo* (an after-dinner liquor thought to aid in digestion). These **meals** can be expensive (€15-25+). To save money, you can pick and choose à la carte or buy groceries from local shops. Though accommodations with **kitchens** are not particularly common, you can occasionally cook your own evening meal. On maps in this book, we do not distinguish between bars/cafés and restaurants, as both normally offer drinks and food.

TRAVEL ON THE WAY

On most days, **count on packing and carrying snacks and lunch**, since supermarkets and cafés can be few and far between. Any grocery store should sell the ingredients to make simple sandwiches (bread, meat, and cheese—all of which can be purchased by weight from the deli section or in prepackaged containers). Hard salami and hard cheeses tend to keep well even on warm days. Even small grocery stores generally have an assortment of cookies, chocolate bars, crackers, and other quick snacks. Shops and produce stands sell fruit and vegetables. You might also consider carrying pizza or pre-made sandwiches from a morning bar/café stop. On many days, you won't find a place to eat between your start and end point. In towns, restaurants and cafés are usually available. Some very small towns do not have shops or restaurants, but here accommodation owners are usually able to coordinate meals with advance notice.

Vegetarian, Vegan, and Gluten-free Options

While traveling can be difficult for people with dietary constraints, it's possible to maintain a vegan, vegetarian, and/or gluten-free diet with some creativity—in fact, it may be easier in Italy than in many countries. Salads and vegetable side dishes are common, and most first courses (*primi piatti*) are vegetarian and/or vegan. Similarly, olive oil, not butter, is the fat of choice in Italian restaurants, increasing the number of vegan-friendly dishes in restaurants. If preparing your own meals, you should not have trouble finding good protein alternatives, such as nuts, beans and cheese, and in larger towns tofu and hummus. For a gluten-free diet, the pervasiveness of pasta and pizza is daunting, but because gluten-rich dishes are so common, there's more public awareness about celiac disease in Italy than in many countries. The Italian government actually offers citizens with celiac disease vouchers to buy gluten-free food. In larger towns, the stores and restaurants often have gluten-free groceries and meals.

WAY OF ST. FRANCIS

Transportation
Getting to the Way of St. Francis

First fly into a major **airport** hub near the Way of St. Francis and take regional or local transit to your starting point. Rome's main airport, Fiumicino (FCO), is the largest airport close to the route and has the most international airline connections. Public transit runs regularly between the airport and major bus and train terminals in Rome, which have connections to cities and towns along the Way of St. Francis. Florence also has a small international airport (FLR) with service to European airline hubs. In unfavorable weather/wind, inbound planes are sometimes diverted to Pisa. The T2 light rail runs frequently between the airport and Florence's Santa Maria Novella train station (€1.50, ⏲5am-12am). **Train stations** in Rome and Florence also have connections to cities throughout Europe.

To Florence

From Rome's Fiumicino Airport, trains leave regularly for Florence's Santa Maria Novella train station. Two high-speed trains daily leave directly from the airport, while others require a connection at Rome's Tiburtina or Termini train stations. Depending on connections, the trip takes 2-3 hours. Tickets range from €35-50. Buses from Rome's Tiburtina bus station also go regularly to Florence. The bus is cheaper than the train but takes longer.

To La Verna

From Rome: Regular inter-regional trains go from Rome to Arezzo. From Arezzo, local Tuscan trains going in the direction of Stia connect to Bibbiena, where you can catch a local bus to Chiusi della Verna. The Sanctuary of La Verna is a 1.3km uphill walk from Chiusi della Verna. Alternatively, there is one daily afternoon bus from Rome's Tiburtina bus station to Pieve Santo Stefano (company Sulga, sulga.eu). Since the bus drops you off at a highway gas station just outside of town, you'll have a short taxi ride or tricky walk in the dark to the town center. Buses from Pieve Santo Stefano go three times a day to Chiusi della Verna; but if you take the bus from Rome, you'll have to spend the night in Pieve Santo Stefano before catching the bus the next morning. From Florence: Regular trains connect Florence to Arezzo. From Arezzo, follow the same local train and bus connections as above.

To Assisi

From Florence and Rome:
Regular trains connect to Assisi. Assisi's main train station (Santa Maria degli Angeli) is located in the valley, a 2.8km walk from the historic hilltop town of Assisi. Buses also go regularly from the entrance to the train station to a bus

TRAVEL ON THE WAY

stop just below the Basilica di San Francesco. Assisi is also served by a very small airport in Perugia: Perugia "San Francesco d'Assisi" (PEG) ✈. There are few airline connections. Buses from the airport to Perugia and Assisi are somewhat infrequent.

Along the Way of St. Francis, public buses 🚌 and **trains** 🚆 are available.

🚆 **Train**: TrenItalia (trenitalia.com) operates across Italy and connects to many towns along the Way of St. Francis including: Florence, Pontassieve, Assisi, Spello, Foligno, Trevi, Spoleto, Marmore, Rieti, and Monterotondo. Other notable TrenItalia hubs with local train and/or bus connections to smaller towns on route are: Arezzo, Perugia, and Terni. Smaller regional trains operate in Tuscany and Umbria. There is a trainline that connects Stia to Arezzo via Bibbiena, particularly useful to reach various towns on route in Tuscany. Consider the Trenit app (see below) for train schedules and ticket purchases.

🚌 **Bus**: Private companies run inter-regional bus lines, while local, intra-regional bus lines operate within Tuscany, Umbria, and Lazio. In the Tiber Valley from Pieve Santo Stefano to Perugia, public buses are the most convenient form of transportation, despite the fact that Sansepolcro and Città di Castello have train stations.

TrenItalia ticket machine

Transport company websites have the most current information on rates and schedules. Third-party websites/applications like **Rome2Rio** (rome2rio.com) or **Trenit** (trenit.app) aggregate information on timetables and prices and link out to relevant company websites to purchase tickets—useful for comparing several options at once. Staff at tourism offices and accommodations also offer helpful advice regarding transport. *Tabacchi*—short for tabaccheria (literally "tobacco shop")—are small convenience shops, common in cities and towns throughout Italy, where you can buy bus and tram tickets.

Business Hours & the *Riposo* ☺

Throughout Italy, most businesses (with the exception of cafés/bars) close from around 1/1:30-4/5pm in a break known as the *riposo* (similar to the *siesta* of Spanish fame). On Sundays, businesses close for the riposo and don't open again until Monday morning. In smaller towns, businesses may close entirely on Sundays. Plan your shopping around these breaks. Larger chain supermarkets sometimes operate without the riposo, though they are likely to still close on Sunday afternoon. In large cities, some supermarkets are open seven days a week, morning-night, without an afternoon break.

Money, Costs and Budgeting €

The unit of currency in Italy is the euro, made up of 100 euro cents. The best way to obtain euros is to use an € **ATM/cash machine**, which are available in all cities and most towns. Travelers' checks are a hassle to cash. You can carry dollars or other currency and change them into euros, but the exchange rate will not be as good as by ATM. Smaller accommodations often work on a cash-only basis, though many hotels, restaurants, stores, and other services do accept credit cards. Remember that most credit cards charge a foreign currency conversion fee of about 3%, so consider applying for a card with no fee. Visa is the most-accepted credit card in Italy, followed by Mastercard.

Currency:
EU €1 ≈ USD $1.00
EU €1 ≈ GBP £0.87
EU €1 ≈ CAD $1.33

Daily costs for most pilgrims are simply lodging, food/drink, and sometimes first aid supplies. By the standards of any European trip, the Way of St. Francis is relatively inexpensive beyond the costs of airfare and transportation and can be adapted to a variety of budgets.

For those who wish to stay in dorms/shared rooms and lower-priced accommodations, €60 a day is a **realistic average budget** (€30 for accommodations/breakfast, €10 for lunch and snacks, €15 for dinner, €5 miscellaneous). It's possible to travel on a slightly lower budget by seeking out parochial hostels whenever available, splitting hotel rooms, eating from grocery stores rather than restaurants, etc, but traveling on a shoestring budget simply isn't as feasible as on the Camino de Santiago where there are many inexpensive lodging options. Those who prefer private rooms and/or higher quality accommodations and food will likely need a higher daily budget. Whatever your daily budget, make sure you have some extra padding in case of emergency. If you would become too injured to walk, consider transportation and accommodation costs to leave the route. Gear might need to be replaced. Leave room for the occasional splurge, like a more-expensive room or meal occasionally.

Most travelers keep valuables in a travel wallet (money belt or neck pouch) that can easily be concealed when in crowded places. As a precaution, make photocopies of your important documents (passport, driver's license, health insurance) and also email them to yourself so you can print them in case of theft. Write down phone numbers from credit cards in case they are lost or stolen. Call your bank and let them know you will be traveling, so they don't put a hold on or cancel your ATM card when they see "suspicious" activity in Italy.

TRAVEL ON THE WAY

Laundry

Some accommodations, particularly those that are oriented toward pilgrims, have clothes-washing sinks with washboards and clotheslines. Often, however, a regular sink is the only option for handwashing clothes, and you'll need your own clothesline and clothespins to hang your laundry to dry.

Bigger towns and cities have coin-operated self-service laundromats (accommodation owners will be able to give you directions), and some hotels and other private accommodations offer laundry service. In either case, combining your dirty clothes with other pilgrims' laundry can save water, energy, and cost.

Phones and Internet

Two main options for mobile phone coverage are with international roaming on your home mobile phone plan or purchasing a local **SIM card** (requires unlocked GSM phone). International roaming on many US and Canada based plans can be quite expensive, but is a good solution if only used for emergencies. T-Mobile has free international data (at metered speeds) and text on some US plans.

Buying an **Italian SIM card** and a pay-as-you-go phone plan is likely the most affordable way to make calls in Italy. TIM, Vodafone, and Wind are well-known mobile service providers in Italy, with TIM offering the best reception in rural areas. Prepaid plans with SIM cards start from around €20 and increase in cost depending on the number of minutes or amount of data you choose. Calling and messaging apps like WhatsApp, Viber, or Skype allow you to make calls via Wi-Fi or a mobile data connection.

TIM (mobile phone service provider)

Italy's country code is (+39). All phone numbers listed in this guide are written without the country code. After the country code, mobile numbers start with 3, while land lines start with 0. To dial Italian numbers from a US phone number or when using one of the aforementioned calling apps, you'll have to include Italy's country code at the start of the phone number.

To call Italian numbers (+39) from a US phone number: +39 - XXX-XXX-XXXX
To call the USA and Canada (+1) from abroad: +1 - XXX-XXX-XXXX

Wi-Fi is increasingly available along the route, and many accommodations and cafés offer free access.

WAY OF ST. FRANCIS

Post Offices/ *Poste Italiane*

Stamps can be purchased either at the post office or at tabacchi (small convenience shops). If you have packed items you are not using, you can mail them back home, though postage is expensive to destinations outside of Europe, and the Italian postal system has a reputation for being slow and unreliable.

It is possible to send items ahead to your endpoint or other city along the route by addressing with your full name, "*Fermo Posta*" and the city name and postal code of the destination. Be sure to write your name as it appears on your passport and bring ID to pick up, and don't send anything you'd be devastated to lose.

Bathrooms, Toilets, *Il Bagno*, WC, the Loo

Finding a restroom when necessary can be a challenge. Public bathrooms are few and far between. Buy a little something in a cafe and use their facilities. When the call of nature comes at an inconvenient time far from any town, be responsible with how you go in nature. Walk at least 30m (100ft) from the trail and any water source. Carry out used toilet paper in a plastic bag to dispose of in the nearest trash can. Toilet paper takes a long time to decompose, and wind often carries it out onto the trail. For solid waste, find a private spot and dig a 15-20cm (6-8in) cat hole using a stick or trowel. Cover your deposit with dirt and pack out your toilet paper.

Luggage Transfer & Tours

A network of tour operators and drivers provides transfer services to pilgrims throughout central Italy, including luggage transfer, bike rental/transfer, and transportation. Prices vary and are based on volume. The lowest price for luggage transfer is **€10 per bag (per day)** and increases in price from there. Transfer services are available year-round and for other pilgrimage routes in the region (Via Francigena, Cammino di San Benedetto, etc.). Call **Pellegrino Support Services** for more information (3319077671). Accommodations can also help organize luggage transfer, though prices are generally higher. For a list of services, see our website.

All packed to hike

TRAVEL ON THE WAY

Medical Care ✚

Italy has good medical care that is free or low-cost for citizens of countries with reciprocal agreements. Citizens of Great Britain, Ireland, and the EU need a European Health Insurance Certificate (EHIC). Non-EU citizens are recommended to have private health and travel insurance. Carry an emergency contact card with known allergies, pertinent medical history, and information that is helpful to medical staff if you are unable to communicate. Dial ✆112 to reach emergency services. Pharmacies are well stocked and readily available in cities and larger towns.

Safety Issues ⚠

Italy has low crime rates, and violent crime is rare. It is always good to remain aware of your surroundings, not leave valuables unattended, and report any incidents to the police by dialing ✆112. Pickpocketing is more likely in touristy, urban settings. Be extremely careful when walking along roads. Always walk on the left side opposite traffic and remain alert. Avoid walking after dark. Aggressive dogs are not common but may be encountered. Carrying a walking stick can enhance confidence when encountering animals.

Beware of cats!

Though not a backcountry wilderness trail, parts of the Way of St. Francis are quite **remote without car access or mobile phone service**. If traveling on your own, share your intended itinerary with a family member or close friend and communicate with them regularly. Make sure they know which emergency number to call if they don't hear from you. Consider walking with a satellite communication device (like a Garmin InReach or SPOT) that can track your location and allow you to contact emergency services when out of mobile phone service.

Take measures to prevent **hypothermia** by wearing appropriate layers and rain gear. Don't walk high mountain passes in wet weather, and avoid dehydration by carrying sufficient water (up to 3L of water over longer stretches in the summer months) and wearing sun protection (sunscreen, hat, etc.).

Pilgrim Associations

Pilgrim associations offer support regionally. ***La Via di Francesco in Toscana*** (laviadifrancescointoscana.it) provides information and helps maintain the trail in **Tuscany**. A volunteer association in **Gubbio** sends out pilgrim credentials for the Via di Francesco and helps pilgrims find lodging, particularly from Pietralunga-Assisi (piccolaccoglienzagubbio@gmail.com, ✆3661118386). Along the route, accommodation owners, tourism offices, and parish staff are quick to offer support and advice to pilgrims in need of assistance.

WAY OF ST. FRANCIS

Mountain Biking the Way of St. Francis ⊙

Though biking the Way of St. Francis is not common, cycling is a possible alternative to walking for an intrepid pilgrim who has limited time or just wants to travel more quickly than walking allows. Due to the very steep climbs and technical difficulty of many of the trail surfaces, you should be quite physically fit and have prior mountain biking and unpaved bike touring (bikepacking) experience. Most importantly, you should have a flexible attitude and be ready for a challenging adventure.

The same company that provides luggage transfer (see Luggage Transfer, p. 30), offers **bike (and bike bags) rentals and transfers**. The ideal bike setup for the route is a **mountain bike with bikepacking bags** (seatpost, frame, and handlebar bags), basic bike tools, a tire pump, and a spare inner tubes. Wear a helmet (though this is not required by Italian law) and have a loud bell to alert hikers.

Mountain bikers can, for the most part, follow the same path as walkers—49% of the route is paved—but significant sections, due to surface quality and grade, would force all but the most technically proficient riders to walk at times. For the most difficult sections, it's possible to find serviceable road detours. The ⊙ bicycle symbol represents a bike shop in a town amenity list, in lodging amenities it represents bike storage available. Information at caminocyclist.com, and the Facebook group **Bikepacking the Camino** ⧉

Suggested Mountain Biking Itinerary

This two week itinerary assumes a mountain bike with bikepacking setup and a fit rider with some technical mountain biking experience. We only suggest detours for very technical sections of trail, assuming that riders can successfully manage smooth single track, double track, and dirt/gravel roads.

1. **Florence-Consuma, 39.1km, ▲ +1,750m**
   ⚠ Likely Detour: Stage 2: After Ferrano from 10.5-15.1km

2. **Consuma-Camaldoli, 33.3km, ▲ +1,610m**
   ⚠ Likely Detours:
   Stage 3: Between Il Gualdo and turn-off to Villa, 3.1-8.6km
   Stage 4: Between Lonnano and Casalino, 5.2-7.6km
   Stage 4: CAI 72 from 12.4-16.1km

3. **Camaldoli-Pieve Santo Stefano, 42.4km, ▲ +2,300m**
   ⚠ Likely Detours:
   Stage 5: Camaldoli-Badia Prataglia, 0-8.0km (technical mountain biking)
   Stage 5: Badia Prataglia-Rimbocchi, 8.0-18.6km (technical mountain biking with initial hike-a-bike after Badia Prataglia)
   Stage 6: Follow easier route option (CAI 54) from Rimbocchi, 1.3-4.7km
   Stage 7: Route from La Verna is rideable, but if in doubt, SP-208 is paved to Pieve Santo Stefano; 0-15.0k

TRAVEL ON THE WAY

4. **Pieve Santo Stefano-Sansepolcro, 35.0km**, ▲ +1,570m
   ⚠ Likely Detours:
   Stage 8: 5.1-10.0km; note good gravel road detour
   Stage 8: 10.0-12.4km; paved + gravel road detour
   Stage 8: 18.7-20.8km; easiest way is hike-a-bike along the technical trail
   Stage 9: 1.4-4.5km; if you want to see Montecasale, best to ride what you can and hike-a-bike remainder; alternatively a paved road descends from La Montagna to Val d'Afra
   Stage 9: 5.6-7.4km; follow paved road detour

5. **Sansepolcro-Città di Castello, 32.3km**, ▲ +1,120m

6. **Città di Castello-Gubbio, 56.4km**, ▲ +2,050m

7. **Gubbio-Assisi, 51.2km**, ▲ +1,920m
   ⚠ Likely Detours:
   Stage 14: 1.6-2.3km; no logical detour, hike-a-bike
   Stage 15: 2.0-5.6km; largely rideable with some walking, easy road detour

8. **Assisi-Spoleto, 59.4km**, ▲ +1,960m (low route from Assisi)
   ⚠ Likely Detours:
   Stage 17: 17.3-18.6km; hiking path with loose rock, best to hike-a-bike
   Stage 18: 0-1.6km, follow easy alternative route from Poreta
   Stage 18: 6.4-7.2km, easy road detour

9. **Spoleto-Arrone, 31.3km**, ▲+1,250m
   ⚠ Likely Detours:
   Stage 19: 1.8-3.5km, follow paved road to Monteluco
   Stage 19: 5.9km-11.6km, no easy/direct detour, hike-a-bike, rideable in places with extreme caution

10. **Arrone-Rieti, 51.5km**, ▲ +1,970m
    ⚠ Likely Detours:
    Stage 21: 12.9-14.4km, paved road detour from Faggio di San Francesco

11. **Rieti-Montelibretti, 54.6km**, ▲ +1,680m

12. **Montelibretti-Rome, 50.4km**, ▲ +1,045m

Packing for the Road: Gear, Resupply and Navigation

A light load makes for a happy pilgrim, and weight should be a primary consideration in packing. A popular guideline is to pack no more than 10% of your body weight. Resist the temptation to pack many extras "just in case." Shops are readily available in Italy and most anything lacking can be purchased along the way.

Backpacks: A 30-40L (1800-2500in^3) pack is sufficient. Measure your torso length and choose a pack of the proper size. Get fitted at a knowledgeable outdoor retail store. Aim for a pack that weighs less than 1.4kg (3lbs) empty.

Footwear: Lightweight boots or sturdy trail runners with a stiff or semi-rigid sole offer protection for your feet and ankles against the often hard, rocky, and uneven path (trail surfaces, p. 36). Get fitted for footwear in the afternoon or evening after feet have expanded during the day. Bring lightweight footwear to wear in the evenings, such as flip flops or foam sandals. ⚠ Be sure to thoroughly break in footwear with practice hikes wearing your loaded pack. Invest in wool or synthetic socks (not cotton), which wick moisture away from your skin, dry quickly, insulate when wet, and manage odor better. If you're prone to blisters, experiment with liner socks (wool or polypropylene) for an extra rubbing layer other than your skin.

Clothing: Consider hiking clothes as layers, with inner layers for moisture management, middle for insulation, and outer for weather protection. The general rule for outdoor clothing is to avoid cotton as it does not retain insulating properties when wet and dries slowly. Synthetic materials (polyester, nylon, spandex) and wool (especially merino) are preferred, especially in cold and wet weather. In warm seasons, choose lightweight, breathable clothing that provides sun protection. Be prepared for the sun with a wide-brimmed hat and **sunglasses,** and use **sunscreen** regularly. Bring a **lightweight rain jacket** with a waterproof breathable membrane, or use a poncho that can also cover your backpack. Bring a waterproof pack cover or line your pack with plastic garbage bags to keep your gear dry. Pack electronics in zippered plastic bags or small dry bags to protect against moisture.

Sleeping Bags: A lightweight, mummy-style, 1-season summer sleeping bag (rated $^+$40+°F/$^+$5+°C) is adequate for the spring, summer, or fall. Some opt for only a sleeping bag liner, as many accommodations provide blankets, even if they don't supply sheets. If planning to stay mostly in private rooms and only an occasional dorm, a liner is sufficient. For the cool edges of fall and spring, it's wise to have a 3-season bag (rated $^+$15-$^+$35°F/$^-$10-0°C), especially if you sleep cold. Buy the lightest bag you can afford within your desired temperature range. If planning to stay in dorms regularly, consider carrying a pillow case, as pillows cases are often not provided. A spare T-shirt can also be stretched over the pillow as a makeshift case.

PREPARING TO WALK

Trekking Poles: Used correctly, trekking poles can reduce impact on joints by up to 25%, particularly on rocky descents. In wet, slippery conditions, they improve balance. Look for telescoping aluminum or carbon poles. Carbon is lighter than aluminum and does a better job dampening vibration. Removable rubber caps for pole ends reduce clicking on pavement.

Water and refills: While water is readily available most days, it's not uncommon to have to walk 10-15km without a refill. Always carry at least one liter, and refill often. Carry two liters or more in more remote areas and up to three on hot days. Reliable water refill sites are marked on stage maps. There are often no signs indicating whether water from a water fountain is drinkable (potable) or not. When in doubt, continue walking to the next store/café. Tap water in Italy is treated and potable. Most historic springs are not potable, since they're not treated or tested. Bottled water is widely available, but less environmentally friendly than refillable bottles. Some towns have water refill stations with still or sparkling water.

Dehydration can lead to fatigue, headaches, **heat exhaustion, and heat stroke** (a dangerous and life-threatening condition). Be sure to eat foods that help to replenish electrolytes and consider an electrolyte drink on hot days. If you become dehydrated and overheated and are unable to cool down, take a break in a cool, shady place, rehydrate with electrolytes, and cool yourself with a wet cloth or fanning until you feel better. **Hypothermia** is possible in wet, cool weather, so be prepared with a dry set of clothes (socks included) for after a rainy day, and bring one insulating warm layer.

Fitness and Training: The length of the Way of St. Francis, the distance walked day after day and challenging ascents and descents all take a toll on the body. By taking the time to practice before beginning the journey, you will greatly reduce possible injuries. Training walks will help you get used to your hiking gear and the weight on your feet and shoulders. Get used to full-day walks, taking 2-3 shorter walks per week and one full-day walk weekly with your loaded pack. For this route in particular, it's useful to practice climbing and descending rocky trails with a loaded pack. Check with your doctor if you have concerns about your health or fitness level.

Blisters: This common injury may seem minor, but can have trip-ending consequences as blisters can be extremely painful and are prone to infection. **For prevention from home,** choose properly fitting footwear. Try on many options before buying (foot should not move or slip when walking on various terrain). Use wool socks and liners. Break in footwear by taking hikes with a loaded pack.

WAY OF ST. FRANCIS

For **on the trail prevention,** keep feet cool and dry, take off shoes and socks for breaks, wash feet and socks daily, use liner socks. For **blister treatment,** take a break, remove socks to let feet cool and dry out. Check for hot spots and address by applying moleskin, Compeed®, or duct tape to create an additional rubbing surface to protect the hot spot. If a blister forms, use a sterilized needle to puncture its edge near the skin and drain using sterile materials. Air dry and re-dress blister with sterile bandages. If the blister or surrounding area becomes infected over the course of several days (increasing red appearance, tenderness, pus, red streaks), see a doctor.

For **dry and cracked feet**, consider wearing socks all the time to keep moisture in, allowing cracks to heal. For severely painful cracks, a tiny bit of super glue can be helpful to hold the crack together, but make sure to clean the area thoroughly with soap, water, and antiseptic. **Impact-related injuries** are common on the high amount of paved surfaces on the way. If your feet and joints are taking a pounding, consider reducing your daily distance or adding walking poles and/or thicker socks.

The Trail

The paths in this book of the Way of St. Francis span roughly 750km (537km main route plus 210km of alternative stages). These trails vary greatly in surface, grade, landscapes, ecosystem, and climate. Rocky mountain trails through mossy forests give way to dirt roads through rolling olive terraces as you make your way from Florence to Rome. Proportionately, the Way of St. Francis has more paved surfaces than some hikers expect, contributing to more stress on feet and joints (49% paved, 51% unpaved). P Paved/ U Unpaved designations in this book refer to most obvious walking surface. There may be unpaved shoulders or faint footpaths along paved roads.

Route Finding, Trail Markings, Maps and GPS

The Way of St. Francis is relatively well marked, though the variations in quality, style, and frequency of markers sometimes make navigation confusing. The most common waymarks are painted yellow/blue stripes and the yellow T or *Tau*. Depending on the route, you may also see green arrows, dancing saint stickers, or red/white GR-style marks, among other waymarking (see p. 12). On each day stage, we include details about the waymarking you should follow for that particular day. Navigation through large cities can be difficult, as markers are less frequent and compete with other signs. For this reason, we've included detailed city maps throughout this book, though note that maps are representative and not exhaustive, without every street name. This book also includes zoomed-in maps to aid in navigation outside of cities when necessary.

With navigational challenges on the Way of St. Francis, we recommend using GPX tracks and a navigation app on your smart phone or GPS device along with this book. When searching navigation apps, be sure it enables downloading base maps

PREPARING TO WALK

for offline use, as you will be out of mobile phone reception for parts of the route. The GaiaGPS app is recommended, and its subscription level provides various offline basemaps and allows you to overlay GPX tracks on these basemaps. (OSM Outdoors is a good basemap layer for hiking in Italy.) Instructions for downloading GPX tracks and using GaiaGPS are available online. **Free GPS files for the route are available at <caminoguidebook.com>.**

Daily Stages and Regional Sections

This book organizes the Way of St. Francis into 27 daily stages averaging around 20km per day, with an additional nine alternative stages. The page spreads introducing each stage include a stage map, elevation profile, total distance, total ascent and descent in meters (▲/▼), paved/unpaved (P/U) percentages, difficulty level (see below), time estimate (☺), and a list of towns with accommodation.

Stages begin and end at the town center of the beginning and ending locality whenever possible. For mid-stage towns, measurements are taken from the town center or main church, whichever is prominent or closest to the marked route. Cumulative stage distances are noted on the stage maps and correspond to distances listed in town listings and elevation charts. Distances for off-route accommodations or points of interest are indicated with a plus symbol (+1.3km). Town boxes list resources available, all the dorm accommodations, and a selection of private accommodations in varying price ranges.

Distances are measured in metric units (kilometers and meters), and elevation in meters (m). In **elevation tables,** note that y-axis intervals vary, and relative scales are indicated with color-coded arrows ⬆⬆⬆, which may not correspond to the stage's difficulty rating color. ☺ Estimated **walking time** for each stage assumes a pace of 3-5 km/hour (1.8-3 mph) with terrain and elevation considered. Factor extra time for breaks and exploration.

Each day's stage route is assigned a **difficulty level** from 1-3. Ratings consider an "average" walker, who is reasonably fit but not necessarily athletic or an experienced hiker. A "Challenging" stage will likely have some characteristics listed below. Exercise more caution in colder months (Nov-Mar) when snow, cold rain and hypothermia are greater possibilities.

Length:
1m ≈ 1yd or 3ft
100m ≈ 100yd
1km = 0.62 miles
10km = 6.2 miles
1.6km = 1 mile

- ▪︎☐☐ **Easy:** Slight elevation change, sturdy footing, water easily accessible
- ▪︎▪︎☐ **Moderate:** More elevation change, steeper grades, longer distance, some challenging terrain
- ▪︎▪︎▪︎ **Challenging:** Significant elevation change, longer distances, some sections of rocky/loose/narrow paths with less stable footing, water sources may be scarce, trail is more remote and exposed (fewer shelter and services nearby in case of bad weather or emergencies)

WAY OF ST. FRANCIS

Hiking Gear Essentials

- ☐ **Backpack** (30-40L)
- ☐ **Sleeping bag or bag liner**, lightweight
- ☐ **Navigation**: guidebook, GPS (optional)
- ☐ **Headlamp** or flashlight/torch
- ☐ **Sun protection**: hat, sunglasses, sunscreen and lip balm
- ☐ **Towel**, lightweight travel type
- ☐ **Water bottles** and/or **hydration system** (2L, 3L in summer)
- ☐ **Waterproof pack cover/poncho**
- ☐ **Emergency blanket** (lightweight, waterproof, heat reflective)
- ☐ **Pocket/utility knife** (checked luggage)
- ☐ **Lighter** or **matches** (buy locally)
- ☐ **Toiletries** (list opposite)
- ☐ **Personal items** (list opposite)
- ☐ **First aid kit** (list opposite)
- ☐ **Insect Repellent**

Take the time to visit a quality outdoor gear shop to get fitted for a backpack that is comfortable and footwear that fits properly.

Footwear & Clothing

- ☐ **Footwear** (boots or trail runners)
- ☐ **Sandals** or flip-flops
- ☐ **Hiking socks** (3 pairs wool)
- ☐ **Sock liners** (1-2 pairs wicking)
- ☐ **Pants** (1-2 pairs quick-drying, zip-offs, or shorts)
- ☐ **Short-sleeved shirts**, tank tops (1-2)
- ☐ **Long-sleeved shirts** (1-2)
- ☐ **Light fleece** or jacket
- ☐ **Waterproof jacket** or poncho
- ☐ **Underwear** (3 pairs)
- ☐ **Sports bras** (2)
- ☐ **Bandana** or Buff
- ☐ **Swimsuit** (optional)
- ☐ **Warm hat***
- ☐ **Insulating jacket***
- ☐ **Long underwear** top/bottom*

*only necessary in cold seasons

Additional Gear (Optional)

- ☐ **Hiking poles**: Used correctly, poles can take up to 25% pressure off of your leg joints. Poles are great for stability, especially going up and down hills, and serve double-duty as a means to chase away dogs. Worthwhile for anyone with joint issues. Inexpensive poles can be purchased in Italy.
- ☐ **Sleeping mat**: A lightweight foam pad can come in handy for sitting on and for sleeping in a pinch.
- ☐ **Pillowcase**: Most dorm accommodations that don't provide linens have pillows but not pillow cases.
- ☐ **Stuff sacks** or (cloth bags with drawstrings) don't weigh much and keep you organized.
- ☐ **Reusable nylon grocery bag**: Comes in handy as a laundry bag, purse and grocery bag.
- ☐ **Clothespins** or safety pins and a cord/line for hanging laundry, recommended.
- ☐ **Travel cooking pot and utensils**: A small plastic bowl and lightweight travel utensils (balsa wood, plastic, or titanium) can be useful when preparing a lunch or dinner from food purchased from the grocery store.
- ☐ **Camping gear:** Lightweight tent (TarpTent) or bivy sack, camping stove, a pot and utensils, and extra water carrying capacity. (See Camping p. 23).

*For recommendations on specific brands and models, visit <u>caminoguidebook.com</u>.
***Decathlon** is a chain of outdoor gear retailers throughout Europe with stores in Florence, Foligno, and Rome.

TOILETRIES

Don't pack too much. Bring small refillable travel bottles of shampoo and conditioner <100mL/4oz. Refill and share.

- **Shampoo/conditioner** (100mL/4oz bottles)
- **Toothbrush** and **toothpaste** (travel sized)
- **Soap**, biodegradable bar or liquid, such as Dr. Bronner's™
- **Laundry detergent** (powder works well and weighs less) or 100mL/4 oz. bottle or solid bar
- **Toilet paper** or tissues
- **Deodorant** (optional, you will stink with or without it!)
- **Hand sanitizer** (optional)
- **Contact solution** (if necessary), replace at pharmacies

FIRST AID/MEDICAL KIT

Supplies are available in pharmacies throughout Italy. It's always best to be prepared with at least a few day's worth of each supply. Keep it light!

- Any **prescription medicine** you need
- Variety of **Band-Aids®/plasters, sterile gauze pads**
- Antiseptic towelettes or **wound disinfectant**
- **Antibiotic ointment**
- **Medical tape**
- **Elastic bandage** (such as ACE™)
- **Pain reliever/fever reducer** (such as acetaminophen or ibuprofen)
- **Antihistamine** (such as Benadryl®)
- **Anti-diarrheal** medicine: loperamide hydrochloride (Imodium®)
- **Blister treatment** (such as Moleskin or Compeed®)
- **Safety pins**
- **Baby powder** (helps with chafing)
- Small **scissors** and **tweezers**

PERSONAL ITEMS (OPTIONAL)

- **Travel wallet**: with passport/ID, health insurance card, pilgrim passport, money, credit cards, ATM card, etc. Stash an extra ATM card or wad of cash somewhere separate from your wallet.
- **Earplugs**: though packed dorms are not common on the way of St. Francis, high quality noise-canceling earplugs can help ensure a good night's sleep.
- **Mobile phone** and **charger** (see Phones and Internet p. 29)
- **Journal with pen/pencil**: highly recommended for remembering the details of each day, reflecting more fully on the experience and recording contact info of new friends.
- **Tablet or e-reader:** useful for checking email and for pleasure reading without carrying heavy books. Photos of family and home are good conversation starters.
- **Book** for pleasure reading (just bring one and trade when you're done)
- **Plug/currency converter** for any electrical appliances (European plugs run on 220V with two round prongs. In Italy a type C plug, as opposed to a type F plug, will suffice in most situations. Most electronics run on 110-220V, labeled on device, requiring only a plug converter and not a current converter.)
- **Zippered plastic bags or waterproof stuff sacks** for keeping electronics and other valuables dry and organized.

1-6 FLORENCE TO LA VERNA

Duomo di Firenze (center) and St. John's Baptistery (right)

Explore Florence, capital of the Renaissance, then journey through the rugged Apennines to La Verna, where St. Francis received the stigmata.

The Way of St. Francis starts in Florence, the capital of Tuscany, a lively tourist city renowned for its rich cultural history. After departing the city itself, the urban hustle and bustle gives way to peaceful pathways through the Arno River Valley to Pontassieve at the confluence of the Arno and Sieve Rivers. Pontassieve historically served as the gateway to northern and eastern Tuscany.

FLORENCE TO LA VERNA

From Pontassieve, demanding climbs into the Apennine Mountains follow old travel and trade routes from one small mountain village to the next. The mountains' moss-covered forests are some of the best preserved in the European continent and, especially in the Casentino Forest National Park, are home to a diverse range of flora and fauna, including rare animal species like wolves (now extinct in other countries in Europe).

Florence: Average monthly temperature range

Florence: Average monthly rainfall

Old and new coincide as the path passes through the Casentino Forest National Park. Modern hikers and mountain bikers on the park's robust network of mountain trails pass ancient hermitages like Camaldoli and La Verna, home to religious monks and ascetics throughout the centuries.

A hundred kilometers after Florence, the Way of St. Francis reaches the mountaintop Sanctuary of La Verna—a site favored by St. Francis for meditation and prayer and the location where Francis is said to have received the stigmata. La Verna is now one of the most important pilgrimage sites in Italy and a fitting, peaceful end to the difficult first leg of the journey to Rome.

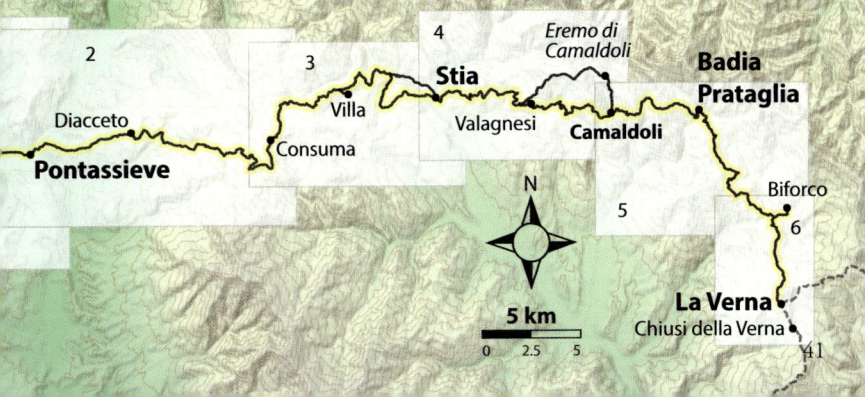

WAY OF ST. FRANCIS

0.0 Florence

1. **7 Santi Hostel** (€25/-/65): Mille 11, ☎0555048452, all year, was a convent
2. **My Friends Hostel** (€25+): Faenza 66, ☎3883403963, all year
3. **Archi Rossi** (€25/55/80): Faenza 94R, ☎055290804, all year
4. **Emerald Fields** (€25/-/85): Guelfa 59, ☎3272604930, all year
5. **Emerald Palace** (€35/-/100): dell'Ariento 2, ☎0554939819, all year
6. **Academy** (€40/-/85): Ricasoli 9, ☎0552398665, all year
7. **Wow Florence** (€25/-/100): Venezia 18/B, ☎055579603, all year
8. **Santa Monaca** (€24/-/60): Santa Monaca 6, ☎055268338, all year
9. **Tasso** (€30/40/70): Villani 15, ☎0550602087, all year
10. **Fiorita** (€55/75): Fiume 20, ☎055283189, all year
11. **Hotel Accademia** (€90/120): Faenza 7, ☎055293451, all year
12. **BB Floralia** (€75): S. Lorenzo 9, ☎055284972, all year
13. **Bavaria** (€60/75): Borgo degli Albizi 26, ☎0552340313, all year
14. **Tourist House Santa Croce** (€85/100): Ghibellina 95, ☎3206230628, all year
15. **Leonardo House** (€65): Trebbio 4, ☎3483409121, all year
16. **Palazzuolo** (€40/55): Palazzuolo 71, ☎055214611, all year
17. **Soggiorno Fortezza Fiorentina** (€60/70): Fratelli Rosselli 61, ☎3427530527, all year

Considered by many to be the birthplace of the Renaissance, **Florence** is one of the world's most beautiful cities and home to countless works of Renaissance art and architecture. Try to allow at least a full day or two to explore Florence.

Originally founded as an army encampment by Caesar on the narrowest part of the Arno River, Florence was a wealthy center of trade and culture by medieval times. As the cradle of the Renaissance, Florence is famous for the many artists and literary figures who resided there. The Florentine dialect used by Renaissance authors was adopted as the standard Italian language, and today the city's many museums house countless works of Renaissance art. (Of the top 15 most-visited art museums in Italy, two-thirds are in Florence).

💡 Florence (Firenze) is an incredibly popular tourist city. There are literally hundreds of lodging options in the city. We list select accommodations; many others are available via online booking sites.

Florence's idyllic historic center was made a UNESCO World Heritage Site in 1982. Here the Santa Maria del Fiore Cathedral, known as the **Duomo di Firenze** (*Duomo* is the Italian word for a church built to serve as a cathedral), rises prominently out of the city center. Begun in 1296, the Duomo was finished in 1436. The cathedral's dome—designed by Brunelleschi, the father of Renaissance Architecture—is still the largest brick and mortar dome in the world. The cathedral entrance is on the west side of the complex.

WAY OF ST. FRANCIS

To climb the 463 steps to explore the dome, visitors must enter on the north side of the cathedral. Giotto's Bell Tower sits just to the south of the Duomo. A long climb to the top of the bell tower (414 steps) yields impressive views of the city. St. John's Baptistery, one of the oldest religious buildings in Florence (dating to 1059), sits across from the main cathedral doors. The Baptistery is renowned for its three sets of bronze doors by Pisano and Ghiberti. The eastern doors, famously called the "Gates of Paradise" by Michelangelo, were created by Ghiberti as part of a commission celebrating the end of the Black Death in Florence.

Of Florence's many art museums, the most famous are the **Uffizi and Accademia Galleries**. Adjacent to the Piazza della Signoria, the Uffizi Gallery is one of the largest and best known in the world and houses a collection of priceless Renaissance artwork, including works by Michelangelo, Raphael, and Botticelli, among many others. On the northern edge of the city center, the Accademia Gallery is home to **Michelangelo's David**. Both galleries are very popular attractions, so be sure to buy tickets in advance (€16 each + €4 advance booking fee, closed Mondays, tickets at www.uffizi.it and galleriaaccademiafirenze.beniculturali.it).

Just west of the Uffizi Gallery, the **Ponte Vecchio** ("Old Bridge") leads over the Arno River, the only bridge in Florence left intact by the retreating German Nazi Army (due to its architectural significance).

Pitti Palace, the largest museum complex in Florence, is located not far from Ponte Vecchio (€16 plus €3 for advance booking, early morning tickets are half price, available at www.uffizi.it). Originally the home of a Florentine banker named Luca Pitti, the palace was later purchased by the powerful Medici family and served as the chief residence of Tuscany's ruling families.

☼ Though there is a ticket office on the south side of the Duomo complex, it's advisable to buy tickets to the various Duomo sites before arriving in Florence; to guarantee your entrance to see Brunelleschi's Dome, you need to reserve a visit time in advance. To purchase tickets and reserve a time to visit the dome, visit museumflorence.com.

An all-inclusive ticket to visit all the Duomo sites (Cathedral, Brunelleschi's Dome, Giotto's Bell Tower, Museo dell'Opera del Duomo, and Crypt of Santa Reparata) costs €30.

FLORENCE TO LA VERNA

Southeast of the Duomo stands the **Santa Croce Basilica**, the largest Franciscan church in the world. According to legend, St. Francis founded Santa Croce himself, though construction of the current building (built over an existing structure) began in 1294. Traditionally the burial place for prominent Florentines, Santa Croce holds the remains of many famous Italians, including Michelangelo, Galileo, and Machiavelli. Many of Santa Croce's sixteen chapels are decorated with frescoes by Giotti, and Franciscan relics are kept in an adjacent convent (€8, ☉Mon-Sat 9:30am-5:30pm, Sun 2-5:30). The bookshop offers a credential stamp.

Beyond Florence's major sites, you can spend hours simply exploring Florence's beautiful narrow streets. If you have the time, venture across the Ponte Vecchio and head southeast, soon following clear signage up a long climb to the **Piazzale Michelangelo overlook**—views are especially nice at sunset.

In Florence, you're sure to eat well as traditional Florentine cuisine grows from a history of hearty Tuscan peasant eating. In local restaurants you might find tripe (*trippa*), sliced bread with chicken liver pâté (*crostini toscani*), or large T-bone steaks (*bistecca alla fiorentina*).

Traditional saltless Tuscan bread is common in soups, such as a vegetable and bread soup (*ribollita*) or bread and tomato soup (*pappa al pomodoro*).

For quick and easy street fare, **All'antico Vinaio** serves some of the best *panini* (sandwiches) in all of Italy.

Entrance way to visit Brunelleschi's Dome

1

FLORENCE TO PONTASSIEVE

18.9km (11.8mi)
▲ 460m / ▼ 410m

⏲ 5.5-7 Hours
Difficulty: 🟧🟧⬜

P 59%, 11.2km
U 41%, 7.7km

D H **Lodging:**
Florence 0.0km
San Jacopo 7.0km
Compiobbi/Ellera 9.km, +1.0km
Pontassieve 18.7km
Diacceto 24.6km
Ferrano 27.4km

🕆 **Waymarking:**
From Florence, as is common through cities, waymarking can be sparse. Look out for Via di Francesco in Toscana stickers and markers, as well as blue arrows and yellow tau symbols.

Leave Florence, and follow the Arno River to Pontassieve, gateway to the Apennines.

The first day from Florence is one of the few relatively flat days on the way to Rome—a good day to get your legs under you before the climbing starts in earnest! From Santa Croce, the route follows a pedestrian and bike path along the Arno River until San Jacopo al Girone. Waymarking is sparse, but navigation along the path is easy. Short climbs from San Jacopo al Girone and again from Compiobbi detour around busier roads in the valley. The climbs offer pleasant views of the Arno River Valley. From Sieci, a mix of rural gravel and

View of Florence from Piazzale Michelangelo

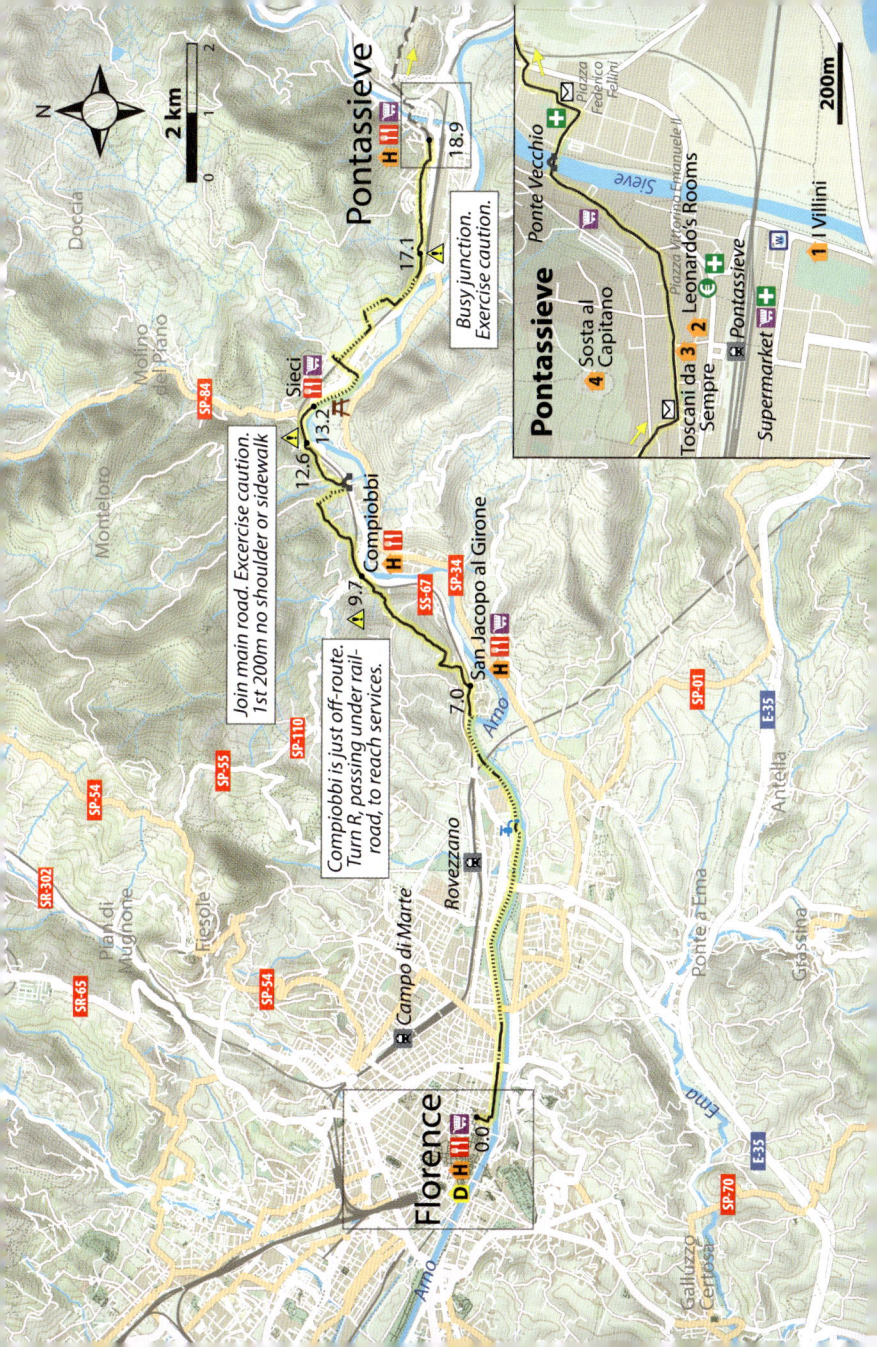

WAY OF ST. FRANCIS

paved roads, as well as one short hiking path, lead to the edge of Pontassieve, where busier roads lead into town.

☼ If you plan to get your credential at St. James Episcopal Church or a stamp at Santa Croce, do so the day before your departure so that you can get an early start as the churches open at 🕘9am and 9:30am respectively.

7.0 San Jacopo al Girone

☼ The small grocery store and shaded bench at the bus stop offer a pleasant spot for a break or lunch. The next store on route is 6.2km ahead in Sieci. On the climb out of San Jacopo al Girone, the route passes two agriturismi:

8.0 Poggiopiano (€90): , Bassi 13, 0556593020/3286767774

8.3 Il Viaio (€90): , Bassi 11, 0556594071

9.7 Compiobbi/Ellera
, café +90m, +1.0km
BB Eridu (€90): , Renato Murri 20a, 3398545141 , prices vary

⚠ The official route skirts the edge of Compiobbi. To reach the café and restaurant in town (or to continue to accommodation in Ellera), turn right, following a larger paved road under the railroad tracks (+90m to services in Compiobbi, +1.0km to accommodation in Ellera).

⚠ Just before Sieci, the route returns to the valley and follows a busy paved road into town. For the first 200m there is no sidewalk. Walk on the left side of the road and exercise extreme caution!

☼ At the entrance to Sieci, continue right onto an unpaved walking path along the Arno River. Shaded tables along the path offer a nice picnic spot. Most services in town are just off route along the main paved road through the center of town.

Leaving Florence along a pathway on the Arno River

FLORENCE TO PONTASSIEVE

When the path ends, turn left following a paved road through a major traffic circle and under the railroad tracks before doubling back R onto a gravel road.

18.7 Pontassieve

1. **BB I Villini** (€32/48): , Armando Diaz 28, 0558368140, all year, budget friendly, accustomed to pilgrims
2. **Leonardo's Rooms** (€45): , Piave 7, 360923824, accustomed to pilgrims, good breakfast for €5
3. **Toscani da Sempre** (€60/70): , Monzecchi 13/15, 3398808658
4. **Sosta al Capitano** (€80/100): , Capitano 18, 3471792675

Pontassieve occupies a strategic location at the confluence of the Sieve and Arno Rivers. Originally called Castel Sant'Angelo after the castle that the city of Florence had built there, the town later obtained the name Pontassieve (literally "Sieve Bridge") from the bridge erected over the Sieve River, which allowed easier access to regions north and east of Florence. The current **Medici Bridge** was built in the 16th century after floods destroyed the older stone bridge. It was restored in 1788 and then again after damage during WWII.

In the 18th century, new roads opened Florence to Casentino and Emilia via Pontassieve. In 1859, the construction of the Florence-Rome railway turned Pontassieve into an important rail junction and industrial center. Due to its importance as a rail hub, the town was bombed repeatedly by Allied planes during WWII. Pontassieve has since been reconstructed, with special attention paid to maintaining the medieval character of the town center.

Basilica di Santa Croce

2

PONTASSIEVE TO CONSUMA

17.3km (10.7mi)
▲ 1159m / ▼ 263m

⏱ **7-9 Hours**
Difficulty: ▬ ▪ ▪

🅿 61%, 10.6km
🆄 29%, 6.7km

D H Lodging:
Diacetto 5.9km
Ferrano 9.4km
Consuma 17.3km
Villa 24.2

✝ **Waymarking:**
Yellow/blue painted stripes, Via di Francesco in Toscana marks, and red/white CAI blazes (see map for specific route numbers).

Passing Il Castello di Ferrano at the entrance to Ferrano

Climb into the Apennines, detour to visit the Santa Maria a Ferrano church, arrive in Consuma, a quaint hamlet on an important mountain pass.

The route climbs steadily upward today, gaining nearly 1200m over 17km, first through rural mountain villages, then through more remote mountain forests. Most of the climbing is on non-technical gravel and paved roads, but between 10.5km and 15.1km, CAI route 11 is steep and rocky in places. Be sure to stock up on food and water in Diacetto, as it is the last town with services before Consuma, which is another 11.4km and 750m of climbing away.

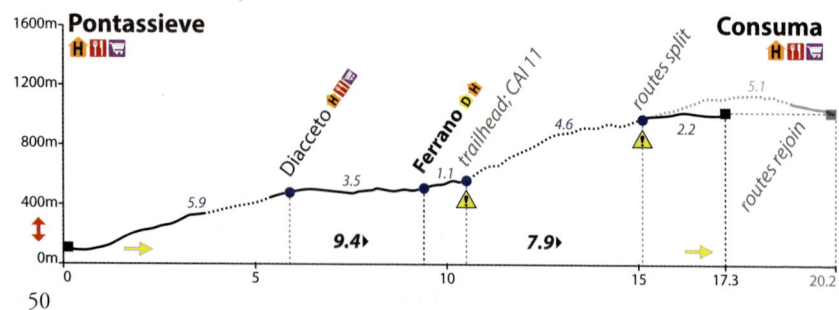

WAY OF ST. FRANCIS

☀ There are several intermediate accommodations along this stage, but since they're fairly remote, be sure to confirm reservations and meal plans in advance.

☀ From Pontassieve's central piazza, go east through the Old City gates and continue on Via Ghiberti across the Medici Bridge (Ponte Mediceo). On the other side of the Sieve River, take the second left onto Via Erice Bettini. Continue through Piazza Federico Fellini. At the far end of the piazza, turn right, cross the main road, and turn left onto a small paved road (Via del Tirolo), now climbing in earnest. Waymarking is good from here.

5.9 Diaccio 🏠🍴🛒 ⚠ Last services before Consuma.
1. 🏠 **Locanda Tinti** (€70/80/110 🛏): 📶⚡, Casentinese 65 📞0558327007 ✉, in town center
2. 🏠 **Altro Pianeta** (€40/60 🛏): 🍴📶⚡, Villini 2B 📞3384980282/3388313498 ✉, 🕒Apr-Oct
3. 🏠 **Podere Castellare** (€100+ 🛏): 🛁🍴📶⚡🚌 Case Spares 12, 📞0558326082 ✉, fancy hilltop agriturismo with rooms and apartments

9.4 Ferrano 🏠🏠
🏠 **Santa Maria a Ferrano** (par, 🛏5+, €20 🛏): 🍴⚡, 📞3386901122/0550456959 ✉, santamariaferrano@gmail.com, beautiful location with welcoming hosts, €5 linens, €10 dinner, hosts groups but keeps beds for pilgrims; must contact in advance
🏠 **Il Castello di Ferrano** (€90): 🛁📶⚡🚌, La Noce 23, 📞3381264968/3345996786 ✉, tours for a fee (call for details)

☀ Even if not staying at Santa Maria a Ferrano, the 1.0km climb to the church is worth the detour. The peaceful location, beautiful church, and hillside views make a nice spot for a break or lunch.

Ferrano is a picturesque hillside village. Il Castello di Ferrano is located at the entrance to the village. On the far end of the village, a 1.0km detour uphill leads to the **Santa Maria Church**. The Romanesque church is around 1,000 years old, with the first documents mentioning the church dating to 1080. Inside the church, a 15th-century fresco shows Mary nursing Jesus. Today the church is used for liturgy and prayer. In 1980, a German sculptor bought the building, restoring it and using the location for spiritual and art retreats. Santa Maria a Ferrano is now associated with the Convocation of Episcopal Churches in Europe and is managed by Rev. Thomas Müller. He and his wife, Paolo, host pilgrims in a building not far from the church.

Santa Maria a Ferrano

PONTASSIEVE TO CONSUMA

⚠ At 15.1km, after the hardest of the climb on CAI 11, reach an asphalt road. Here you have two route options.

❶ ⭐ The shortest option turns left, initially following the paved road toward Consuma.

❷ A longer option goes straight across the paved road onto a gravel road following signs for CAI 60 toward Consuma. This option adds 2.9km and some additional climbing, but it includes more views and less distance on paved roads.

20.2 Consuma 🏨🍴🛒➕🚌

1. 🏨 ⭐ **San Domenico** (€35/45 🛏): 📷 📶, ☎3471993121, elenac71@yahoo.it, triple rooms €60, run by Luca and Elena, both heavily involved in the work of the Via di Francesco in Toscana
2. 🏨 **Miramonti** (€45/66 🛏): 🍴📶◉, Casentinese 61, ☎0558306413, 🕐all year

Passo della Consuma (Consuma Pass, 1,050m) was the favored place to cross the Apennine Mountains on the historical Casentino to Pontassieve route. The little village of Consuma was born as a waystation for travelers passing through. The village's chapel (designed by architect Pare Franci) was built in 1932 over the remains of a 16th-century church.

Arlotto Mainari—better known as Pievano Arlotto (Parish Priest Arlotto)—was a 14th-century Catholic priest famous for his mischievous pranks and bold wit. His hijinks were a favorite subject in Renaissance folk literature, and he was further immortalized by a 17th-century painting by Volterrano (*Una burla del Pievano Arlotto/A Joke by the Parish Priest Arlotto*, now at the Palazzo Pitti gallery in Florence). In a well-known legend, Pievano Arlotto was traveling in heavy rain from Casentino to Florence when he stopped at a tavern in Consuma. Because of the weather, the tavern was full, and all of the seats by the fire were occupied. Arlotto—appearing to converse with the proprietor in confidence, but speaking at a volume clearly audible to the other tavern guests—lamented that he had lost a pouch containing a considerable sum of money along the side of the road when he stopped to relieve himself. Several of the more "altruistic" guests "generously" set out into the rain to search for his lost money. Arlotto promptly settled down in the now-free seats by the warm fire, while the tavern owner, taking pity on Arlotto, offered him a free meal.

💡 The extremely hardy hiker might consider continuing another 7.5km past Consuma to the highly-recommended Rifugio San Jacopo in Villa.

Conversely, staying in the pleasant pilgrim accommodations of Santa Maria (Ferrano) and Rifugio San Jacopo (Villa), allows walking to Stia in three shorter days:

1. Pontassieve to Ferrano, 11.4km
2. Ferrano to Villa, 14.6km
3. Villa to Stia, 11.3km

CONSUMA TO STIA

17.2km (10.8mi)
▲ 570m / ▼ 1140m

⏱ 5.5-7 Hours
DIFFICULTY: ▰▰▱

P 24%, 4.1km
U 76%, 13.1km

D H Lodging:
Il Gualdo 2.2km, +480m
Villa 6.9km, +660m
<u>Stia 17.2km</u>
Lonanno 22.4km
Valagnesi 25.8km
Asqua 29.1km (on main route, CAI 72)

⚑ Waymarking:
Via di Francesco in Toscana markers, yellow/blue painted stripes, as well as red/white CAI blazes (00) in the direction of "Stia."

Follow forested ridgelines to Castel Castagnaio before descending to Stia, a pleasant village on the headwaters of the Arno.

☼ The first half of the day follows hiking paths along forested ridgelines and valleys. The first few kilometers along the ridge from Passo della Consuma are poorly marked, but the 4x4 trek along the ridge is easy to follow. After Il Gualdo, the hiking path passes through a tight valley and dense undergrowth, though the way is well marked. After a steep climb to another

View of Castel Castagnaio and the Casentino Valley

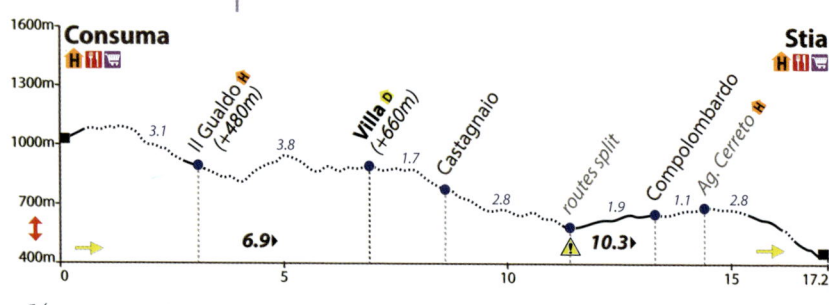

WAY OF ST. FRANCIS

⚠ There are no resupply points between Consuma and Stia, so carry your food and water for the day. The public fountain in Villa is +660m meters off route, roughly ⅓ of the way through the day. If you choose to refill here, continue on the paved road to reconnect with the official route at Castel Castagnaio without backtracking.

ridge, the way opens up a bit, eventually offering spectacular views of Castel Castagnaio and the surrounding mountains. The day's final kilometers roll through pleasant countryside before descending steeply to Stia in the Casentino Valley.

⚠ Waymarking is sparse along the ridge after leaving Consuma before reaching Il Gualdo: follow the ridgeline along a clear dirt road then rough 4x4 track. At points, other 4x4 tracks leave the ridge to the right and left—do not leave the ridge left or right. After descending a rocky 4x4 track to a saddle at a junction of several larger dirt roads at 2.2km, stay straight across the dirt road. Follow clear signs for "Il Gualdo" and "Stia" along a dirt path going downhill. From here, waymarking is better.

To reach the Il Gualdo Horse Farm, turn right at the junction at 2.2km, following the gravel road downhill. Ahead the road turns into rough asphalt. The accommodation is +480m from the junction.

2.2 🛏 **BB Il Gualdo** (€75): 🍴📶⊙, Gualdo 46, ☎3314645799/0575554057, horse farm, +480m

Country roads between Campolombardo and Stia

CONSUMA TO STIA   3

💡 At 6.9km, a clearly marked detour to
⭐Rifugio San Jacopo descends from the ridgeline to the tiny hamlet of Villa. From Villa, you can reconnect to the official Way of St. Francis route by continuing on the paved road nearly the whole way to Castel Castagnaio.

6.9 Villa, D, +660m

⭐ **D Rifugio San Jacopo** (📞6, 25/40 🛏):
🍴 W 📶 ⊙, 📱3471993121 📝, 🕐Apr-Oct,
elenac71@yahoo.it, six twin beds in three rooms, meals by donation, hospitable family
(same owners as San Domenico in Consuma)

💡 At 8.6km, reach a paved road with the community of Castagnaio to the left. The official route turns right following the paved road before soon making a left down a rocky 4x4 track. At the paved road, a short detour left through the village brings you to **Castel Castagnaio**. The castle, dating back to 1050, was a strategic outpost overlooking the Casentino Valley and ancient routes between Casentino and Florence. A pilgrim's hospital (hostel) was located near the castle, and the 16th/17th-century St. Bartolomeo Church sits at the edge of the castle remains.

Yellow tau and CAI waymarking between Consuma and Villa

💡 At 11.4km, there are two ways to Stia.

❶⭐ Option 1 winds along the mountainside through farmland and small villages before descending steeply to Stia's center. While longer than the second way, this route has more walking on unpaved surfaces and avoids walking on the Landa-Stia provincial highway into Stia.

❷ Option 2 is more direct, shaving 2.6km from the day's total distance. However, there is more walking on a busier, less-safe paved road.

WAY OF ST. FRANCIS

Casentino Valley on the descent to Stia

17.2 Stia

1. **Borgo Vecchio** (€35/50): Borgo Vecchio 36, ©3394978807/3384340194, lacasinadiborgovecchio@virgilio.it, vacation apartment with double rooms and shared kitchen
2. **La Piazza UNO e DUE** (€45): Piazza Tanucci 24, ©3357242405, olgafiorini1947@gmail.com
3. **BB La Guardia** (€65): Piazza Tanucci 59, ©3470180074, all year, overflow in separate vacation apartment on Piazza Tanucci
4. **Albergo Falterona** (€60/90): Piazza Tanucci 85, ©0575583545
5. **Brilli** (€100): Adamo Ricci 1, ©0575583108, all year
6. **Canto alla Rana** (€35/60): Campo Sportivo 11, ©0575583661/3395355984

CONSUMA TO STIA

Stia, often called the "source of the Arno," is the first village in the upper Arno watershed and is located on the confluence of the Arno and Staggia Rivers. Stia grew up as a market town below the Guidi family castle in Porciano. Nestled in the fertile Casentino Valley, Stia prospered along with other towns in the area.

During the Medici period, timber exports were important for shipbuilding, and later wool was an important export. Wool was first produced by nuns and monks in the area, but by the industrial revolution, factories employing over 500 works produced 700,000 meters of cloth annually. The **Museo dell'Arte della Lana** on the northern edge of town documents the history of wool production in Stia (€5, hours vary seasonally: check museodellalana.it/en for current info). Today the town is a vacation hub for tourists visiting **Casentino Forest National Park**.

The Way of St. Francis enters the main square (Piazza Tanucci, named after the Italian statesman Benardo Tannucci) through the Vicolo San Francesco, passing under a fresco of St. Francis. Just south of the fresco, in the main square, is the **Santa Maria Assunta Church**, which was commissioned in the 12th century by Guidi counts. The church's facade was demolished in 1776 and rebuilt in its current Baroque style, but the interior contains Gothic and Romanesque features dating back centuries. The **Parco del Palagio Fiorentino** has a contemporary art museum with 200+ pieces of art (sculptures, paintings, and drawings).

Inside the Santa Maria Assunta Church in Stia

4

STIA TO CAMALDOLI

16.1km (10.1mi)
▲ 1040m / ▼ 670m

🕐 **5.5-7 Hours**
Difficulty: ▬ ◼ ◼

🅿 42%, 6.8km
🆄 58%, 9.3km

D H Lodging:
Lonnano 5.2km
Valagnesi 8.6km
Asqua 11.9km (on main route, CAI 72)
Camaldoli 16.1km
Badia Prataglia 24.1km

✝ **Waymarking:**
VF in Toscana markers, CAI 72 all the way to Camaldoli.
❷ to Camaldoli Hermitage: see map for CAI route numbers after split.

Mountain views from the Camaldoli Hermitage

Explore the Casentino Forest, climb to the Camaldoli Monastery and its community dating to the 11th century.

💡 The day begins with a long climb out of the Casentino Valley following CAI 72 through several mountain villages. A technical section of hiking trail with exposed drops between Lonnano and Casalino requires care. ⚠ Shortly after Casalino, the routes split—one option going directly to Camaldoli via CAI 72, the other arriving at Camaldoli after a visit to the Eremo Camaldoli (hermitage). Both options are lovely, passing through the old growth forests of the Casentino Forest National Park.

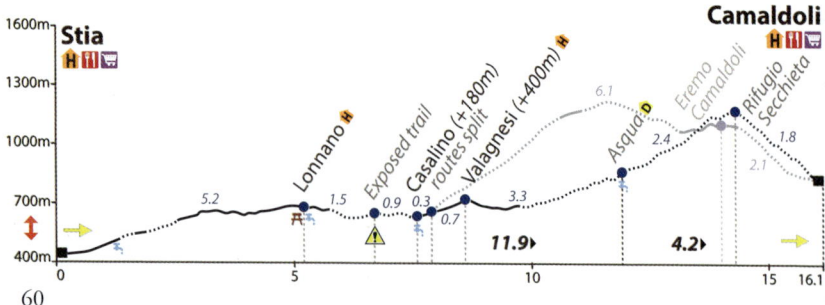

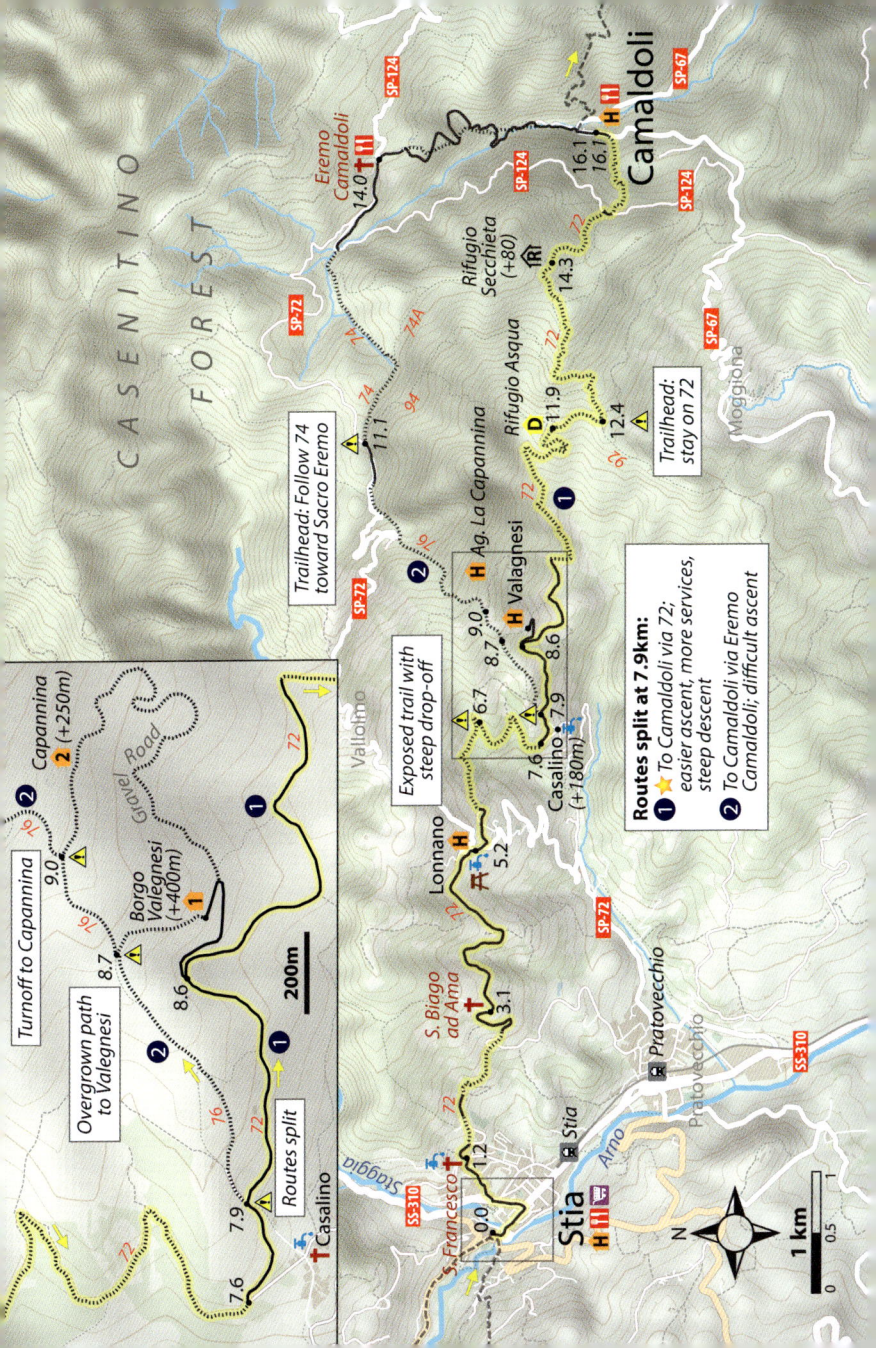

4 WAY OF ST. FRANCIS

The ascent from Stia

Country tracks on the outskirts of Lonnano

💡 There are no resupply points between Consuma and Camaldoli (and no grocery store in Camaldoli, though there are restaurants and cafes), so carry plenty of food and water. Fountains in Lonnano and Casalino and outside Rifugio Asqua allow for water refill periodically.

💡 If you're very ambitious (and very fit), you can add another 8.0km and 500m+ of climbing to reach Badia Prataglia (Stage 5), where there are more accommodations and other services. This leaves roughly 17.0km to La Verna the following day, shaving a day from your overall itinerary.

Shortly after Casalino, the Way of St. Francis enters the **Casentino Forest National Park** and largely remains within the park boundaries until Chiusi della Verna. The park covers 368 square kilometers along the border of the regions of Tuscany and Emilia-Romagna. Old-growth forests consisting of beech, maple, oak, and pine trees cover the majority of the park, which is home to a wide range of wildlife, including Apennine wolves, boar, deer, foxes, eagles, and owls, among others. Criss-crossed by a well-marked network of CAI routes, the park is also popular with hikers, trail runners, and mountain bikers.

⛱ The picnic table and fountain at the sports center (*centro sportivo*) in Lonnano make a nice break spot.

5.2 Lonnano 🏨

🏨 **La Casina di Lonnano:** 🅁, Casato 43, ☎3407418991, spacious garden with view, email for pricing: mcparigi@gmail.com

STIA TO CAMALDOLI

☀ At 7.6km, there is a paved road at a switchback after a section of technical trail. The official route continues uphill on the paved road. A short detour downhill brings you to Casalino, where there is a water fountain across from the church.

⚠ At 7.9km, the route splits at a junction marked by several trail signs.

❶★ The official route continues to follow CAI 72 all the way to Camaldoli. This route continues to Rifugio Asqua following a mix of paved and gravel roads with good walking surfaces. Shortly after Rifugio Asqua at 12.4km, the route turns left, following hiking trails marked CAI 72 to Camaldoli. There are several trail junctions, so keep a sharp eye out for CAI 72 markers toward Camaldoli. The final descent to Camaldoli is quite steep.

❷ From the 7.9km junction, the second option ascends steeply—first for a short distances on a gravel double track, then a rocky path—following CAI 76 and signs saying *"La Via dei Legni Giogo Secchieta."* Near the top of the climb, you reach a paved road (SP 72), which you follow uphill to a pass and three-way trail junction. Here, take the second right, following CAI 74 toward "Sacro Eremo." Ahead stay left on CAI 74 toward "Sacro Eremo" while 74a goes straight toward "Cassotto Secchieta" (a primitive rifugio). Descend along a valley to a paved road, which you follow to the Camaldoli Hermitage (Sacro Eremo or Eremo di Camaldoli). From the Camaldoli Hermitage you can follow red/white GR blazes along a hiking path directly to Camaldoli, but following the paved road for this descent is much easier on the knees.

The route options are equal in distance and similar in total ascent. The first option follows slightly easier trail surfaces and is closer to people and car access; as such, it's the route we recommend. However, if you want to visit the more ascetic Camaldoli Hermitage (p. 65), take the second option.

WAY OF ST. FRANCIS

8.6 Valagnesi
1. **BB Borgo Valagnesi** (€45/60), Valagnesi 27, 0575509038/3335278965
2. **Podere Capannin** (€50), 3804520062, ivanagrofi@gmail.com, €5 for linens, country home in peaceful mountainside location, cost includes home-cooked dinner and breakfast, best accessed from route option 2 (clear signs)

11.9 Rifugio Asqua (rif, 25, €35), Asqua 12, 3395644292/3277176235, Mar-Oct (call for availability in off season), dinner €15, peaceful location

16.1 Camaldoli
Foresteria di Camaldoli (par, €45/55), 0575556013, all year, dinner €10
Albergo/Ristorante Camaldoli di Tassini (€50/65), Camaldoli 11, 0575556019
Locanda dei Baroni (€50/65), Camaldoli 5, 0575556015
Camping Camaldoli (€45/50 for bungalows), €20 for rental tent & mattress Camaldoli 12, 0575556202, campingcamaldoli@itrebaroni.it, campingcamaldoli.it

The **Benedictine monastic community at Camaldoli** was formed in the early 11th century by St. Romuald and strictly follows the rule of St. Benedict. Located high in the Casentino Forest, the community is split between an upper hermitage and lower monastery, which represent two important dimensions of monastic life: solitude and communal life. The monastery is separated from the hermitage by a steep 3km climb.

The Camaldoli community occupies land donated by a wealthy patron, Count Maldolo, and the name Camaldoli may derive from an appropriation of *Campo Malduli* (literally, "Madolo's field"). The Camaldoli Hermitage was built from scratch, while the monastery (originally known as Fontebuono for the spring that supplied water to the monastery) was built upon one of the Count's hunting residences.

The monks in Camaldoli have long enjoyed a symbiotic relationship with the surrounding forest. Early on, monks introduced fir trees into the forest to take advantage of its lumber, and the community has long produced herbal remedies, sold in traditional pharmacies at both the hermitage and

The fountain outside Rifugio Asqua is a good place to refill water.

Outside the Camaldoli Hermitage

STIA TO CAMALDOLI

monastery, using resources from the forest. Cognizant of the value of the surrounding forest, the Camaldoli monks have long sought to protect it, even developing a full code of forest preservation in 1520.

In lower Camaldoli, the monastery church, pharmacy, and *foresteria* (guesthouse) are regularly open to visitors. A tourist info office has very abbreviated hours (◷10am-1pm, weekends and holidays, though hours change by season). Other private cafes, restaurants, and guesthouses operate in the vicinity of the monastery. Several buses run daily from lower Camaldoli to Bibbiena and Poppi. The **Camaldoli Hermitage** (Eremo di Camaldoli, 2.1km above Camaldoli) is more secluded and less touristy. To preserve the solitude of the hermits there, guests are only allowed to enter at pre-scheduled times (◷every ½ hour from 10am-12:30pm and again every ½ hour from 2-5:30pm, though hours may vary seasonally) in the company of a guide (suggested donation €1 a person). A small cafe and pharmacy are open on the outside of the hermitage. For more information on the hermitage contact: eremo@camaldoli.it or ☏0575556021.

Arriving in Camaldoli

5 CAMALDOLI TO BIFORCO

20.1km (12.6mi)
▲ 1230m / ▼ 1380m

⏱ 7-9 Hours
Difficulty: ▬ ▬

P 12%, 2.3km
U 88%, 17.8km

D H Lodging:
Badia P. 8.0km
C. Santicchio 16km
Biforco 20.1km
La Verna 27.4km

✝ Waymarking:
Via di Francesco in Toscana, CAI 72 (Camaldoli-B. Prataglia), CAI 73 (B. Prataglia-Frassineta), CAI 70 (Frassineta-Rimbocchi), intermittent tau markers

Badia Prataglia from the Fonte del Pellegrino

Trek through forested mountains, visit Badia Prataglia's church and arboretum, arrive to the charming village of Biforco.

💡 Another tough day begins with a long forested climb followed by an equally-long descent along beautiful hiking trails to Badia Prataglia, a picturesque tourist town nestled on the mountainside. From Badia Prataglia, more strenuous alpine hiking brings you via Frassineta to Rimbocchi, where a short detour from the main Way of St. Francis route takes you to the quaint village of Biforco. Conversely, you could walk a very short day to Badia Prataglia (8.0km), where accommodations and services are more plentiful.

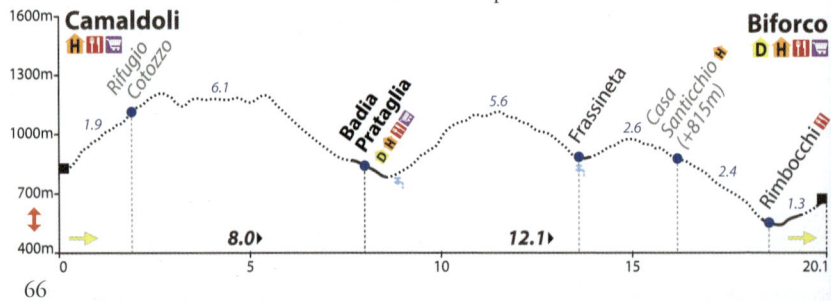

WAY OF ST. FRANCIS

Climbing mountain trails from Badia Prataglia

About 25km and 1,900m of climbing separate Camaldoli from La Verna. We advise against attempting this in one day, due to the difficulty of the terrain. Our itinerary proposes a long (20.1km) challenging day to Biforco (1.3km off route), followed by a more manageable short day (still with significant climbing) to La Verna (7.3km). The short day into La Verna allows plenty of time to explore the sanctuary.

Conversely, you could walk a very short day to Badia Prataglia (8.0km) with its more plentiful accommodations and amenities, followed by a longer day to La Verna (16.8km) with over 1,100m of climbing. This avoids the detour to Biforco but, in turn, means a longer arrival day to La Verna.

Roman-era crypt in Santa Maria Assunta church in Badia Prataglia

Casa Santicchio (16.2km after Camaldoli) offers another intermediate accommodation with good reviews, but be sure to call in advance to make reservations if you plan to stay there as there are no other services in the vicinity.

CAMALDOLI TO BIFORCO — 5

8.0 Badia Prataglia

1. **Casanova** (rif, €65, €40): Casanova 3, ☏3665849069, all year, mountain lodge/hostel on approach to town, prices per person in rooms of 2 or 4, dinner €10
2. **Bosco Verde** (€45/60): Via Nazionale 8/10, ☏0575559017, Apr-Oct
3. **La Foresta** (€45/65): Via Nazionale 13, ☏0575559009, all year, open weekends (weekdays with advance notice)
4. **Giardino** (€40/60): Via Nazionale 15, ☏0575559016, all year, a bit run down, but pleasant
5. **Residence Gloria** (€35): Via Nazionale 47/B, ☏0575559019/3421482953, barvittoria56@gmail.com, rooms in vacation apartment, check-in at Café/Bar Vittoria, good reviews

💡 Stock up on food in Badia Prataglia. While the tiny café/bar in Biforco sells panini and very basic food, Badia Prataglia has the only true grocery store between Stia and Chiusi della Verna.

Badia Prataglia—literally, "Abbey in the meadows"—takes its name from the Benedictine monastery established here in the late 10th/early 11th century. As the monastery grew more important, feuding began with the Badia Prataglia monastery under the jurisdiction of the monastery in Camaldoli. Today the parish church of Santa Maria Assunta and St. Bartholomew is all that remains of the monastery. Particularly noteworthy is a crypt within the church that dates back to Roman times.

Long-sustained by its lumber industry, Badia Prataglia is still known for its artisanal woodworking. Today, situated high in the Casentino Forest, Badia Prataglia's economy is based primarily on tourism. Various vacation homes and hotels are scattered throughout the town serving seasonal residents and tourists.

The **Carlo Siemoni Arboretum and Museum** are located behind the church. Established in 1846 and named after Karl Simon, the

Views on the approach to Badia Prataglia

German forestry engineer who helped rehabilitate and manage the Casentino Forest, the arboretum is the oldest in Italy and contains 139 species of trees. The museum is open regularly during the day but hours change seasonally.

The Casentino Forest National Park Tourist Office offers information about the park and sells high-quality hiking maps of the surrounding area. Open hours are limited and change seasonally, but the office is generally open Fridays and weekends.

At 16.2km, a well-marked detour following CAI 70A leads to Casa Santicchio. Another marked route following a gravel road returns to CAI 70 without backtracking.

16.2 H **Casa Santicchio** (€50/65): 🍴🛜⊙,
📞05751787586, info@santicchio.org,
beautiful hillside location, sauna and hot/cold tub,
good reviews, +815m

🚰 Shortly after passing Frassineta's church to the left at 13.6km, there is a water fountain just off route to the left.

Church in Frassineta

💡 At 18.6km, Rimbocchi has a small restaurant, but don't count on it being open. At 18.8km, on the south side of Rimbocchi, the official Way of St. Francis route reaches a T, continues straight across the paved road following CAI 53, and immediately crosses a stream (no bridge). For much of the year, you can walk across on rocks without getting your feet wet, but in wetter periods (seasons with lots of rain and/or snow melt), a dry crossing may be impossible. ⚠ If you're worried about the stream crossing, a longer, but slightly easier, detour from the T intersection includes a bridge crossing of the stream. (See Stage 6, p. 72, for more.)

CAMALDOLI TO BIFORCO 5

⚠ To go to Biforco, turn left at the T intersection, leaving the official Way of St. Francis route and staying on the main paved road to the next left. There, you go left, uphill, following clear signs for Biforco. You can either follow the paved road all the way to town, or take periodic shortcuts on marked, unpaved paths.

20.1 Biforco D H 🍴🛒

D Locanda Nonna Menica (€20, €28): 🛏, ☏3319667967, rossana.mazzieri@gmail.com, ⊙all year, shared rooms in home with kitchen, pleasant, pilgrim oriented, near bar

H BB da Silva (€40/60): 🛏🍴 W 📶 ⊙, ☏3662283864, silviafranci77@gmail.com, ⊙all year, beautiful country home with very hospitable owner, cost is €10 less without linens

Biforco is a very simple town with few services (the café/bar is the only shop in town and only sells panini and very basic food), but it's very welcoming. A number of different long-distance hiking routes pass through the area, and the locals happily accommodate pilgrims.

Views on the descent to Rimbocchi

BIFORCO TO LA VERNA

7.3km (4.6mi)
▲ 720m / ▼ 260m

⏱ 3-4.5 Hours
Difficulty: ▰▰▱

P 13%, 0.9km
U 87%, 6.4km

D H Lodging:
La Verna 7.3km
Pieve S.S. 22.3km (7)
Chiusi 8.6km (7A)
Caprese 24.3km (7A)

⚑ Waymarking:
VF in Toscana markers, CAI 53 from Rimbocchi to La Verna. Intermittent yellow tau markers. Possible to take CAI 54 for longer, but slightly easier, approach to La Verna (see map: includes a bridge, avoiding stream crossing).

Climb high, amble through an enchanting beech forest on your way to La Verna, a favorite retreat of St. Francis.

💡 A short day, but the climb from Rimbocchi to La Verna is possibly the hardest of the entire route. Take your time and enjoy the periodic views. Shortly before reaching the Sanctuary of La Verna, the route passes through a simply stunning old-growth beech forest dotted with moss-covered boulders.

Mountain trails approaching La Verna

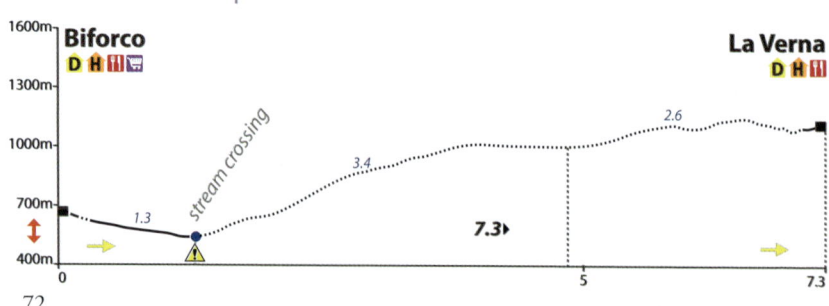

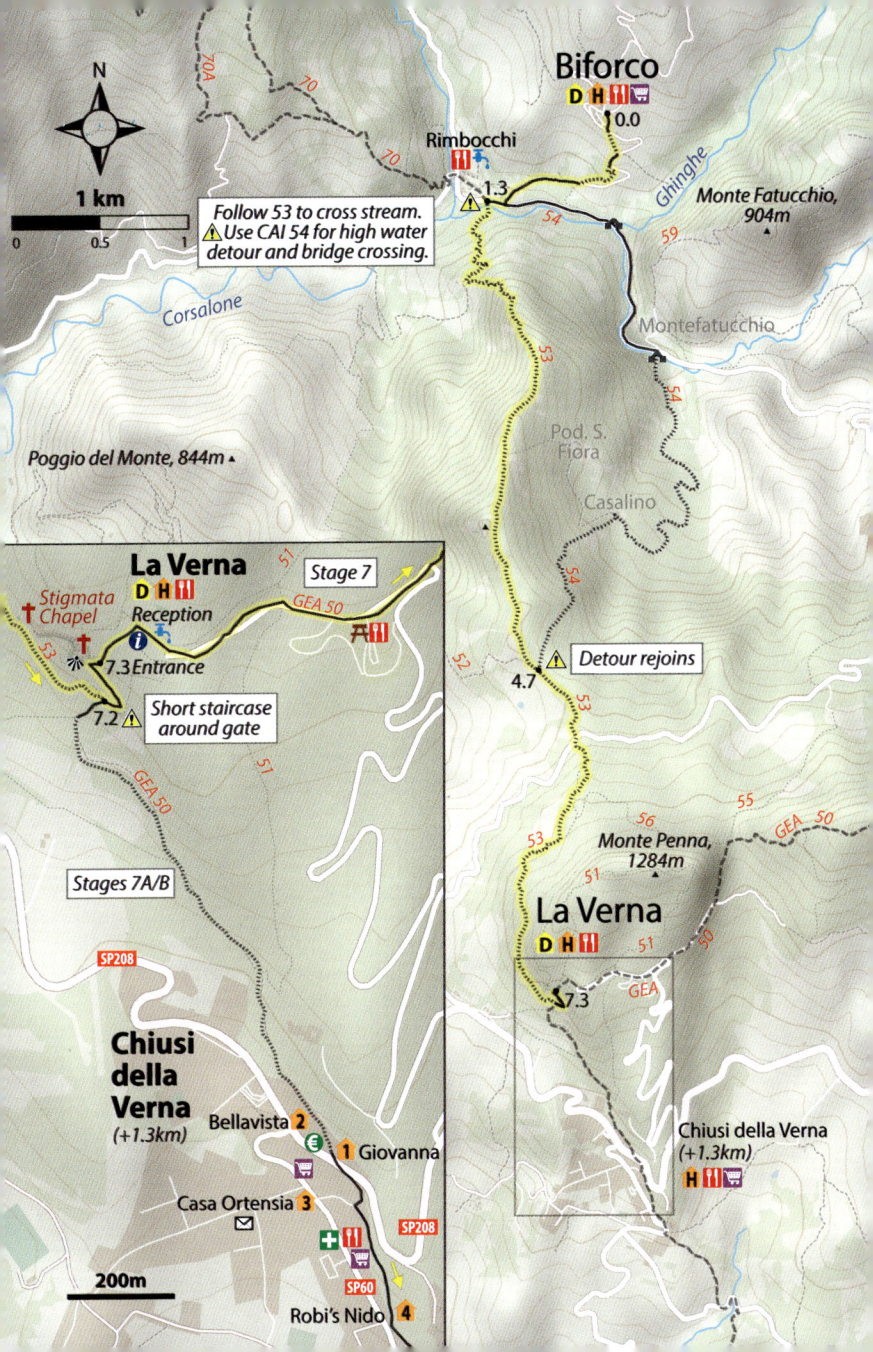

La Verna Sanctuary

Among these very boulders, St. Francis is said to have spent time in prayer and meditation. Views of the Chapel of the Stigmata mean you're close to your destination—one final climb to the La Verna Sanctuary.

💡 It's possible to avoid the stream crossing after Rimbocchi by following CAI 54 along the paved road, heading east from Rimbocchi. After walking 1.7km from the T intersection and stream crossing, you reach a junction below Montefatucchio. Turn right onto a gravel double track, crossing a bridge over the river. From there, continue to follow CAI 54 along the gravel double track, then a hiking path (from Casalino) to return to CAI 53.

💡 If this day seems short, it's possible to combine with it the following stage (Stage 7: La Verna-Pieve Santo Stefano, 15km or Stage 7A: La Verna-Caprese Michelangelo, 17.0km), though either option would make for a very long, challenging day. If you intend to stop at La Verna but don't want to stay in the Sanctuary's foresteria or pilgrim hostel, Chiusi della Verna

BIFORCO TO LA VERNA 6

(+1.3km down the mountain) has several private accommodation offerings, as well as various other services, like bars, small grocery shops, a pharmacy, and ATM.

73 La Verna D H

D H Foresteria and Pilgrim Hostel (13, €25/66/132):
0575534 1/0575534210, all year, check-in at reception, pilgrim hostel just to the right after entering La Verna, private room and pilgrim hostel prices include dinner/breakfast,
⚠ call in advance about status of pilgrim dorm

La Verna Sanctuary, located on the southern face of Mt. Penna, was one of St. Francis' favorite refuges and today is one of Italy's most important Franciscan sites and pilgrimage destinations. The name La Verna comes from the pagan goddess Laverna. In Roman mythology she was the goddess of thieves—one can imagine marauding robbers hiding in the very rocky crevices that St. Francis later used as retreats for prayer.

In 1213, the Count Orlando, impressed with St. Francis' preaching, offered the mountain of La Verna to him as a place of contemplation and prayer. Francis organized the construction of the Santa Maria degli Angeli Chapel and several small hermit cells sometime between 1216-1218, and he regularly visited La Verna throughout his life for prolonged periods of withdrawal. Francis' bibliographers record that during an extended period of fasting and prayer at La Verna in the fall of 1224, Francis received the stigmata. The site was taken under papal protection in 1260, after which several additional buildings, churches, and chapels were erected.

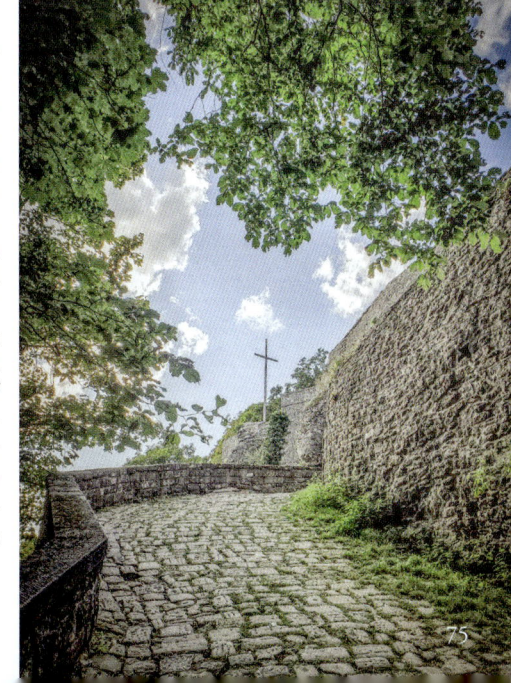

Final cobblestone climb to the La Verna Sanctuary

WAY OF ST. FRANCIS

Just through the Sanctuary's entrance is an open courtyard that offers spectacular views of the surrounding mountains. On the edge of the courtyard is the main Basilica, containing Franciscan relics and terracotta sculptures by Andrea della Robbia. Accessed via the Basilica, the Santa Maria degli Angeli Chapel dates back to St. Francis. From the Basilica, the Hallway of the Stigmata leads to the Chapel of the Stigmata. Along the sides of the hall, frescoes recount the life of St. Francis. Detours to the left and right from the hall lead to the Sasso Spico (literally, "a rock/stone peaking out") where St. Francis prayed in gaps in the rock and a stone grotto where St. Francis slept. Friars at La Verna make processions to the Chapel of the Stigmata twice daily, and large crowds of pilgrims journey to La Verna on September 17 for the Feast of the Stigmata. Time permitting, hiking route CAI 51 makes a 2.5km loop to the peak of Mt. Penna and then back to the Sanctuary.

Approaching La Verna from below the sanctuary

To reach the reception office for check-in and to receive a map and other information about the site, turn right from the entrance to La Verna and go through a hall passing the museum. A special pilgrim mass is held in the morning in the Basilica—ask at the reception for more details.

☀ There are various route options from La Verna. See La Verna to Città di Castello Route Choices, p. 79.

If you intend to walk Stage 7: La Verna to Pieve Santo Stefano, consider making an afternoon trip +1.3km off route to Chiusi della Verna to restock on food, since there are no services in the 15.0km between La Verna and Pieve Santo Stefano.

BIFORCO TO LA VERNA

+1.3 Chiusi della Verna

1. **Da Giovanna** (€50/80): S. Francesco 33, ©0575599275, ⊙Apr-Nov
2. **Bellavista** (€45/65): S. Francesco 17, ©0575599029
3. **Casa Ortensia** (€35/person): XXV Aprile 5a, ©3391478526, saraminelli30@gmail.com
4. **Robi's Nido** (€40): ©3661820872, roberta.migliorini22@gmail.com

💡 Chiusi della Verna is on route if you are following Stage 7A, and is 1.3km from and 180m below the La Verna. By public transportation, Chiusi della the Verna is the closest you can get to the La Verna Sanctuary. Buses arriving in Chiusi della Verna connect to Pieve Santo Stefano (in the valley east of La Verna) and Bibbiena (in the valley west of La Verna).

La Verna Sanctuary from its courtyard

7-15 LA VERNA TO ASSISI

Descending to Pieve Santo Stefano from La Verna

Descend from the Apennines to the fertile Tiber Valley, follow in St. Francis' footsteps to Assisi, the city central to his story.

Between La Verna and Assisi, the Way of St. Francis alternates between the rugged terrain of the Central Apennines and easier stretches through wide valleys. From La Verna, the route descends to the Tiber River that, though only a relative trickle this far upstream, continues all the way to Rome.

From Pieve Santo Stefano, the way crosses the rugged Alpe della Luna, then descends via Montecasale to Sansepolcro. After Sansepolcro, the route crosses the Tiber Valley, passing countless sunflower and tobacco fields along the way to Città di Castello. From here, the way leaves the Tiber and ascends through lesser mountains and rural villages to Pietralunga and Gubbio, a cultural capital of Umbria and home to the oldest surviving text in the Umbrian language. Leaving Gubbio, the route passes through rolling terrain, roughly following a long-used route above the Chiascio River to Assisi.

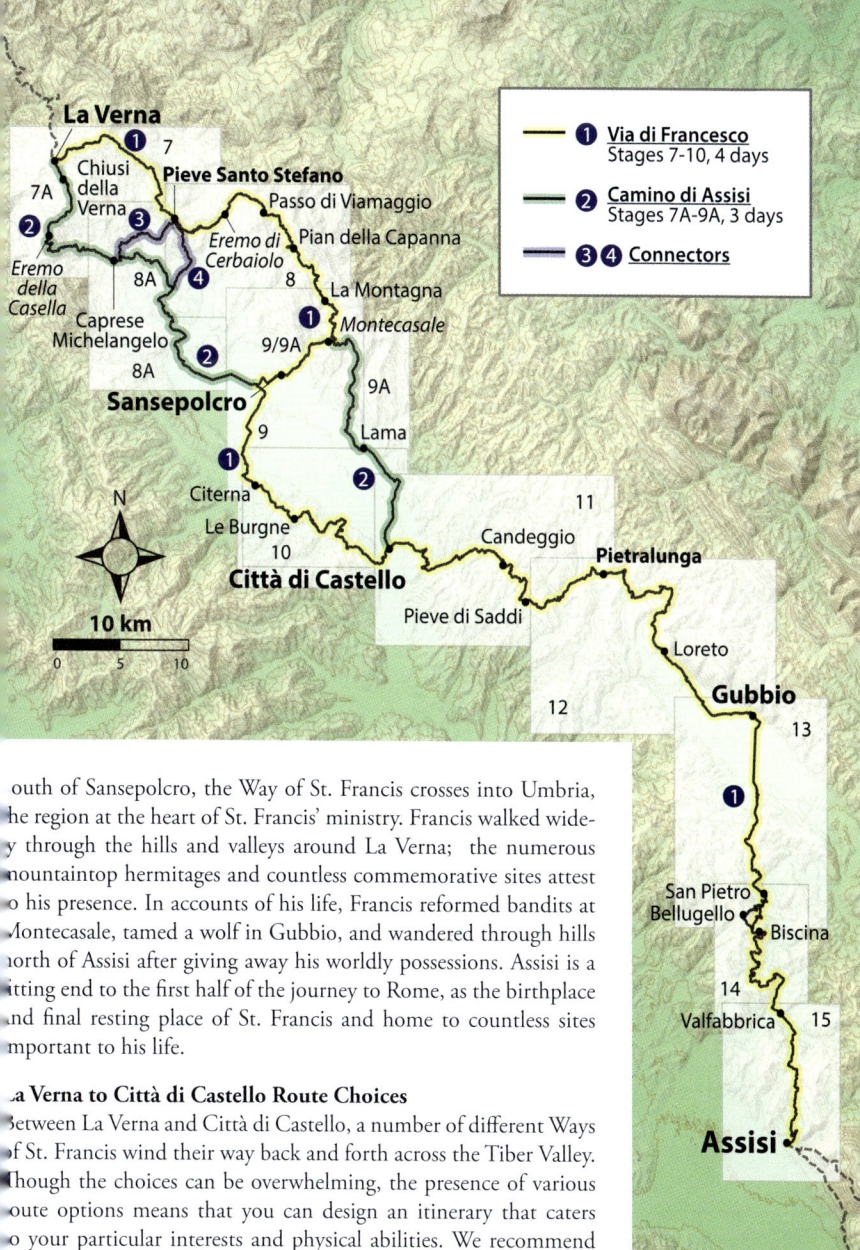

outh of Sansepolcro, the Way of St. Francis crosses into Umbria, he region at the heart of St. Francis' ministry. Francis walked wide-y through the hills and valleys around La Verna; the numerous nountaintop hermitages and countless commemorative sites attest o his presence. In accounts of his life, Francis reformed bandits at Montecasale, tamed a wolf in Gubbio, and wandered through hills north of Assisi after giving away his worldly possessions. Assisi is a itting end to the first half of the journey to Rome, as the birthplace and final resting place of St. Francis and home to countless sites important to his life.

La Verna to Città di Castello Route Choices

Between La Verna and Città di Castello, a number of different Ways of St. Francis wind their way back and forth across the Tiber Valley. Though the choices can be overwhelming, the presence of various route options means that you can design an itinerary that caters to your particular interests and physical abilities. We recommend either of the following two itineraries:

WAY OF ST. FRANCIS

The Via di Francesco roughly follows the ridgeline east from La Verna before descending to Pieve Santo Stefano. From there, a very demanding section of the route ascends steeply back into the mountains, passing the Franciscan hermitages of Cerbaiolo and Montecasale before dropping steeply to Sansepolcro. Going south from Sansepolcro, the route crosses the Tiber Valley and continues through hills on the southern edge of the Tiber Valley to Città di Castello.

The **Camino di Assisi** descends to Chiusi della Verna before climbing to the Franciscan hermitage of Casella and descending to Caprese Michelangelo, Michelangelo's birthplace. From Caprese Michelangelo, the route follows a mix of rural paved and gravel roads to the Tiber Valley and Sansepolcro, arriving to the city from the south. It then climbs from Sansepolcro to Montecasale and crosses another mountain before descending back to the Tiber Valley for the last 12km to Città di Castello.

Not specifically a St. Francis route, the **Grande Escursione Appenninica** (GEA, 425km) traverses the Apennine Mountains in Tuscany and Emilia-Romagna and forms a part of the Norway-Italy E1 European hiking route. In places, this route overlaps with both the Via di Francesco and Cammino di Assisi and is useful for navigation, as it is well marked (mostly with E1 signs, though also occasionally with GEA signs). See stages for waymarking.

❶ Via di Francesco
Stages 7-10 (4 days)
82.3km, ▲ 3030m
Most challenging & beautiful, longest, best marked.

This route is the best marked and includes some of the most beautiful mountain scenery of the entire Way of St. Francis. This option is longer than the second (both in distance and days), and it includes more climbing per kilometer. What's more, the route is both remote and physically challenging between Pieve Santo Stefano and Sansepolcro, with sections following technical trail surfaces (steep, slippery, and/or rocky). ⚠ We advise against walking this route in inclement weather.

If you're up for the challenge, this is our recommended way, with plenty of Franciscan history (hermitages of Cerbaiolo and Montecasale) and stunning natural scenery.

❷ Camino di Assisi
Stages 7A-9A (3 days)
71.0km, ▲ 2130m
More manageable ascents/trail surfaces, beautiful, markings occasionally sparse.

This option is ideal if you're concerned about the difficulty of the Via di Francesco between Pieve Santo Stefano and Sansepolcro. Though the Cammino di Assisi spends considerable time in the mountains between La Verna and Città di Castello, the walking surfaces, with the notable exception of the climb from Chiusi della Verna, are non-technical, made up primarily of jeep tracks, gravel roads, and paved roads. Similarly, no section is quite as remote as on option 1. You miss Eremo Cerbaiolo, the Museum of the Diary in Pieve Santo Stefano, and the lovely mountain town of La Montagna,

LA VERNA TO ASSISI

but add both Eremo della Casella and Caprese Michelangelo. This option is not waymarked as well as the first, and some confusing waymarks closer to Città di Castello present navigational challenges. Also, the approach to Città di Castello follows a busier road than option 1, making the final kilometers a bit less enjoyable.

In the end, both route options have a similar mix of cultural/historical sites and natural scenery. If you're interested in a slightly more beautiful (and challenging) mountain hiking experience, take the first. If you have concerns about the difficulty of the first option, the second way gives you much of the same natural scenery with less climbing and fewer sections of technical trail surfaces.

> ☀ While the Via di Francesco and Cammino di Assisi overlap in Sansepolcro, we don't recommend switching routes there. In other words, if you arrive to Sansepolcro from the south, continue on the Cammino di Assisi north from the city; and if you arrive to Sansepolcro from the north, continue on the Via di Assisi south from the city—this avoids unnecessary backtracking.

Trail connectors allow for other route combinations; less recommended itineraries have their advantages.

❸ Stage 7A, Caprese-Pieve connector, Stages 8-10 (4 days)
92.7km, ▲ 3720m *(long/hard, includes maximum historical/cultural sites)*

This combination follows the Cammino di Assisi to Caprese Michelangelo. Shortly after Caprese Michelangelo, T signboards and yellow tau markers follow the E1/GEA route to Pieve Santo Stefano, connecting with the Via di Francesco there. Though circuitous and not for the faint of heart, this itinerary maximizes beautiful mountain hiking and passes the most notable Franciscan (and other) sites, visiting Eremo della Casella, Caprese Michelangelo, Pieve Santo Stefano, Eremo Cerbaiolo, and Eremo Montecasale. A wonderful itinerary, but longer and challenging!

❹ Stage 7, Pieve-Cammino di Assisi connector + Stage 8A, Stage 9A (3 days)
68.2km, ▲ 1960m *(least amount of mountain walking, misses sites)*

This route follows the Via di Francesco from La Verna to Pieve Santo Stefano. From Pieve Santo Stefano, a marked connecting route meets the Cammino di Assisi on Monte Fungia and then the Cammino di Assisi the rest of the way to Città di Castello.

This is the shortest itinerary, and has slightly less climbing than option two, but not enough to represent a meaningful difference. Consider this itinerary if you're more interested in visiting the Museum of the Diary in Pieve Santo Stefano than in visiting the Michelangelo Birthplace Museum in Caprese Michelangelo. <u>Unfortunately, this route skips the notable Franciscan hermitage at **Montecasale**.</u>

7

LA VERNA TO PIEVE SANTO STEFANO

15.0km (9.4mi)
▲ 350m / ▼ 1040m

⏱ 4.5-5.5 Hours
Difficulty: ▮▮▯

🅿 21%, 3.1km
🆄 79%, 11.9km

D H Lodging:
Pieve S.S. 15.0km
Passo V.M. 25.0km

✝ Waymarking:
Yellow tau and arrow markers indicate the way to Pieve Santo Stefano. GEA/E1 passes through La Verna. Signage for GEA/E1 routes until 4.9km. Also follows various CAI routes, including: CAI 56, 50, 66, and 75 (see map for details).

Pilgrims descending from Monte Calvano

**Follow forested ridges,
descend to the headwaters of the Tiber,
explore the "City of the Diary."**

💡 Today's route follows mountain ridgelines, steadily descending to the Tiber River and Pieve Santo Stefano. The day begins with a short but substantial climb to Monte Calvano, with expansive views of the surrounding mountains. From here, it's predominantly downhill to Pieve Santo Stefano, a small town on the Tiber River, which is home to the Italian National Archive of Diaries.

Leave from the reception side of La Verna, pass a statue of St. Francis preaching to doves, and follow E1 signs and yellow tau markers along the main road with car access to La Verna. Shortly after passing the main parking lot and touristy

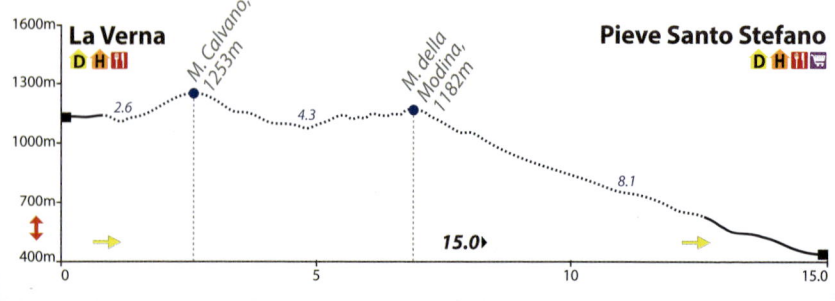

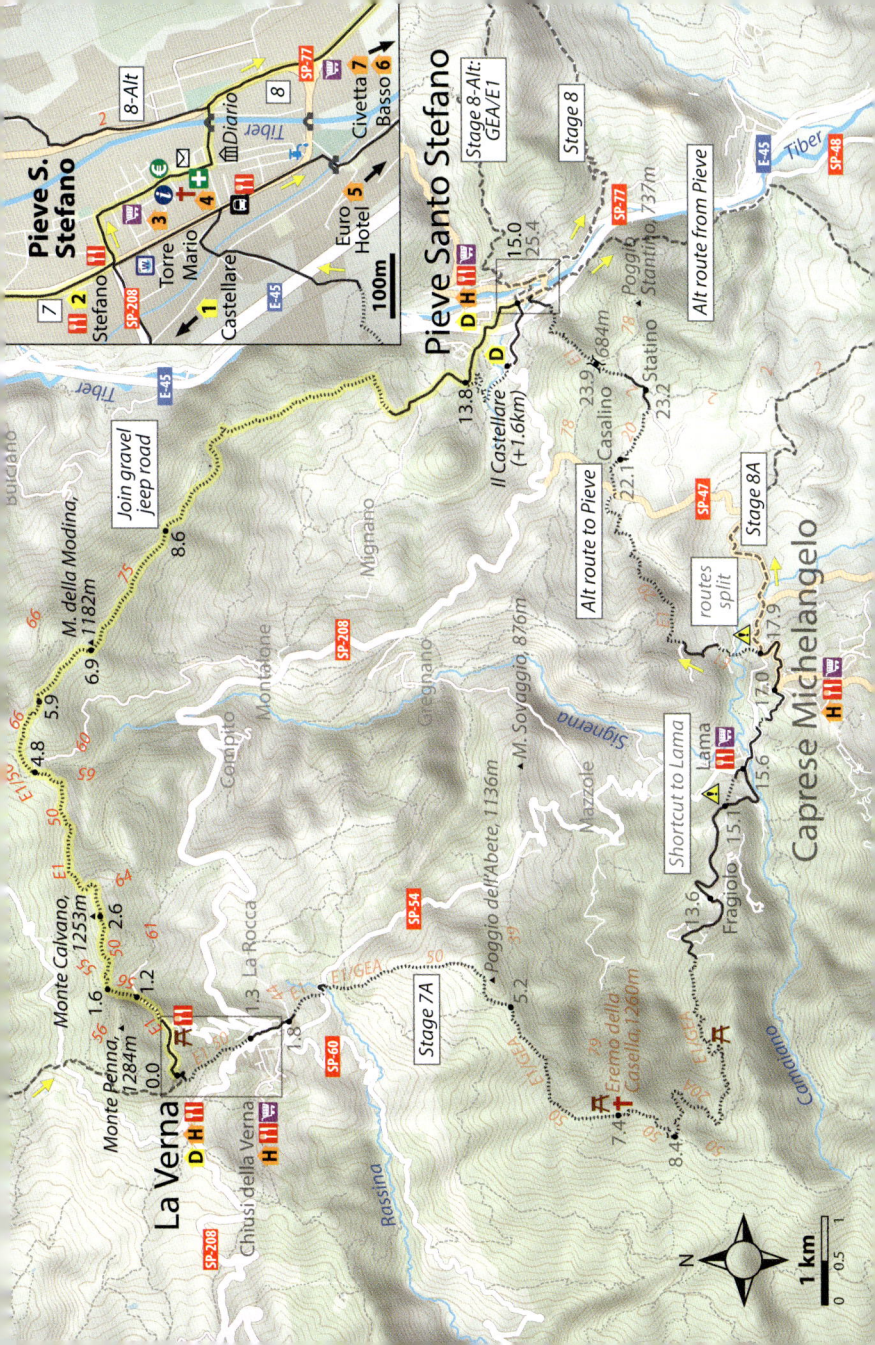

WAY OF ST. FRANCIS

> There are no services between La Verna and Pieve Santo Stefano, so be sure to carry sufficient food and water from La Verna.

café, continue straight onto a gravel road as the paved road switches back. See map and CAI trail #s from here; notable junctions are:

- At 1.2km, the 4x4 track you've been following continues as CAI 61, while you turn left on CAI 56.
- At 1.6km, there is a 4-way junction. You go right on CAI 50/E1. CAI 55 goes straight, and CAI 56 goes left.
- At 2.9km, stay straight on CAI 50/E1 as CAI 64 goes right.
- At 4.8km, stay straight as CAI 65 goes right toward "Compito." Just ahead stay straight on CAI 66 toward "Pieve Santo Stefano" as CAI 60 goes right ("Montalone") and CAI 50/E1 goes left ("Mandrioli")
- At 5.9km, turn right, following a gravel hiking path following signs for "Pieve Santo Stefano," while signs for "P. So Gualanciole" point straight
- At 8.6km, join a gravel 4x4 road and continue downhill (soon pass an "18% grade" sign). The road improves progressively as you approach Pieve Santo Stefano.

15.0 Pieve Santo Stefano

1. **BB Castellare** (13, €20/30/50): SP 208 della Verna 13, 3393463117/0575799393, all year, on the outskirts of town w/clear detour from 13.8km, can follow SP 208 to Pieve S. Stefano to avoid backtracking
2. **Hotel Santo Stefano** (4, €25/55-65/85-90): Tiberina 95, 0575797129, all year, breakfast €5 if in dorm, 10% private room pilgrim discount
3. **Casa di Mario** (€30/50): Tiberina 50, 0575799272/3335806242, all year
4. **La Torre di Pieve** (€56): Piazza delle Oche 5, 3313075005, private rooms in apartment
5. **BB Dagnano Basso** (€45/60): Dagnano 26, 3386101569, Via Dagnano south of town off SP-77
6. **Euro Hotel** (€55/65): E45 km 150, 0575797055, on the E45 highway south of town, bus stop to Rome here and bus stop from Rome on opposite side of highway
7. **Camping la Civetta** (€25/40): Civetta 11, 3336546145, bungalows with kitchenette, 4 person €55, shared bathrooms, well south of town off of SP-77

A pilgrim on a CAI trail outside of La Verna

LA VERNA TO PIEVE SANTO STEFANO

Pieve Santo Stefano is a small town located on the Upper Tiber River, not far from the river's headwaters. The history of civilization in Pieve dates back centuries. During Roman times, a route connecting Arezzo to Rimini passed through Pieve Santo Stefano and over the Passo di Viamaggio. As early as the 8th century, records documenting the gift of the Cerbaiolo Hermitage to the Benedictine Order refer to the town as "Pieve." Despite its long history, little ancient architecture remains. Floods in 1855 damaged much of the city, and the Nazi Army mined and destroyed the city while retreating from Allied Forces in 1944.

More recently, Pieve has gained fame as the "City of the Diary." Italian journalist Saverio Tutino was inspired to collect and remember the stories of ordinary Italians, and in 1984 he established the Italian Archivio Diaristico Nazionale (National Diary Archives) in Pieve Santo Stefano. Every year, the archives invite ordinary Italians to submit autobiographical material and awards the *Premio Pieve* (Pieve Award, award ceremonies take place in mid-September) to each year's best diary, which is then published. To date, the archives have collected over 8,000 diaries, letters, and other autobiographical material. The lovely **Little Museum of the Diary** holds various creative audio/visual diary exhibits (many of which have been translated into English) that provide a window into the daily life of ordinary Italians (€5, ☺Mon-Fri 9:30am-12:30pm, 3-6pm, weekends and holidays 3-6pm).

💡 Buses from Pieve Santo Stefano go to Chiusi della Verna and Sansepolcro. Tickets can be purchased at Bar Jepson, just to the east of the bus stop.

Crossing the headwaters of the Tiber River in Pieve Santo Stefano

8 PIEVE SANTO STEFANO TO LA MONTAGNA

23.4km (14.6mi)
▲ 1110m / ▼ 870m

⏱ **8-10 Hours**
Difficulty: ▬▪▪

🅿 11%, 2.5km
U 89%, 20.9km

D H Lodging:
P. Viamaggio 10.0km
Pian Cap. 16.9km
Il Palazzo 22.4km
La Montagna 23km
Val d'Afra 30.8km

✝ **Waymarking:**
Blue/yellow stripes, GR-style stripes, and yellow tau markers for the entire day except for 1.6km around Eremo Cerbaiolo. E1/GEA markers for much of the day. CAI 2, 00, 8, and 6. Map has more notes.

Ascend to the "Alp of the Moon," visit an idyllic hermitage, continue to a picturesque mountain village.

💡 Prepare for a long, demanding climb onto the Alpe della Luna (Alp of the Moon), a beautiful Apennine Mountain massif that is home to the Franciscan hermitages at Cerbaiolo and Montecasale. Eremo Cerbaiolo and Passo di Viamaggio split up the climb and offer pleasant break spots, though the 2.5km after Passo di Viamaggio follow very steep and potentially slippery hiking paths. A long stretch of rolling

Tiber Valley from the Cerbaiolo Hermitage

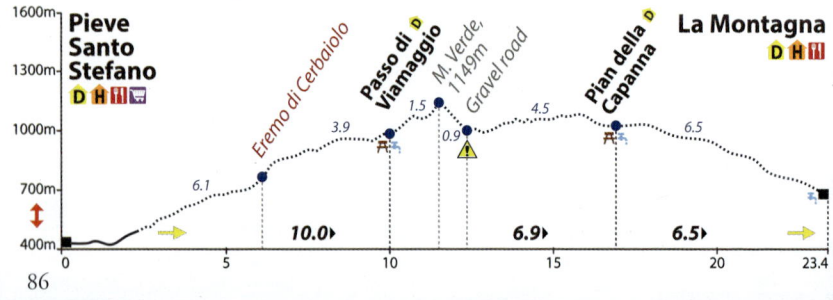

WAY OF ST. FRANCIS

💡 Between Pieve Santo Stefanovic and Sansepolcro the path is physically challenging and remote and there are no grocery stores, though there are several reliable water refill points: Ca La Fonte (+320m, fountain behind the main building), and Pian della Capanna (water fountain outside main entrance).

⚠ To walk this route option, you should be comfortable navigating in the mountains. Not recommended in bad weather.

Hiking trail after Passo di Viamaggio

gravel road below the ridgeline offers splendid views of the surrounding countryside and Tiber Valley. At 18.7km, a final rocky hiking trail leads to another gravel road and the idyllic mountain villages of Il Palazzo and La Montagna.

Alternative Itinerary Options:

💡 Though it adds another day to your overall itinerary, it's easy to split the challenging two-day Pieve Santo Stefano-Citerna section into three days:

- Pieve Santo Stefano-Pian della Capanna (16.9km, ▲ +1,036m)
- Pian della Capanna-Sansepolcro (18.1km, ▲ +535m)
- Sansepolcro-Citerna (12.2km, ▲ +337m, or +5.0km to Le Burgne)

In addition to the more manageable distances, this itinerary allows for a night in Sansepolcro, a notable and very pleasant city worth exploring. This stage breakdown leaves 12.1km to Montecasale from Pian della Capanna, meaning that without an early start, you're likely to arrive at Montecasale when the hermitage is closed for its afternoon riposo (🕐12-3:30pm).

💡 Starting on the east side of the Tiber River, the day's route follows blue/yellow marks south along the main road (SP-77) out of Pieve Santo Stefano for 1.4km, before turning left onto a smaller paved road (following signs for "Cerbaiolo") and ascending. SP-77 is a larger road, though not particularly busy, but you should walk carefully. Alternatively, to exit Pieve Santo Stefano avoiding SP-77, follow CAI 2/E1/GEA from the city. On the east side of the Tiber River, this route option goes north, soon climbing, then continuing onto unpaved hiking trails, reconnecting with the official route after 6.8km (at 7.2km on our recommended route) above Eremo Cerbaiolo (possible to detour to visit the hermitage). Though there's less paved walking, the trail surfaces are more technical and challenging on the E1 option from Pieve Santo Stefano than on the route we recommend, which follows paved/gravel roads all the way to Eremo Cerbaiolo.

PIEVE SANTO STEFANO TO LA MONTAGNA 8

☼ At 5.1km, at a Y intersection, the main route follows the left gravel road option, while another gravel road goes right. Though not an official route, the right gravel road option climbs all the way to Passo di Viamaggio, bypassing all hiking trails before Passo di Viamaggio.

☼ At 5.6km, the blue/yellow painted stripes and yellow tau markers go left following a gravel hiking track in the direction of "Passo di Viamaggio," while the gravel road continues straight toward Eremo di Cerbaiolo. Here we recommend continuing straight to Eremo di Cerbaiolo. From Eremo di Cerbaiolo, a hiking path marked with red/white GR stripes and signage for "Passo di Viamagio" and "Panoramica" climbs to a viewpoint with a cross, then follows the ridgeline uphill, reconnecting with the main route at 7.2km. Following this route allows a visit the Cerbaiolo Hermitage and reconnects with the official Via di Francesco without backtracking.

☼ Another route from Pieve Santo Stefano connects with the Cammino di Assisi on Monte Fungaia. See Stage 8A (p. 108)

The **Eremo di Cerbaiolo** was built in the 8th century for the Benedictine Order. By the 1200s, the hermitage was no longer inhabited, but on a journey to La Verna, St. Francis learned of the hermitage's existence. From 1216-1783, the hermitage was inhabited by Franciscans, and the Benedictines transferred the hermitage to the Franciscan Order in 1303. Unfortunately, Eremo di Cerbaiolo was destroyed by the German Army retreating at the end of WWII. In the 1960s, however, Sister Chiara Barboni of the Piccola Compagnia di Santa Elisabetta found the ruins of the hermitage and dedicated the rest of her life to restoring it (she died in 2010). Nestled on the mountainside, the hermitage boasts beautiful views of the valley and Lago di Montedoglio. According to a local saying: "Whoever has seen La Verna but not Cerbaiolo has seen the mother but not the son."

CAI signage between Passo di Viamaggio and Pian della Capanna

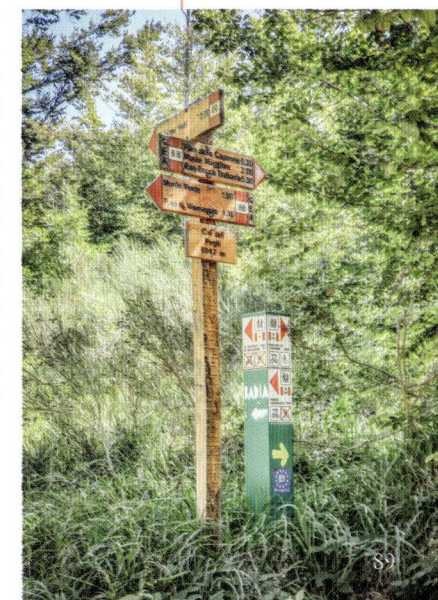

WAY OF ST. FRANCIS

10.0 Passo di Viamaggio D H

hotel off-route in Valdazze

D Ca La Fonte (rif, 10, €20): , Alpe 11, ☏3393028614, calafonteimperatore@gmail.com, all year, lovely mountaintop rifugio, also has larger building (30) for groups, for €5/person can provide food to cook dinner, good reviews

Picnic tables and water fountain (behind larger building) make Ca La Fonte a pleasant picnic spot, even if you're not staying there.

From Passo di Viamaggio, the route follows narrow hiking trails over Monte Verde (1,146m) to a gravel road 2.4km past Passo di Viamaggio. At times, the trail is quite steep and could be very slippery in wet weather. It's possible to detour around this section of trail on an unmarked gravel/dirt road. From Passo di Viamaggio, continue 1.1km south on the main paved road (SP-258), before turning left and following the gravel/dirt track over a lower part of the mountain to the good gravel road on the other side. (Only recommended with GPS navigation.) This adds about 1.0km to the day's total distance.

Between Pieve Santo Stefano and Sansepolcro, the Way of St. Francis traverses the **Alpe della Luna** (Alp of the Moon). The name may have been derived from the Ripa della Luna (bank of the moon), the exposed, sickle-shaped mountain face of Monte dei Frati, visible from the northeast side of the mountain. The Alpe della Luna Nature Reserve encompasses much of the mountain and is home to a range of diverse flora

Gravel road descending to Il Palazzo and La Montagna

PIEVE SANTO STEFANO TO LA MONTAGNA 8

and fauna. Beech and holly trees, crocus, and cyclamen cover the mountainside; the purple blooms of the appropriately named lunari flowers dot the mountain's pastures. Also in the reserve are the remains of the "Gothic Line," German military bunkers established along the Central Apennine ridgelines during WWII.

16.9 D **Rifugio Pian della Capanna** (rif, 🛏20, €25 🛌): 🍴⊙, ☏05755750000/3335956500 📧, prenotazioni@fattoriadigermagnano.it, ⊙Apr-Nov

Welcoming visitors to the Rifugio Pian della Capanna

💡 A water faucet outside the mountain hut has potable water. On the exterior of the main building an enclosed structure with a fireplace and benches serves as simple shelter (much like Rifugio Secchieta or Rifugio Cotozzo). The rustic no-services emergency shelter is open year round (whether or not the official mountain hut is open) and is a good refuge from the elements.

At 18.7km, the route leaves the good gravel road and turns left, continuing to follow CAI 6, now along a gravel hiking track. If you reach Rifugio La Spinella, you've gone too far (note that Rifugio La Spinella is open only to groups). Ahead on CAI 6, a somewhat technical rocky descent could be tricky in wet weather. 2.1km after leaving the good gravel road, you reach a 4x4 track that leads to Il Palazzo and La Montagna.

22.4 Il Palazzo D H

D H BB **Il Palazzo** (🛏9, €25/-/65-80 🛌): 🐕 W D 📶 ⊙, ☏3477817173 📧, ⊙all year, beautiful country home
D BB **Ritmo dei Passi** (🛏6, €25 🛌): 🍴W 📶 ⊙, Il Palazzo 54, ☏3381899137 📧, ⊙May-Oct, beautiful country home & garden

23.4 La Montagna D H 🍴

⭐ D H BB **Alla Battuta** (🛏7, €20/person 🛌): W 📶 ⊙, Frazione Montagna 46, ☏3493829435/0575749352 📧, a.puleri@gmail.com, ⊙all year, hospitable, idyllic location, beds in double/triple rooms, dorm overflow in local church
H BB **Antico Passo del Pellegrino** (€30 🛌): 🐕 📶 ⊙, Frazione Montagna 44/A, ☏3356953624 📧

💡 Both Il Palazzo (just a few houses) and La Montagna are pleasant mountain villages with lovely little bed and breakfasts. Either are highly recommended places to end the day.

9

LA MONTAGNA TO CITERNA

23.8km (14.9mi)
▲ 800m / ▼ 990m

⏱ **7.5-9.5 Hours**
DIFFICULTY: ▬ ▬ ▬

P 55%, 13.1km
U 45%, 10.7km

D H LODGING:
Val d'Afra 7.4km
Sansepolcro 11.6km
Zoccolanti 23.0km
Citerna 23.8km
Le Burgne 28.8km

♱ WAYMARKING:
Blue/yellow stripes, yellow taus, Via di Francesco/Via di Roma signboards begin after crossing into Umbria, CAI 6, 6A, and 4

Descend to a Franciscan hermitage, visit Sansepolcro and its peace-inspiring art, end your day in a pleasant hilltop village.

☀ Today's route descends from the mountains and crosses the flat, expansive Tiber Valley, leaving Tuscany to enter Umbria. The first 5km to Montecasale mostly follow rugged hiking trails with wonderful views of the surrounding hillsides. The beautiful Franciscan hermitage at Montecasale is a perfect location for an early morning pause. From Montecasale, a very steep, tough descent leads to the valley floor. If you're worried about your knees, the paved road to the valley offers a less demanding descent and connects with the official Via di Francesco in the valley. Sansepolcro, home to Piero

Tiber Valley from the Montecasale Hermitage

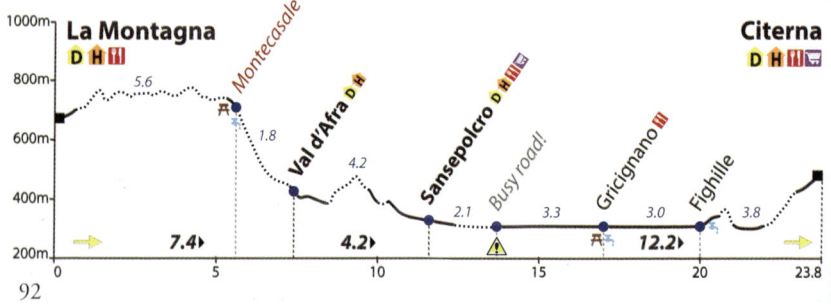

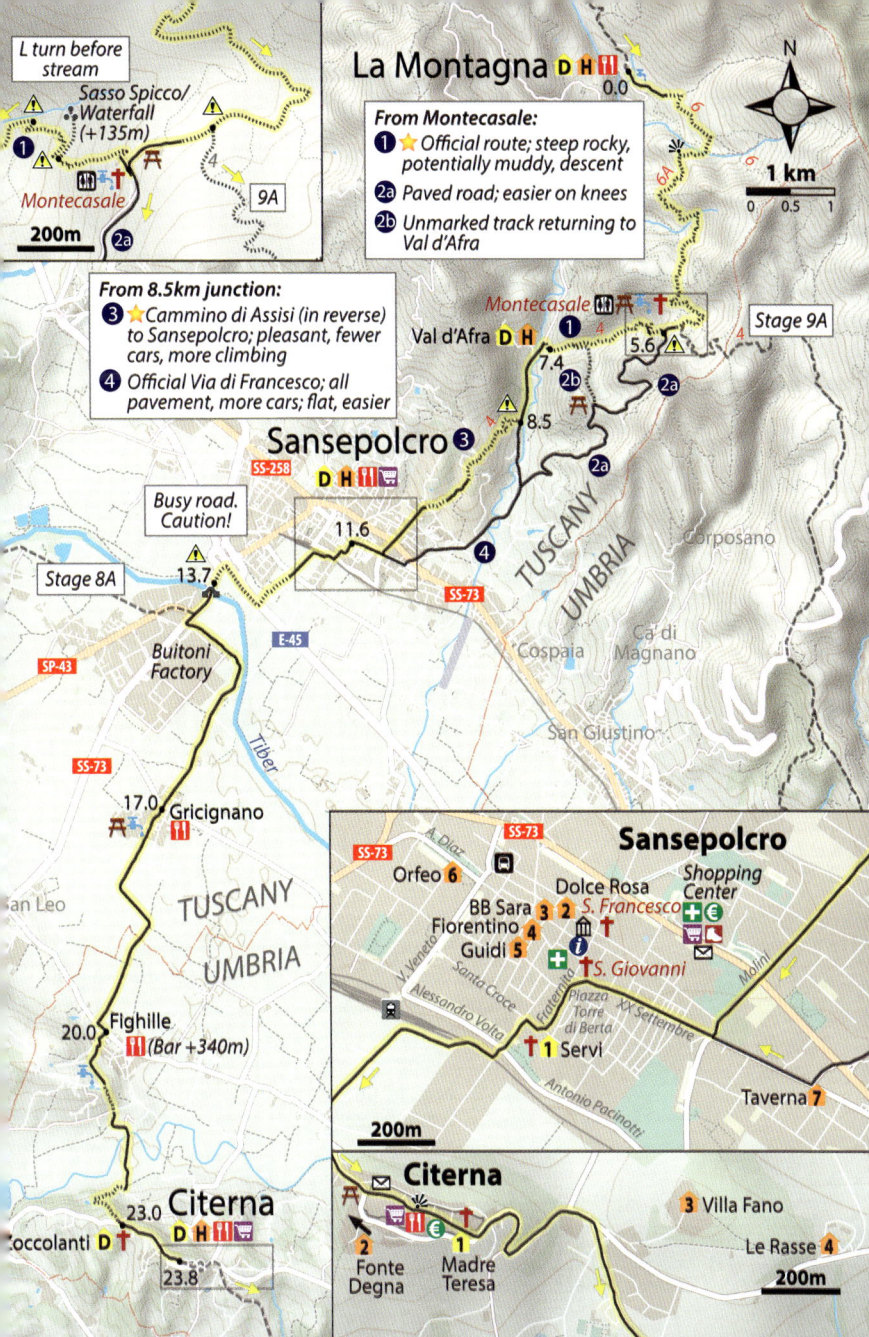

WAY OF ST. FRANCIS

Rocky hiking trail on the outskirts of La Montagna

Chapel inside the Montecasale Hermitage

della Francesca's Resurrection, is worth a longer visit if you have the time. From Sansepolcro, the miles pass quickly as you cross the fertile Tiber Valley, passing countless sunflower fields. The final climb to Citerna, a lovely little hilltop town, is hard but short.

5.6 Montecasale

The **Eremo di Montecasale** is a famous Franciscan hermitage on the mountainside above Sansepolcro. The Monastery dates to 1192, when the Camaldolese built a small hermitage and hospice that served pilgrims crossing the Alpe della Luna. In 1213, the Camaldolese gave the hermitage to St. Francis, who then visited frequently throughout his life. Later, St. Bonaventure resided here while writing his biography of St. Francis.

Two famous St. Francis stories have a connection to Montecasale. In one account, two wealthy men from Sansepolcro approached Francis, hoping to become members of the Friars Minor. Francis received them warmly, then directed them to plant cabbage upside down in the hermitage's garden. One man dutifully obeyed, while the other, confused, attempted to inform Francis that this was not, in fact, the correct way to plant cabbage. Francis noted that this man might be ill-suited to the unorthodox Franciscan way of life, while accepting the first, obedient man into the order.

A second story recounts interactions between the friars at Montecasale and three thieves who harassed travelers on the mountainside. Occasionally, the thieves would descend to Montecasale to beg for bread. One of the friars refused to give food to the robbers, citing the hardship they caused to people in the area. Francis, hearing this, rebuked the friar, noting that sinners were reformed by kindness, not reprimands. He commanded the friar to take wine and bread to the robbers and beg their forgiveness. Moved by the friar's kindness, the thieves joined the Franciscan brotherhood at Montecasale.

LA MONTAGNA TO CITERNA

Upon entering the hermitage, there is a small chapel. Behind the chapel is the choir room (where monks chant and pray) with original plainchant books. Nearby, you can visit the cells that Francis and his brothers are said to have slept in. To the right of the chapel, through a stone corridor (with a sign for Oratorio di S. Francesco) you come to the oldest part of the hermitage and a shrine with the skulls of the famous thieves. On the trail descending from Montecasale, a short detour takes you to the Sasso Spicco (literally, "jutting out rock") below a small waterfall. St. Francis spent time in prayer and meditation here.

A small courtyard at the bottom edge of the hermitage is a nice spot for a morning break, and it has a water fountain and bathroom open to the public whether or not the hermitage is open. The hermitage itself is open ☺Mon-Fri 9am-12pm, 3:30-7pm, weekends and holidays 11am-6pm. Abbreviated hours in the winter.

💡 <u>After Montecasale, there are several route options</u>
❶⭐ The primary option follows a steep, and at times rough, hiking trail to Val d'Afra. The trail surface is not particularly worse than other technical sections of the route encountered up until this point, but you can skip it by following the paved road downhill from Montecasale.

❷ₐ The first detour option follows the paved road all the way to the valley bottom, reconnecting with the Via di Francesco there.

❷♭ The second option descends on the paved road, then turns right from the paved road onto a small, unmarked hiking/MTB track just before reaching a picnic area. This track follows a more-manageable descent than the official hiking trail and reconnects with the Via di Francesco just before Val d'Afra.

Montecasale Hermitage

WAY OF ST. FRANCIS

Statue of St. Francis above the Montecasale Hermitage

There are two more route options in the valley just south of Val d'Afra (if you followed route option 1). At 8.5km, a gravel road joins from the right.

Option ❸⭐ goes right onto this gravel road, following CAI 4 and the Cammino di Assisi in reverse to Sansepolcro. This adds more climbing than just following the paved road but also uses more unpaved surfaces and stays further away from vehicle traffic.

Option ❹, the official Via di Francesco, continues straight along the main paved road into Sansepolcro.

7.4 Val d'Afra D H

D H San Martino (🛏12, €25/person 🌐): 🍴💧📶🌐🍳, ☎3497834112/3492136154 🔗, 🕐all year, beds in double/triple private rooms, possible overflow cots in church, substantial breakfast (pancakes or bacon!), owner very knowledgeable about Montecasale and surrounding area.

11.6 Sansepolcro D H 🍴🛒🚌⛪➕€ℹ🏧🚉

💡 Stock up here. Last reliable services until Citerna.
1. ⭐ **D Santa Maria dei Servi** (par, 🛏22, €17): 📶🌐, Matteo di Giovanni 2, ☎3396246194/3505372385, 🕐reception: 2:30-6:30pm, mid-Apr to mid-Oct, €3 for sheets, open in winter for groups staying 2 nights or more, simple, but a true pilgrim hostel!
2. **H Dolce Rosa** (€45/60): 📶, Niccolo' Aggiunti 74, ☎3663973527 🔗
3. **D H BB Sara** (€18/30/55 🌐): 🍴💧📶🌐, Luca Pacioli 72, ☎05751610292 🔗, possibility of twin beds in shared room
4. **H Fiorentino** (€55/80 🌐): 📶🌐, Luca Pacioli 56, ☎0575740350 🔗, 🕐all year
5. **H Guidi** (€55/80 🌐): 🍴📶🌐, Luca Pacioli 46, ☎0575736587
6. **H Orfeo** (€25/50): 🍴📶🌐, Armando Diaz 12, ☎0575742287, 🕐all year
7. **H Taverna** (€35/55 🌐): 🍴📶🌐, Anconetana 27, ☎0575742575 🔗, 🕐all year

Sansepolcro, originally Borgo Santo Sepolcro (literally, "Town of the Holy Sepulchre"), traces its origins to the 9th century, when a pair of pilgrims who had traveled to the Holy Land returned to the region, built a chapel to Saint Leonard, and began a monastic life. According to their travels accounts,

LA MONTAGNA TO CITERNA

they brought a stone from the Church of the Holy Sepulcher in Jerusalem, leading to the name of the town. Sansepolcro, located on several trade routes, later became a market town.

The **Basilica di San Giovanni Evangelista**—Sansepolcro's main cathedral, built in Gothic-Romanesque style—now sits on the original chapel of the two pilgrims. The **Chiesa di San Francesco** is several blocks north. Outside of the church is a statue of Luca Pacioli, a Renaissance mathematician known as the "Father of Accounting and Bookkeeping" in Europe for his work on double-entry bookkeeping systems. Later Pacioli became a Franciscan monk. One of his Sansepolcro contemporaries was Piero della Francesca, also a mathematician and geometer, but today more famous for his art, which is known for its accurate perspective and serene humanism.

One of Piero della Francesca's most famous works, a fresco painting called The Resurrection, is located in Sansepolcro's **Museo Civico** (€11, ☉June 10-Sep 24 10am-1:30pm and 2:30-7pm, Sep 25-Jun 9 10am-1pm and 2:30-6pm). In a 1925 essay, British author Aldous Huxley called it "the greatest picture in the world."

During World War II, British artillery officer Tony Clarke saved the city, and likely the painting, from destruction because of Huxley's words. Ahead of the Allied infantry advance on Sansepolcro, the British artillery was ordered to shell the city, but Clarke, an art lover, remembered Huxley's essay and risked court martial by ordering his troops to hold fire.

⚠ On the south side of Sansepolcro, use extreme caution when walking along SS-73. Since there is only one bridge crossing over the Tiber in the vicinity, you're forced to walk along this very busy road for a short stretch. Walk on the left side of the road and be vigilant.

Basilica di San Giovanni Evangelista

WAY OF ST. FRANCIS

23.0 Zoccolanti D

D Monastero del SS. Crocifisso e S. Maria (par, 5+, don): ⬛, Zoccolanti 8, ☎3662969218/0758592126, ⏱9am-2pm/3:30-6pm, all year, pleasant, peaceful lodging run by nuns, dinner by donation with advance notice, beds in several double rooms

23.8 Citerna D H ⬛

1. **D Madre Teresa** (par, 3, don): Garibaldi 3, ☎3333695662, keys across square at S. Michele Arcangelo or nursing home, very simple room with three beds and shower, welcoming, but should really be seen only as overflow option—the monastery in Zoccolanti is better set up to host pilgrims
2. **H Fonte Degna** (€45/70): ⬛, Eroi 15, ☎3317431965
3. **H Villa Fano** (€50/70): ⬛, ☎3470834295, info@poggiovillafano.it, ⏱all year
4. **H Le Rasse** (€70): ⬛, ☎3939324922
5. **H Agriturismo Draghi** (€30/50-70): ⬛, Pocaia 64, ☎3393959147, in Monterchi (off-route), owner can pick up in Citerna, good reviews

Citerna is a small but beautiful hilltop town on the south side of the Tiber Valley. Dating to the 13th century, the town was built at the site of a previously-existing fortress that overlooked the valley. Worth visiting is the **Chiesa di San Francesco** (not far from the town center), which was once a Franciscan monastery.

View of the Tiber Valley from Citerna

LA MONTAGNA TO CITERNA

A recently-discovered terracotta Madonna by Donatello is displayed within. Check in at the town's info point for access (⏱weekends and holidays 10am-12:30pm and 3-6:30pm, weekdays call ☎3388817814 or 3398445619 in advance). According to local stories, St. Francis stayed on the hilltop and blessed it. Since then, it's said, Citerna has been largely spared from the earthquakes that have plagued towns in the valley.

💡 Most of the accommodations listed are outside of town. The local grocery (in the town center) is quite small, but it has everything you need. Expansive views from the central piazza stretch across the Tiber Valley.

💡 If you have the energy, consider continuing on to ⭐Agriturismo Le Burgne, which is very accommodating to pilgrims.

Citerna center

10

CITERNA TO CITTÀ DI CASTELLO

20.1km (12.6mi)
▲ 770m / ▼ 950m

⏱ **6-8 Hours**
Difficulty: ▭▭▭

🅿 46%, 9.3km
Ⓤ 54%, 10.8km

D H Lodging:
Le Burgne 5.0km
Città di Castello 20.1km
Candeggio 34.9km

🏳 **Waymarking:**
Blue/yellow stripes, yellow taus, Via di Francesco/Via di Roma signboards

Duomo di Città di Castello

Stroll through rolling countryside, pass one of St. Francis' refuges, descend to the city where St. Francis cast out a demon.

💡 Though no single climb is particularly long, three 200m+ climbs throughout the day mean you'll have earned your evening meal upon arriving in Città di Castello. Passing through agricultural countryside on the southern edge of the Tiber Valley, the day has a distinctly different feel from the alpine walking of days prior. Still, regular hilltop views keep the walking from becoming a slog. Though services are sparse, a grocery store and café located roughly halfway through the day in Lerchi make resupply manageable.

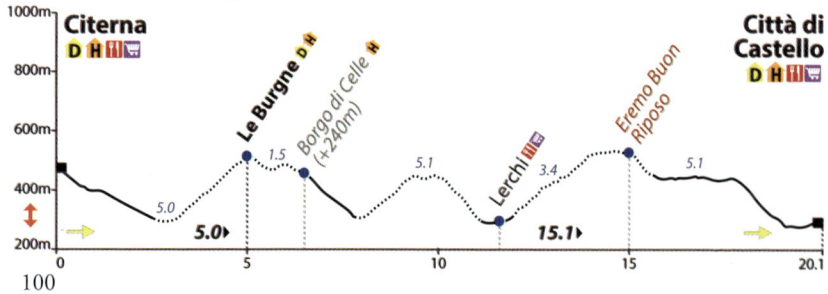

10 WAY OF ST. FRANCIS

Hilltop pool in Le Burgne

Hiking trail above Lerchi

5.0 Le Burgne D H

⭐ D H **Agriturismo Le Burgne** (6, €25/60/85): 🍴🛏️💧📶, Burgne 12, ☎3290192923, 🕐Mar-Nov, beautiful accommodation in peaceful hilltop location, very hospitable with good food, if owners are in, you can order food from menu even if not staying

H **Hotel Borgo di Celle** (€60/75): 🍴🛏️💧📶, Celle 7, ☎0758510025, 1.5km past Le Burgne and +240m off route

Eremo Buon Riposo is a small hermitage located on the side of Monte Cicerone, 5km from Città di Castello. A group of natural caves existed at the location before the hermitage was built, and St. Francis frequently stopped here on his way to and from La Verna, calling the place *Buon Riposo*, or "Good Rest." On one occasion, after receiving the stigmata, St. Francis fled to this hermitage in order to hide his wounds from crowds eager to see him.

A convent and church were added to the hermitage in later years, but during Italian state confiscation of religious property in the late-19th century, the hermitage was turned over to private owners. The current owner can facilitate visits. (Call ☎3355407782 in advance).

CITERNA TO CITTÀ DI CASTELLO

20.1 Città di Castello D H ¶ ▯ ⊕ ⊖ ℹ ▯ ▯

1. **D Monastero delle Clarisse Urbaniste di Santa Cecilia** (par, 🍴15, €12): ¶ ⊙, Fraternità 1, ☏3711886742, ⊙2:30-7pm, twin beds in shared rooms, dinner €12
2. **H Umbria** (€35/55 ▯): 📶⊙, Sant'Antonio 7, ☏0758554925 ✉, ⊙Mar-Nov, convenient, accommodating, pilgrim-oriented
3. **H Tiferno** (€75/110-120 ▯): 🅆 🅳 📶⊙, R. Sanzio 13, ☏ 0758550331 ✉, ⊙all year
4. **H Residence San Bartolomeo** (€56/74): 🏠📶⊙, San Bartolomeo 4, ☏3271111363 ✉, apartments for 2+
5. **H Antica Canonica** (€70): 🏠📶⊙, San Florido 23, ☏390758523298/3471564910 ✉
6. **H Mattonata** (€35/50): 📶⊙, Mattonata 3/a, ☏3899622407/3298995234 ✉
7. **H Le Mura** (€45/70 ▯): ¶📶⊙, Borgo Farinario 24, ☏0758521070 ✉

Città di Castello was founded some 2,500 years ago by Umbri and Gallic tribes. Known in Roman times as Tifernum Tiberium, the city was destroyed by the Goths in the 6th century before being rebuilt by Bishop Florido around a fortress, the source of the town's current name: Città di Castello ("City of the Castle"). Of particular note in Città di Castello is the **Pinacoteca Comunale**, an art museum that houses works by Raphael, Signorelli, della Robbia, and Ghiberti, among others (€6, ⊙10am-1pm, 2:30-6:30pm).

Eight centuries ago, Francis would have passed through Città di Castello. According to his follower and biographer, Thomas of Celano, it was here that Francis cast a demon out of a possessed woman. Locals of the town pleaded with Francis to help the woman, who was causing disturbances in town. Francis first sent one of his brothers to see if the woman was a fraud, or actually possessed. She recognized that this was not St. Francis and began to mock the brother. Francis then arrived and cast out the demon.

City streets in Città di Castello

7A LA VERNA TO CAPRESE MICHELANGELO

17.0km (10.6mi)
▲ 670m / ▼ 1190m

⏱ **5.5-6.5 Hours**
Difficulty: ▭▭▭

🅿 30%, 5.0km
🆄 70%, 12.0km

D H Lodging:
Chiusi Verna 1.3km
Caprese M. 17.0km

Waymarking:
Cammino di Assisi marks (green arrows, dancing saint stickers, red/green/white wooden arrows), E1/GEA, CAI routes 50 and 20A

A foggy morning at the mountaintop Eremo della Casella

Follow forested trails to a mountaintop chapel, continue through hillside villages to Michelangelo's birthplace.

💡 After descending to Chiusi della Verna, the route climbs back into the mountains, first following a rugged hiking trail, then 4x4 tracks. After passing the Eremo della Casella, the route descends through small alpine villages to Lama before making a short climb to Caprese Michelangelo, Michelangelo's birthplace. For those hoping to reconnect with the Via di Francesco in Pieve Santo Stefano (instead of in Città di Castello), an alternative route leaves the Cammino

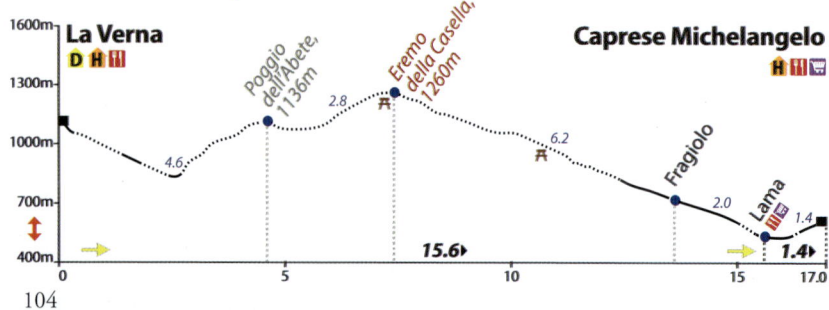

7A WAY OF ST. FRANCIS

di Assisi just after Caprese Michelangelo, following the GEA/E1 to Pieve Santo Stefano.

💡 Navigation is relatively straightforward, following the GEA/E1 route and Cammino di Assisi marks to Chiusi della Verna then on to Caprese Michelangelo.

💡 900m after Caprese Michelangelo, a 7.5km detour leaves the Cammino di Assisi and follows the GEA/E1 (as well as yellow tau markers and markers for REV19 and CAI 20), reconnecting with the Via di Francesco in Pieve Santo Stefano. Walking from La Verna to Pieve Santo Stefano via this route in one day is manageable, but it is a long, hard day (25.4km, ▲ 1040m / ▼ 1730m). If you follow this route, continue with Stage 8 (p. 86).

After 7.4km reach **Eremo della Casella**, a small Franciscan chapel at the top of Monte Foresto. According to tradition, St. Francis left La Verna on September 30, 1224 after receiving the stigmata and traveled toward Assisi via a route crossing Monte Foresto. At a place called La Casella at the top of the mountain, Francis turned back in the direction from which he'd come and bid farewell to La Verna for the last time. The first records of the hermitage date to September 30, 1228, the four-year anniversary of the departure of St. Francis from La Verna, and local villages have long-considered the chapel a true Franciscan sanctuary. On June 29 every year, locals gather in the meadow by the chapel to celebrate St. Peter and Paul's Feast Day.

Cobbled streets in Caprese Michelangelo

LA VERNA TO CAPRESE MICHELANGELO 7A

17.0 Caprese Michelangelo 🏠🍴✚€🚌

1. 🏠 **La Pecora e l'Agnello** (€39/65-70): Capoluogo 72, ☏3473484549
2. 🏠 **Buca di Michelangelo** (€45/70): 🍴📶⊙, Capoluogo 51, ☏0575793921, ⊙all year except for mid Jan-mid Feb
3. 🏠 **La Casina del Prete** (€50/90): 🧺📶⊙, Ca' di Franca 279, ☏3473484589, well outside Caprese, call about shuttle options
4. 🏠 **Agriturismo Borgo di Faeta** (€80): 🍴🧺📶⊙, Strapolino 109, ☏3397853334/3381673113, well off route

Bust in the museum at Michelangelo's birth home

Caprese Michelangelo is a small village in the Valtiberina ("High Tiber Valley") that is the birthplace of Michelangelo Buonarroti (born in 1475), one of the most famous artists in history. Michelangelo's father was a noble and magistrate of Caprese (now Caprese Michelangelo) and Chiusi della Verna. Michelangelo loved drawing as a child, and later in life he claimed that because his wet nurse's husband was a local stone cutter he was drawn to sculpture. By age 12, Michelangelo was apprenticing in Florence to become an artist. The rest is history.

The original **Buonarotti House** and castle complex have been turned into a museum (€4, ⊙ 10am-1pm and 3-5:30pm, reduced hours in winter, casanatalemichelangelo.it).

While there are no original Michelangelo pieces in the museum, there are a number of copies and casts, as well as art by other sculptors. It's also possible to see the **Chiesa di San Giovanni Battista**, the church where Michelangelo was baptized. Coordinate entry with the museum staff.

Michelangelo's birth home

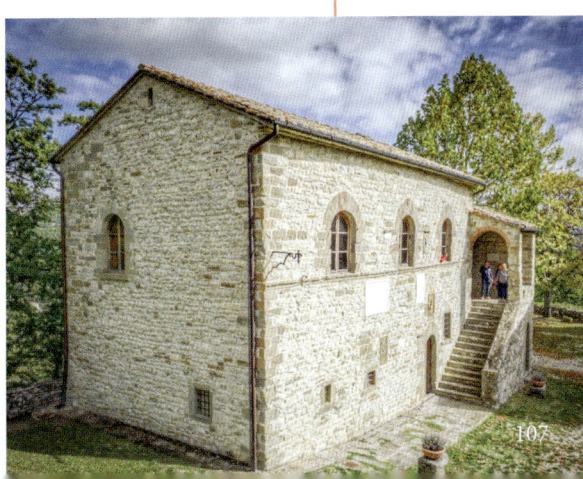

8A
CAPRESE MICHELANGELO TO SANSEPOLCRO

25.0km (15.6mi)
▲ 500m / ▼ 790m

⏱ **7-9 Hours**
Difficulty: ▭▭▯

🅿 39%, 9.8km
Ⓤ 61%, 15.2km

D H Lodging:
Sansepolcro 25.0km
Val d'Afra 29.2km

✝ **Waymarking:**
Cammino di Assisi marks, very intermittent marks for CAI 2 and 14 (details on map)

Caprese Michelangelo on the descent from the village

Descend from the Apennines, cross a floodplain to Sansepolcro, a town famous for its peace-inspiring art.

💡 The way to Sansepolcro continues down out of the mountains and into the Tiber Valley. The first half of the day passes through rolling countryside. After descending to Lago di Montedoglio, the routes flattens and continues through the countless tobacco fields in the fertile floodplain below the reservoir dam. The last few kilometers into Sansepolcro are less entertaining, as you traverse an industrial zone and walk briefly on a busy road. The distance passes quickly, and Sansepolcro provides a interesting endpoint to explore.

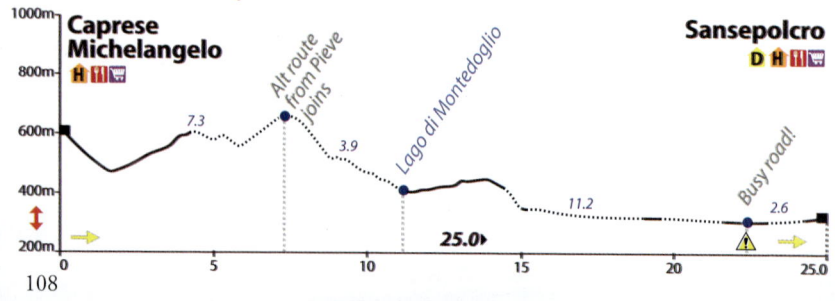

8A — WAY OF ST. FRANCIS

⚠ There are no certain places to for water/food resupply between Caprese Michelangelo and Sansepolcro. Be sure to carry plenty of food and water.

Starting from Caprese Michelangelo, the route follows SP-47 for 3.0km before turning right onto a smaller paved road in the direction of "Casina Baroti." Ahead, the road turns to gravel, climbing to a hilltop. After passing a large electric pylon, the route turns right and continues on a gravel road across the ridge, while another gravel road descends to the left. At 7.3km, an alternative route from Pieve Santo Stefano joins.

At 11.2km, before a larger intersection, the route turns left onto a dirt road, which quickly becomes a dirt path, cuts a corner, and descends to a series of gravel roads that cross the floodplain and tobacco fields below Lago di Montedoglio. Keep a sharp eye out for Cammino di Assisi marks at intersections, as they're easy to miss.

⚠ Use extreme caution when turning left onto SS-73 at 22.4km. Because there is only one bridge over the Tiber in this area, you must walk this road to cross the river. This is a very busy road, so stay on the left side of the road and remain alert. After crossing the Tiber, cross to the right side of the road (using a crosswalk) after passing gas stations to the right and left. From here gravel roads take you under the limited-access highway and into town.

Lago di Montedoglio

CAPRESE MICHELANGELO TO SANSEPOLCRO 8A

☼ Though it makes for a long day, walking an additional 4.2km to the very pleasant San Martino accommodation in Val d'Afra shortens the next (long) day to Città di Castello. An early enough start from Val d'Afra the subsequent morning means that you can feasibly arrive at Montecasale for morning mass. (Inquire at San Martino about current morning mass times.)

25.0 Sansepolcro D H 🍴 🛒 ⊕ ✚ € 🛈 🏧 🚻

See Stage 9, p. 96 for accommodation details.

☼ An alternative route from Pieve Santo Stefano joins the Cammino di Assisi on Monte Fungaia. From Pieve Santo Stefano red/white CAI 22 marks and blue/yellow marks head south on the west side of the Tiber River. Soon the route passes under the limited access highway. Just after the underpass, the route leaves the gravel road, continuing past an abandoned farmhouse onto a hiking path. After 2km on this hiking path, pass a quarry, and continue on a paved road passing a police equestrian school. A half kilometer after the equestrian school, turn right on a gravel road gong uphill, then 1.1km ahead ignore a left turn toward "Sigliano" and continue straight toward "Poggio Rosso." At the top of the climb, the route joins the Cammino di Assisi.

Passing through old city walls into Sansepolcro

9A SANSEPOLCRO TO CITTÀ DI CASTELLO

29.0km
(18.1mi)
▲ 960m / ▼ 990m

⏱ 9-11 Hours
Difficulty: ▪▪▪

🄿 44%, 12.6km
🅄 56%, 16.4km

D H Lodging:
Val d'Afra 4.2km
Agri. Somaia 15.7km
Selci-Lama 19.3km
<u>Città Castello 29km</u>

✝ Waymarking:
Cammino di Assisi
marks, CAI 4, 101A,
and 101 (details on
map)

Abandoned buildings in the mountains above Montecasale

Climb to a famous Franciscan hermitage, cross a mountain pass, descend to the city where St. Francis cast out a demon.

💡 Leaving the Tiber Valley and returning to the Apennine Mountains, the day begins with a tough climb to the famous Franciscan Hermitage at Montecasale. From the hermitage, another 10km of very pleasant mountain walking follow. The second half of the day follows smaller dirt and paved roads through farmland on the northern edge of the Tiber Valley, while the final 4km follow busier roads into Città di Castello.

⚠🍴🛒 There are no services until Celalba, 16.8km away. Be sure to carry plenty of food from Sansepolcro.

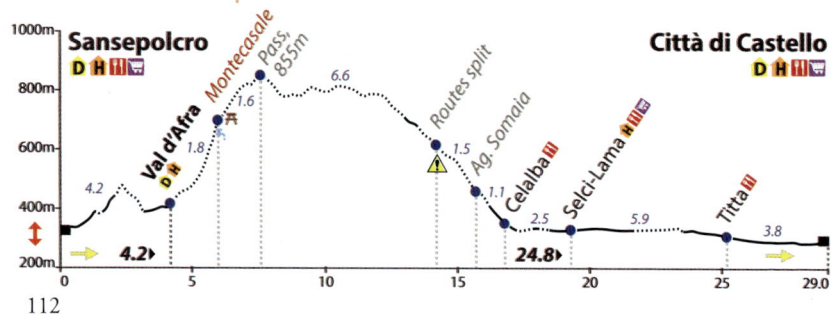

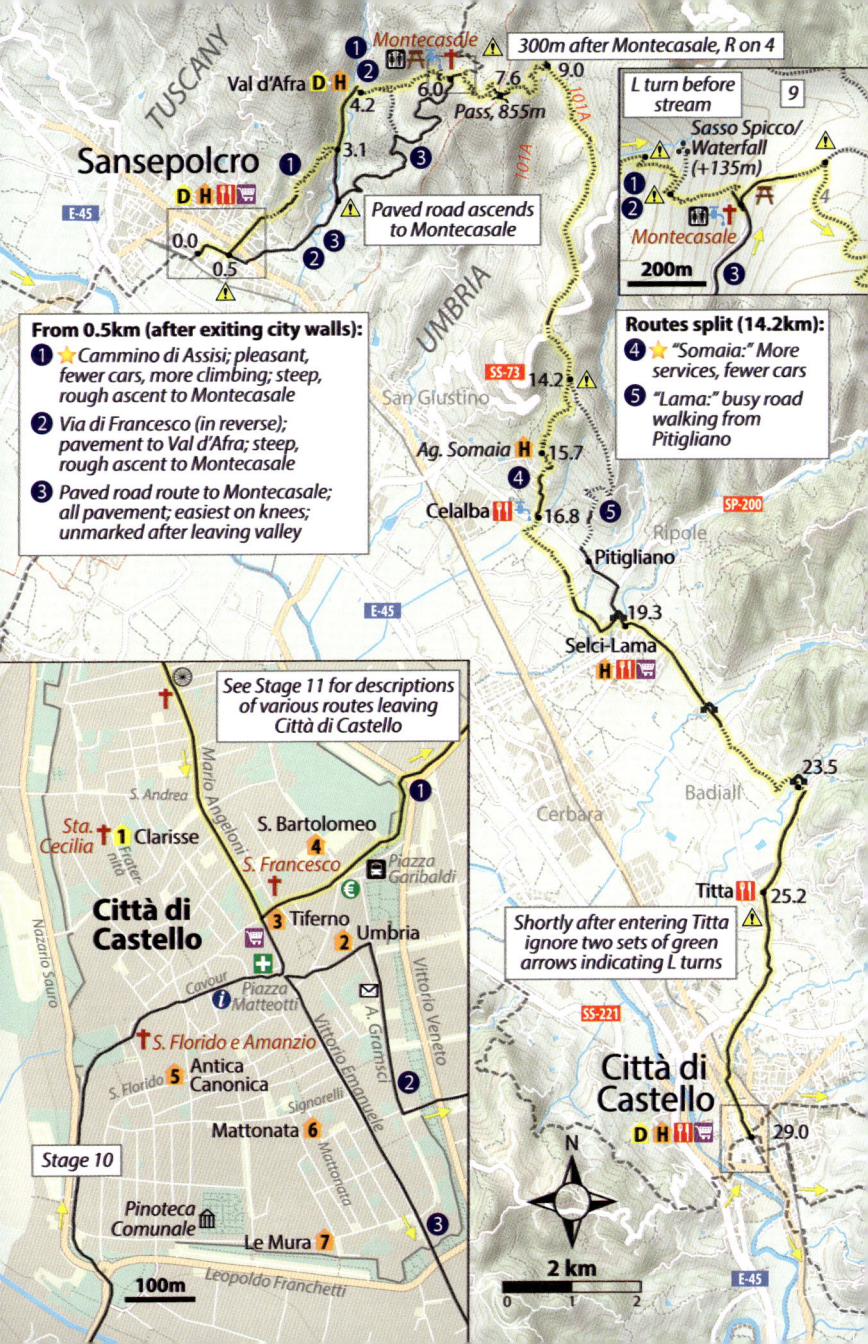

Farmland outside of Sansepolcro

There are several options for leaving Sansepolcro.

❶⭐ follows the Cammino di Assisi. From Piazza Torre di Berta, follow Via XX Settembre east, exiting the Old City walls and turning L on Via dei Molini. Ahead continue to follow signs for REV 10 and CAI 4 toward Montecasale.

❷ also exits the Old City following Via XX Settembre and continues straight nearly the whole way to Albergo Ristorante Taverna, then turns left on Via Dogana Vecchia. Ahead the route crosses SS-73 and continues on Via della Montagna toward Montecasale. At the turnoff you can either take option ❸ and follow the paved road to the right all the way to Montecasale or option ❷ and continue on Via della Montagna to Val d'Afra. Both these options follow paved roads that have more traffic than option ❶.

💡 **Alternative Itinerary:** You can split this long day into two short days by staying in Agriturismo Somaia or Selci-Lama.

4.2 Val d'Afra D H
(see Stage 9, p. 96)

6.0 Montecasale
(see Stage 9, p. 94)

💡 300m after Montecasale, turn right on CAI 4. Continue to a high point at 7.6km. (At a T intersection before the high point, go right following a sign for MTB 2.) On the other side of the high point, continue on a good 4x4 double track. At 9.0km follow CAI 101A toward "Celalba."

SANSEPOLCRO TO CITTÀ DI CASTELLO 9A

☀ At 14.2km the route splits, with two options descending the mountain to the valley below. At a Y intersection arrows point toward both ❹ "Somaia" and ❺ "Lama." Take the right option toward Somaia. Celalba has more services than Pitigliano, and the walking from Celalba to Selci-Lama follows much less lighter traffic roads than the Lama alternative.

15.7 H **Agriturismo Somaia** (€40/80 🛏): 🍴📶⊙, Somaia 1, ☎3397125463 🔗

19.3 Selci-Lama H🍴🛒⊕€🚌
H **La Rotunda** (€20+ 🛏): 🛁📶⊙, Togliatti 4/a, ☎0758582494 🔗, various accommodation options including B&B for pilgrims, prices/amenities vary

Directions to an agriturismo on the descent to Celalba

☀ At 25.2km, turn left onto the main road in Titta. Just ahead, at two consecutive intersections, green arrows indicate left turns.

⚠ Disregard these arrows, and continue straight on the main road into Città di Castello. (Cammino di Assisi marks pick up again shortly after the erroneous turns.)

29.0 Città di Castello D H🍴🛒⊙⊕€ℹ🚌🅿
(See stage 10, p. 103)

Farm tracks on the way to Selci-Lama

115

11
CITTÀ DI CASTELLO TO PIETRALUNGA

30.3km (18.9mi)
▲ 1170m / ▼ 900m

⏱ **9-11.5 Hours**
Difficulty: ▬ ◼ ◼

🅿 72%, 21.9km
🆄 28%, 8.4km

D H Lodging:
Candeggio 14.8km
Pieve de' Saddi 20.5km
Pietralunga 30.3km

✝ **Waymarking:**
Blue/yellow stripes, yellow taus, Via di Francesco/Via di Roma sign boards

Views of Pietralunga

Wander undulating hills, visit a chapel commemorating early Christian martyrs, explore the fortress and palaces of mountaintop Pietralunga

💡 After a potentially confusing exit from Città di Castello (three possible routes leave the city), a very long day through hilly terrain and rural countryside follows. Despite the day's length, non-technical trail surfaces (well-maintained gravel and paved roads) allow for making good time to Pietralunga, yet another idyllic hilltop town. If you're worried about the distance, lovely pilgrim hostels in Candeggio and Pieve de' Saddi make good intermediate stopping points.

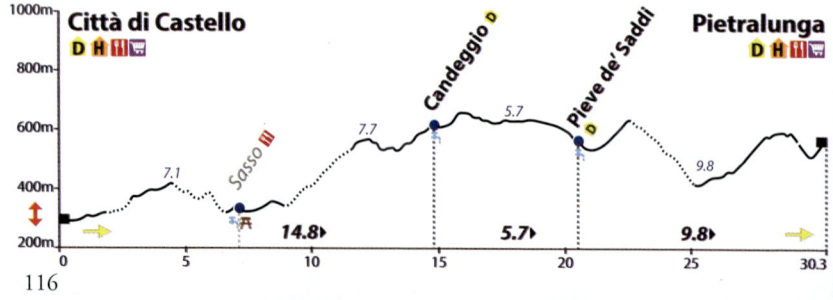

WAY OF ST. FRANCIS

⚠ **Flooding in 2022 made large portions of the route impassable from Città di Castello-Pietralunga-Gubbio (Stages 11-12).**

Local authorities recommend using bus services to **skip** these stages or **detouring** using provincial roads:
- SP-106 between Città di Castello and Pietralunga
- SP-205 between Pietralunga and Gubbio

For up-to-date information about route conditions, consider the following authorities:
- **Città di Castello Tourism Office** (city map, p. 113)
- **Gubbio pilgrim infoline:** ☏3661118386 (info on p. 124)
- **Municipality of Pietralunga Office of Public Relations:** ☏759460721
- Local accommodations on-route

Alternative Itinerary:

💡 The next two days to Gubbio cover 56.4km with a considerable amount of elevation gain. If this feels difficult, consider covering the distance in three days:

- Città di Castello-Pieve de' Saddi (20.5km, ▲ 749m)
- Pieve de' Saddi-Loreto (25.4km, ▲ 1073m)
- Loreto-Gubbio (10.6km, ▲ 227m): though short, this half day allows time to visit Gubbio's many notable sites.

Waymarking on the approach to Pietralunga

To walk this itinerary, be sure to call ahead about accommodation in Loreto, as it is sometimes limited.

⚠ There are few services between Città di Castello and Pietralunga, so carry plenty of food. 🚰 Reliable water fountains are located in a park across from Bar Sasso, at the turn-off to Candeggio, and at the pilgrim hostel in Pieve de' Saddi. Bar Sasso is the only place to buy food before Pietralunga, but it has variable hours, so don't count on it being open.

CITTÀ DI CASTELLO TO PIETRALUNGA 11

There are three possible ways to exit Città di Castello:

❶ ⭐ The first follows the Via di Francesco, avoids car traffic, and is by far the best waymarked. This way is far better, even if slightly longer than both other options. Walk to the east end of Piazza Garibaldi and follow blue/yellow marks and yellow taus out of the city.

❷ The second follows very intermittent Cammino di Assisi marks before rejoining the Via di Francesco not far out of Città di Castello. From Piazza Matteoti, walk east on Via Sant'Antonio to Viale Antonio Gramsci, where you turn right. Continue to Via Lampa (on the right) and turn left, going through a parking lot and passing a park on your left. Continue across railroad tracks, then immediately after turn right on Galileo Galilei. Continue to follow this road until SP-106. Turn right onto SP-106, then make an immediate left onto a smaller paved road, following Cammino di Assisi marks and a sign for Agriturismo San Giovanni. Just before reaching the agriturismo, turn right onto a dirt double track. Follow it as it turns left and climbs to a better dirt road, where you turn right, rejoining the Via di Francesco. This route option is slightly more direct than the first, but waymarking is poorer. ⚠ GPS navigation is recommended for this way.

❸ The third is the most direct, but least appealing and not marked. Leave Piazza Matteotti following Vittorio Emanuele. Exit the Old City walls and continue straight. Ahead follow the road as it angles left to a traffic circle, passing a park (Laghetto dei Cigni) to the right. Turn right, following the main road past a Eurospin grocery store. Ahead, turn left, following signs for Pietralunga and Sasso. Cross under the railroad tracks, and turn right at the T intersection on the other side, now following SP-106. Continue on this road, rejoining the Via di Francesco just before Sasso. We do not recommend this route as SP-106 is somewhat busy near Città di Castello and has no shoulder. While this route is included in other guides and on the Via di Francesco website, there's little-to-no waymarking to be found.

Interior of the chapel at Pieve de' Saddi

14.8 Candeggio D

D Rifugio Candeggio (par, ⌂25, don 🛏): 🏠🍴🇼📶⊙,
📞3295620677, ⌚all year, dinner/breakfast by donation

20.5 Pieve de' Saddi D

⭐ **D Pieve de' Saddi** (par, ⌂16, don 🛏): 🏠🍴🇼📶⊙,
📞3295620677/3805158248, ⌚Mar-Oct, dinner/breakfast by
donation, beautiful restored church building in peaceful location,
welcome to stop for a break and a drink

Pieve de' Saddi is the location where one of the first Christian communities in the Upper Tiber region formed. The church dates back to the 5th century and was built on the former site of a Roman temple. The name Pieve de' Saddi, a contracted form of the name Pieve dei Santi ("Parish of the Saints"), points to the various saints connected with the place. Most famous was Saint Crescentinus (or St. Crescenziano), a 3rd/4th-century Roman soldier who is said to have converted to Christianity. Fleeing Diocletian, the Roman emperor known for his persecution of Christianity in the early Roman Empire, Crescentinus and his companions traveled

Country views from Pietralunga's central piazza

CITTÀ DI CASTELLO TO PIETRALUNGA

to Umbria, specifically the region around Tifernum Tiberinum (modern day Città di Castello). There they successfully grew a Christian community. Crescentinus is venerated as a warrior saint, and is said to have slain a dragon—a "rib" of the dragon (possibly a mammoth tusk) is on display in the Diocesan Museum in Città di Castello. Crescentinus was eventually captured and beheaded at Pieve de' Saddi. Today a simple but lovely pilgrim hostel is located at the church complex. Even if not staying there, it's worth a detour to visit the church and see the 8th-century fresco depicting St. Crescentinus killing a dragon.

30.3 Pietralunga D H 🍴🛒➕€🅿

1. **D Betania** (par, 🛏19, don): ☎3280338261, central location with peaceful garden, behind main church, 🕘all year
2. **H Tinca** (€30/60 🛏): 📶🅦🛜⊙, G. Marconi 7, ☎0759460057, 🕘all year
3. **H BB Gaigo** (€20/40 🛏): 🅦🛜⊙, Roma 55, ☎3498709198, nico.ortali@gmail.com, €60 for 4-person room
4. **H Villa Ginevra** (€35 🛏): 🅦🛜⊙🍴, Falani 3, ☎5743249/0759462077, bebginevra@gmail.com, 🕘all year
5. **H Borgo** (€50/74 🛏) 🛜⊙, Roma 139, ☎0759460798, 🕘Mar-Nov

Pietralunga is an ancient hilltop town whose founding dates to 2nd/1st century BCE Umbrians. There are significant Roman remains in the area: ruins of villas, aqueducts, and roads. Today the town retains much of its medieval character. The parish church of Santa Maria, which rises proudly from the central piazza, is particularly worth visiting.

Portraits of pilgrims in Pietralunga

12

PIETRALUNGA TO GUBBIO

26.1km (16.3mi)
▲ 880m / ▼ 940m

⏱ **7.5-10 Hours**
DIFFICULTY: ▬ ▬

🅿 59%, 15.3km
U 41%, 10.8km

D H LODGING:
Loreto 16.1km
Gubbio 26.1 km
*Various Agriturismi
32.3-34.3km*

⚑ WAYMARKING:
Yellow/blue stripes
and yellow taus

Views from the mountains above Pietralunga

⚠ No food services are directly on route, but at 17.3km, a short detour (+600m) to Mocaiana brings you to a grocery store and café.

Enjoy expansive mountain views, plod through a long, wide valley, finish in one of Umbria's most idyllic cities.

☀ After Pietralunga, several significant climbs separate you from Gubbio, though none are technically challenging. At the day's second pass, stop for a moment to take in the wide-ranging views of the mountains and valleys ahead. After finally descending into the valley plain that stretches west from Gubbio, roughly 9km of flat, monotonous walking follow. Gubbio, an exquisitely-preserved medieval Umbrian town, makes an excellent day's endpoint. Intermediate accommodation in Loreto allows you to break up the day.

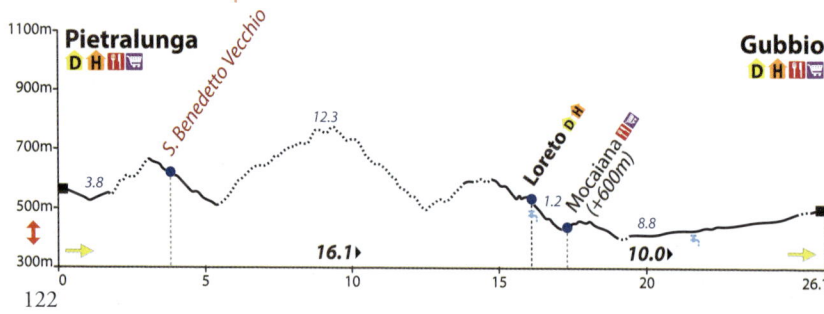

122

⚠ **Flooding** in 2022 made large portions of the route impassable from Città di Castello-Pietralunga-Gubbio (stages 11-12). See details on p. 118.

12 WAY OF ST. FRANCIS

16.1 Loreto D H

- **D** Ostello Parrocchiale (par, 35, don): Jun-Aug, 3460899676
- **H** BB di Valle (12, €35): Loreto 27, 3479768879, country home with wonderful views, beds in private rooms in apartments, good reviews

26.1 Gubbio D H

1. **D** S. Francesco (par, 25, don): Piazza Quaranta Martiri, 3703490485, accoglienzasanfrancescogubbio@gmail.com, best economical parochial option in Gubbio
2. **D** S. Ubaldo (par, don) Monte Ingino 5, 0759273872, f.panfili@tin.it, accessed by cable car and hiking trail
3. **D** Istituto Maestre Pie Filippini (par, 16, €31): Giuseppe Garibaldi 100, 0759273768, maestrepiefgubbio@virgilio.it, all year, twin beds in private rooms, pleasant
4. **D** S. Secondo (par, don): Tifernate, 0759273869, biblioteca.steucco@libero.it
5. **D** S. Marziale (par, don): Appennino, 3297199958, (Sister Daniela), pictestn1@gmail.com
6. **D** S. Agostino (par, don): Porta Romana 7, 0759273814, marcodibenedetto12@gmail.com
7. **D** Madonna del Prato (par, don), Perugina 94, 0759274574, madonnadelprato@gmail.com
8. **D** Oratorio don Bosco (par, groups only, price dependent on group size): Massarelli 4, 3339389999 (Anna), oratoriodigubbio@libero.it
9. **H** Grotta dell'Angelo (€36/52): Gioia 47, 0759271747, Feb-Dec
10. **H** Piccardi (€30/50): Piccardi 12, 0759276108, Apr-Dec
11. **H** Porta Marmorea (€50-55/65): Mazzatinti 12, 0759222680, all year
12. **H** Hotel S. Marco (€45/55): Campo di Marte 5, 0759220234, all year
13. **H** Bosone (€60/80): XX Settembre 22, 0759220688, all year
14. **H** Relais Ducale (€70-85): Piazza Grande 5, 0759220157
15. **H** Locanda del Duca (€60): Piccardi 1, 0759277753
16. **H** Logge (€40/50): Piccardi 7, 0759277574
17. **H** Hotel Gattapone (€45/60): Beni 11, 0759272489

☀ There are an impressive eight parochial pilgrim accommodations in Gubbio, the most convenient of which are San Francesco (donation dormitory in central location) and Istituto Pie Filippini (twin beds in private rooms). Also notable is Sant'Ubaldo, located on Monte Ingino, looking out over Gubbio (accessible by cable car).

⭐☀ **Piccola Accoglienza, the pilgrim association for the Way of St. Francis** that sends out credentials is located in Gubbio. The association operates a pilgrim infoline offering information about the route and assistance in finding pilgrim lodging in Gubbio (Baldassini 22, 3661118386, piccolaccoglienzagubbio@gmail.com).

⚠ **Some pilgrim accommodations in Gubbio may be intermittently open**, check with the Pilgrim Association for latest openings.

🛍 Though not a full gear store, a small athletic shoe store ("Athlete's Foot") on the southern edge of the city has basic footwear supplies.

PIETRALUNGA TO GUBBIO

Gubbio is an idyllic Umbrian town built into the side of Mount Ingino. The hills above the town were settled as early as the Bronze Age. The city itself was established by the Umbrian people. By the Roman Age, Gubbio (then known as Iguvium) had become an important Roman town. The Roman amphitheater, visible on the approach to the city from the south, is one of the largest surviving Roman amphitheaters in the world. In the Middle Ages, Gubbio continued to prosper, sending 1,000 knights on the First Crusade. According to local legend, knights from Gubbio were the first Crusaders to enter the Church of the Holy Sepulchre in Jerusalem.

In 1444, the Iguvine Tablets were discovered in Gubbio. These tablets represent the largest and most complete surviving example of the Umbrian language, and their content provides insight into ancient religious practice in Europe and the Mediterranean. The tablets are displayed in the Civic Museum in Palazzo dei Consoli (€7, ☉Apr-Oct 10am-1pm and 3-6pm, Nov-Mar 10am-1pm and 2:30-5:30pm).

On May 15, Gubbio celebrates Saint Ubaldo Day, with the spectacle of the *Corsa dei Ceri* ("Race of the Candles"). On this day, local teams celebrate Saints Ubaldo, George, and Anthony by racing up Mount Ingino to the Basilica di Sant'Ubaldo. Each team carries a statue of their saint fixed

Hillside city of Gubbio

atop a wooden pillar measuring 4m tall and weighing around 280kg. Thousands of visitors from throughout Italy travel to the town to take part in the celebrations.

Also notable is Gubbio's annual Christmas tree. Since 1981, members of the town have strung Christmas lights stretching from the top of Monte Ingino down to Gubbio, forming the shape of a Christmas tree. The tree is over 650m tall and made up of hundreds of lights. The Guinness Book of World Records recognizes this as the world's tallest Christmas tree.

Palazzo dei Consoli and Museo Civico

PIETRALUNGA TO GUBBIO — 12

Many stories also connect St. Francis to Gubbio. After renouncing his inheritance and removing his cloak in front of the Bishop of Assisi, Francis fled to Gubbio via Valfabbrica. In Gubbio, he was welcomed by friend and fellow cloth merchant Giacomo Spadalunga, who gave Francis the cloak and belt that would become the typical Franciscan habit. Also in Gubbio, Francis served in a leper house and was inspired to make aiding lepers a key part of Franciscan life.

Perhaps most famously, legend has it that Francis tamed a wolf in Gubbio that had been terrorizing the town. The wolf had been eating livestock and attacking people, and the terrified townsfolk begged Francis to intervene on their behalf. Francis agreed and went to find the wolf, approaching the wolf's hideout. When the wolf came toward Francis with his teeth bared, Francis made a sign of the cross. Then, saying that he came in God's name, he asked the wolf not to harm any people, including "Brother Ass" (referring to himself).

At this, the wolf became calm and sat quietly at his feet while Francis spoke to the wolf, making an agreement with him: if the wolf would repent from his marauding, the townspeople would feed him regularly so that he never went hungry. Francis and the wolf then walked together back into town, and when Francis announced the agreement he had made with "Brother Wolf," the wolf held out his paw to cement the pact. Today a statue commemorating Francis and the wolf sits across from the small Vittorina Chapel on the way out of town.

There's much to see in Gubbio. Here are just a few sites that should be on your visit list: In the lower part of town are the Roman amphitheater and Chiesa di San Francesco, the latter built on the site of the Spadalunga family house. Higher, midway to the top of the town is the Palazzo dei Consoli and Museo Civico. At the top of the town are the Cathedral of Saints Mariano and Giacomo and, across from it, the Palazzo Ducale. You can walk or take a cable car all the way up to the Basilica di Sant'Ubaldo on Monte Ingino, where the remains of St. Ubaldo are kept (cable car: ☉10am-7pm, one way €4, round trip €6).

13

GUBBIO TO SAN PIETRO IN VIGNETO

16.3km (10.2mi)
▲ 460m / ▼ 510m

⏱ **4.5-6 Hours**
Difficulty: ▬▬□

P 57%, 9.3km
U 43%, 7.0km

D H Lodging:
Various Agriturismi
6.2-13.1km
San Pietro 16.3km
*Bellugello 18.6km,
+2.6km
Biscina 22.3km*

Waymarking:
Blue/yellow stripes,
yellow taus, Via di
Francesco/Via di
Roma sign boards

Pilgrims on gravel
roads in the hills south
of Gubbio

Follow a well-trod route through the hills above the Chiasco River, arriving at a pilgrim hostel famous for its foot washing.

💡 Finally, a short day provides respite for weary legs, while the foot washing ceremony at San Pietro in Vigneto offers refreshment for dusty soles. From Gubbio, the route passes the statue commemorating St. Francis' negotiations with the Wolf of Gubbio and continues south another 8km through the flat valley, passing Ponte d'Assi and its café and grocery store. Soon the route climbs into the low hills south of Gubbio, which are dotted with agriturismi. The day ends at a pilgrim dorm in a peaceful church complex at San Pietro in Vigneto, where gracious hosts provide lodging and meals. If the dorm

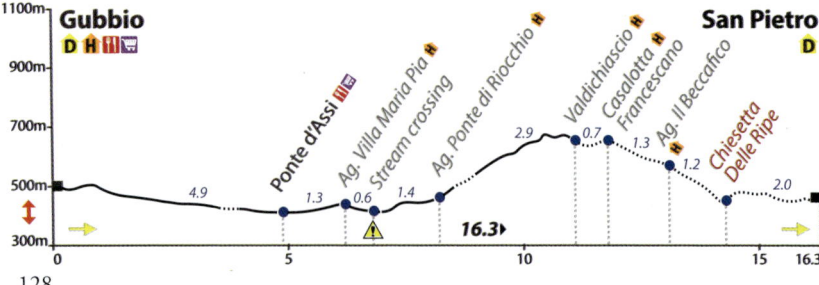

13 WAY OF ST. FRANCIS

Statue of St. Francis and the wolf of Gubbio

at San Pietro in Vigneto is full, there are various other accommodation options in the surrounding 5km.

⚠️ There are no places to buy groceries before Valfabbrica (37.9km from Gubbio) after passing Ponte d'Assi. Stock up on food in Gubbio or in Ponte d'Assi, and be sure to confirm meal plans with accommodations on your first night after Gubbio. Most of the agriturismi can provide meals and/or groceries, but they require advance notice. The pilgrim hostel in San Pietro serves dinner and breakfast on a donation basis.

💡 The pilgrim hostel in San Pietro has only 12 beds, so call ahead to confirm your arrival. If full, several other agriturismi and B&Bs are located within 5-6km of San Pietro.

6.2 🛏 **Agriturismo Villa Maria Pia** (€70): 🐕📶⊙🍴, ☎3398110234, apartments for two, extra person €15, breakfast €3.50

8.2 🛏 **Agriturismo Ponte di Riocchio** (€55/person 🍴): 🍴📶⊙🍴, ⊙all year, ☎0759222611, ⊙all year, price is per person including dinner and breakfast (reduced price without meals)

11.1 🛏 **Vadichiascio** (€50/80 🛏): 🍴📶⊙🍴, Valdichiascio 1, ☎075920251/3476511520, beautiful/peaceful location with nice garden

11.8 🛏 **Casalotto Francescano** (€35/person 🛏): 🐕🍴W📶⊙, Valdichiascio 3, ☎3473643807, ⊙all year, basic cooking supplies in kitchen, with 3-day advance notice can provide groceries, additional, simpler apartment at the back of the property (€25 + €15 for each additional person, + cost of heating), €18 pilgrim menu

13.1 🛏 **Agriturismo Il Beccafico** (€50 🛏): 🍴W D📶⊙, ⊙all year, price per person including dinner and breakfast, preferably more than one person

GUBBIO TO SAN PIETRO IN VIGNETO 13

16.3 San Pietro in Vigneto D

⭐ **D Eremo San Pietro in Vigneto** (par, 📷12, don 🛎️):
🏠🍴📶⊙, ✆339450501/334274023,
sanpietroinvigneto@confraternitadisanjacopo.it, true pilgrim dorm in lovely, peaceful location, meals by donation, footwashing ceremony, call ahead

The hermitage at San Pietro in Vigneto is situated along the Roman-era route from Assisi to Gubbio. Dating to the 13th century, the church would have existed in St. Francis' time. The religious complex served as a residence for Benedictine monks and as a pilgrim hostel. Today the pilgrim hostel at San Pietro is run by the Perugia Chapter of the Confraternity of St. James. Inside the church, frescoes date to the 15th century.

Pilgrims enjoying a peaceful evening at the pilgrim hostel in San Pietro in Vigneto

14

SAN PIETRO IN VIGNETO TO VALFABBRICA

21.6km (13.5mi)
▲ 890m / ▼ 1060m

⏲ **7–8.5 Hours**
Difficulty: ▬▬ ▬

P 22%, 4.8km
U 78%, 16.8km

D H **Lodging:**
Bellugello 2.3km,
+2.6km
Biscina 6.0km
Valfabbrica 21.6km
Assisi 34.9km

✝ **Waymarking:**
Blue/yellow stripes,
yellow taus, Via
Francesco/Via di
Roma signs

Mountain road above Valfabbrica with views of the Chiascio Valley

Climb hills, visit remains of an imposing castle, descend to a town where a destitute St. Francis met a miserly welcome.

☀ Though not a particularly long day, a steep climb to Biscina and a series of short and steep ascents and descents make today's walk a demanding one. Enjoyable views of the Chiascio River Valley and Lago di Valfabbrica (formed by a dam on the Chiascio River) are present all day, and the Biscina Castle is worth a visit despite its disrepair. Two unmarked paved road shortcuts allow you to significantly ease the day's overall difficulty, if you so choose, though they also miss some nice sections of the route.

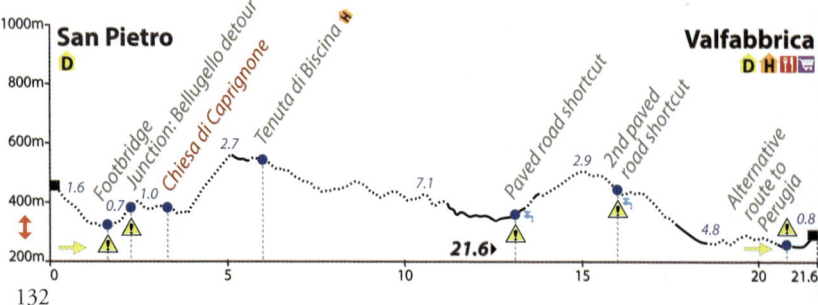

WAY OF ST. FRANCIS

Narrow trail below Biscina

Castello di Biscina

A similarly-distanced detour passes through Bellugello with its accommodations, and returns to the main route on another path, not adding many kilometers. At 2.3km at a T with a gravel road, a sign points R to Bellugello while the official route goes L. From Bellugello, you can return to Biscina along a paved road without backtracking.

2.3 Bellugello, +2.6km

1. BB Bellugello (€40/60): ☎3331722906, ⊙Mar-Nov, apartments for 2 and 4 people, +€15 for each additional person above 2
2. Agriturismo La Sosta di San Francesco (€35/60): ☎075920035/3333838769, direzione@lasostadisanfrancesco.com, ⊙Mar-Dec

The now-abandoned **Church of Caprignone** sits on the hillside above the Chiascio Valley. The church was built on the remains of an existing pre-Christian temple, and in the 13th century Franciscans built a larger church (visible today) and monastery (in ruins). According to tradition, the church hosted the first Franciscan chapter established outside of Assisi.

6.0 Agriturismo Tenuta di Biscina (€60/100):
☎0759229730, ⊙Apr-Nov, apartments for 2 and 4 people, €40/person in 4-person apartment, dinner €20, owner can provide groceries with advance notice

The hilltop **Biscina Castle** overlooks the Chiascio Valley. The origin date of the castle is unknown, but it certainly existed in St. Francis' time and was an important fortification on the road between Assisi and Gubbio. Because of its strategic location, the castle was often a point of contention between Gubbio and Perugia during conflicts between the two cities.

💡 There are two possibilities for shortening the day with paved road detours. The first stays on the paved road in the Chiasco Valley instead of climbing to the right at 13.1km. This option misses some nice views from the mountaintop. The second possible detour follows a paved road to the right at the second of two successive T intersections with paved road at 16.0km, just before reaching the Pieve di Coccorano chapel.

SAN PIETRO IN VIGNETO TO VALFABBRICA   14

21.6 Valfabbrica D H 🍴🛒➕€🏠

1. **D** **Betania** (par, 🛏29, don): 🎒🛜🖥, Piazza S. Sebastiano 3, ☎075901619 ✉, betaniavalfabbrica@gmail.com, 🕑all year, pleasant, central option
2. **D H** **Ostello Francescano** (🛏30, €15-20/-/43): 🍴🧺🛜🖥, Piave 3, ☎075901195, 🕑Mar-Nov (all year for groups), dinner €20, beautiful garden
3. **D** **Santa Maria** (par, 🛏30 don), 🎒🖥, Mameli 20, ☎075901155 ✉, valfabbrica@diocesiassisi.it, simple
4. **H** **Affittacamere Sui Passi** (€26/40): 🍴🧺, Castellana 21, ☎3466156189 ✉, 🕑all year, apartments for 2-4 people (triple €60, quad €72), reception and pilgrim menu in restaurant around corner
5. **H** **Camere Villa Verde** (€25/50): 🛜🖥, Roma 1, ☎0759029013/3385824259 ✉, 🕑all year
6. **H** **Agriturismo Il Pioppo** (€25 🛏): 🍴, 🛜🖥🛏, ☎0759029400/3343696948 ✉, price per person in rooms, possibility of discount with sleeping bag, **+1.8km**

After giving up his family inheritance, Francis wandered the hills north of Assisi joyfully singing songs of praise in French. Not far from Valfabbrica, Francis was accosted by thieves who demanded to know who he was and what he was doing. Francis responded, confidently, that he was the "herald of the Great King." Unperturbed, the thieves robbed Francis, beat him, and threw him in a pit of snow. After the thieves had gone, Francis picked himself up and made his way to Valfabbrica (other sources say Coccorano or Caprignone) where he sought out the charity of a local monastery. Unimpressed with the bedraggled Francis, the monks offered him little help, forcing him to serve as a kitchen boy in return for a meager broth. Still only clothed in a ragged shirt, Francis eventually left, out of necessity, for Gubbio. Later, after Francis had become famous, the abbot of the monastery, remembering Francis, asked Francis for forgiveness.

Valfabbrica formed around the Benedictine Abbey of Santa Maria and was an important town on the route between Assisi and Gubbio. The town's name alludes to its strategic location at a crossing of the Chiascio River. (Valfabbrica was originally called Vado Fabricae, or "Fabricae Ford.")

☀ At 20.8km, an official Via di Francesco alternative route stays straight, going to Perugia (not covered in this guide). Turn left here, heading into Valfabbrica. A day trip to Perugia from Assisi can easily be made by public transportation.

Pieve di Coccorano

15

VALFABBRICA TO ASSISI

13.3km (8.3mi)
▲ 570m / ▼ 500m

⏱ **4-5 Hours**
Difficulty: 🟧🟧⬜

P 53%, 7.1km
U 47%, 6.2km

D H Lodging:
Agr. Il Pioppo 1.8km
Agr. La Pieve 6.9km
Assisi 13.3km
Spello 26.1km

✝ **Waymarking:**
Blue/yellow stripes, yellow taus, Via Francesco/Via di Roma signs

Approaching Assisi with views of the Basilica di San Francesco in the distance

Enjoy a short day to Assisi, the birthplace of St. Francis and a city overflowing with Franciscan history.

💡 After 15 days, Francis' birthplace and home base of Assisi makes a fitting end to the first half of the journey to Rome and constitutes an important pilgrimage destination in its own right. At only 13.3km, the day's walk to the Basilica di San Francesco is quite short, though there's one punchy climb after Valfabbrica. Arrive early, register for a testimonium document, and explore the city. The nightly pilgrim mass in the basilica is worth prioritizing.

6.9 H **Agriturismo La Pieve** (€25/40): 🐕 W 📶 👁,
Pieve S. Nicolo, ☎3338178150/0758199018 📝, breakfast €5

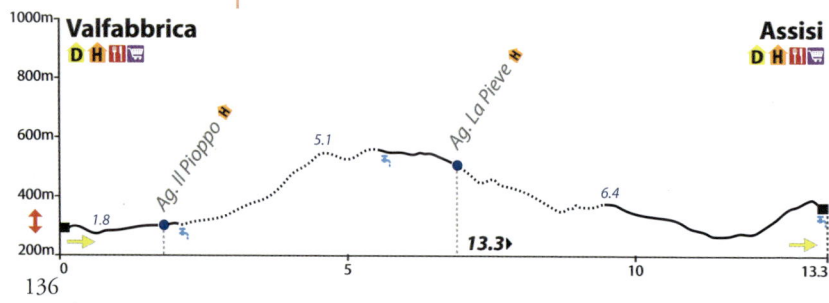

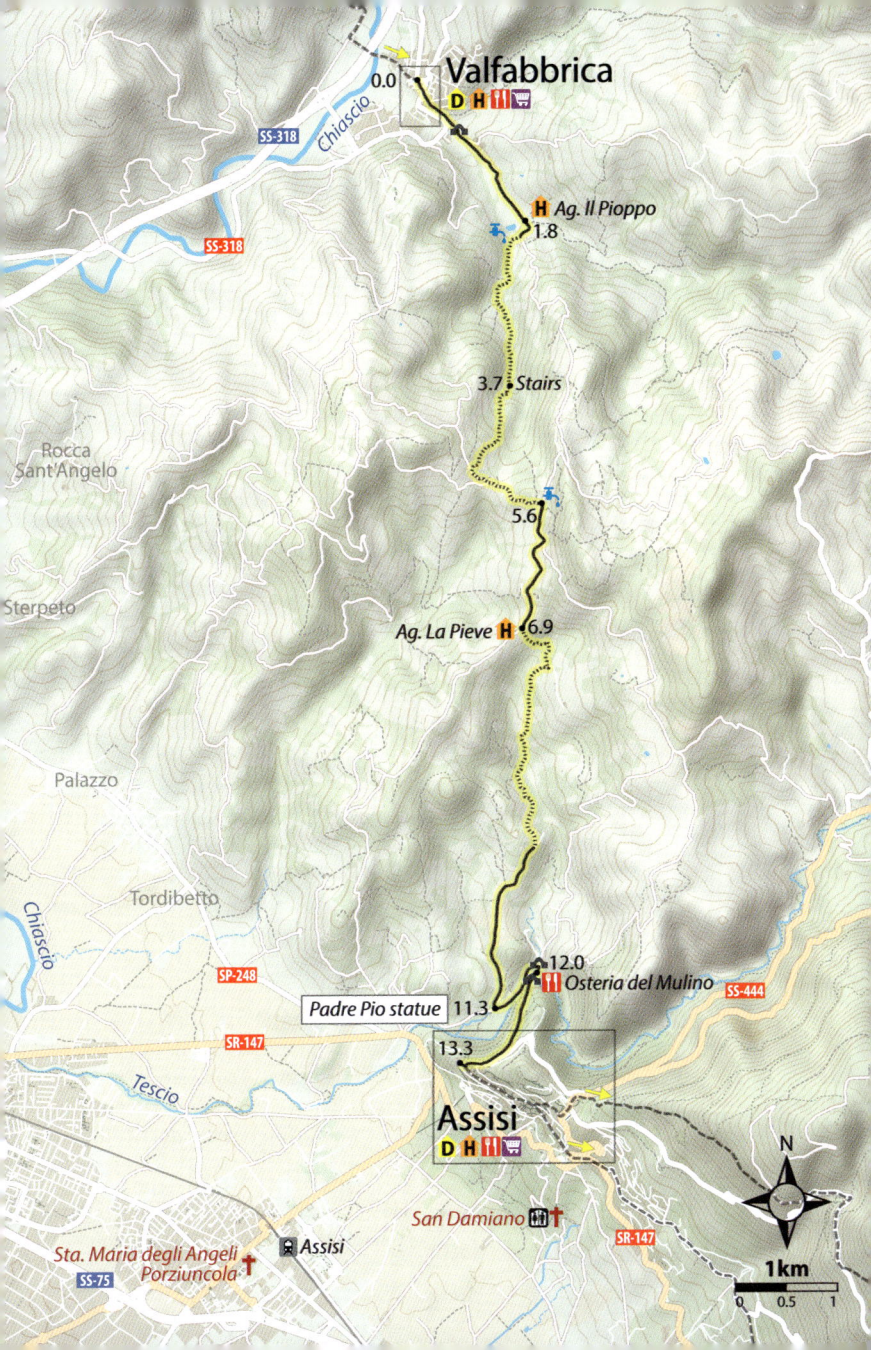

15 WAY OF ST. FRANCIS

13.3 Assisi D H 🛒 ➕ € 🛈 🚻 🚉 ✈

1. **D Camping Fontemaggio** (€22/28/48): 🍴 W D 📶 ⓘ, Via Eremo delle Carceri 24, 📞075813636/075812317, ⓒall year, 2.5km from Basilica di San Francesco
2. **D H Casa Francesca** (🛏15, €20/person 🍴): 📶 ⓘ, San Pio X 7, 📞0758043670, www.assisicasafrancesca.it, ssmassisi@gmail.com, ⓒall year, +**3km off route in lower city near Basilica di Santa Maria**
3. **H Posta Panoramic** (€45/65 🍴): 🍴 📶 ⓘ, S. Paolo 11, 📞075812558, ⓒall year, rooms with great views, owners are very accommodating to pilgrims, good reviews
4. **H Camere Martini** (€20/40): W 📶 ⓘ, S. Gregorio 6, 📞3479085212/075813536, pleasant, economic
5. **H Camere Calocci** (€60): 📶, Macelli Vecchi 11, 📞3703757684
6. **H Pax** (€50/80 🍴): 🍴 W D 📶 ⓘ, Sant'Antonio 14, 📞075816297
7. **H Camere Santa Chiara** (€40/60): 🅿 📶 ⓘ, Arco Sant'Antonio, 📞075815220, ⓒMar-Nov
8. **H Alter Ego BB** (€55 🍴): 🅿 W D 📶, S. Gabriele d'Addolorata 14, 📞3312538401
9. **H Camere Carli** (€45/60): 📶, Piazza S. Rufino, 📞075812490
10. **H Vico del Poeta** (€60-65 🍴): 🅿 📶, Jorgensen 6, 📞0758064135, 2 apartments
11. **H Cittadella Ospitalità** (€37/54 🍴): 🍴 📶 ⓘ, Ancaiani 3, 📞075813231, ⓒall year
12. **H Il Palazzo** (€60/95 🍴): 📶, S. Francesco 8/E, 📞075816841
13. **H Giotto** (€105/112+ 🍴): 🍴 📶 ⓘ 🛏, Fontebella 41, 📞075812209, ⓒMar-Dec
14. **H Berti** (€45/76 🍴): 🍴 📶, Piazza S. Pietro 24, 📞075813466
15. **H BB A Casa Tua** (€70 🍴): 📶, Piaggia di Porta S. Pietro 9, 📞3297741497
16. **H Minerva** (€50/75 🍴): 🍴 📶 ⓘ, Piazza Ruggero Bonghi 7, 📞075812416, ⓒMar-Nov
17. **H Sorella Luna** (€63/90 🍴): W D 📶, Frate Elia, 📞075816194
18. **H Porperzio** (€48/80 🍴): 📶, S. Francesco 38, 📞075815198
19. **H San Giacomo** (€90): 🍴 📶, San Giacomo 6, 📞075816778
20. **H Porta Nuova** (€74 🍴): W D 📶, Umberto I 21, 📞075812405

☀ Assisi receives thousands of visitors annually. As such, there are a multitude of accommodation options, though surprisingly few economical pilgrim accommodations. We include a list of pilgrim-oriented accommodations, as well as a selection of other private accommodations that receive consistently-positive reviews.

ⓘ **Statio Peregrinorum ("Pilgrim Office")** is located directly across from the lower entrance to the Basilica di San Francesco. The office issues testimonia (certificates of completion) to pilgrims who have traveled at least 100km on foot, or 200km on bicycle, to visit the tomb of St. Francis. ⓒMon-Sat 10am-12:30pm and 3-6pm, Sun 10am-12:30pm

✝ A **special pilgrim mass** is held Mon-Fri at ⓒ6pm in the lower basilica. Check at the pilgrim office for more information.

WAY OF ST. FRANCIS

The Saint's hometown was the center of the Franciscan movement. Francis' initial conversion took place here, and it's where the first small Franciscan communities were established. Though Francis' fame grew as he traveled widely, he always returned to his home. Memories of St. Francis permeate Assisi, and many sites commemorate various parts of his life. The hilltop town has retained its medieval character and is a major tourist and pilgrimage destination, with thousands visiting annually. The more modern (less touristy) town of Assisi is located in the valley bottom.

Plan to spend at least a day in Assisi—that's the minimum necessary to visit the major sites connected to St. Francis—though you can easily spend more time wandering through the city's lovely narrow streets. This book covers a few of Assisi's main attractions, and additional information is available in the tourist office. Entire guidebooks are dedicated to the city of Assisi itself.

Sunset over the Basilica di San Francesco

VALFABBRICA TO ASSISI

On your way to Assisi from Valfabbrica, the **Basilica di San Francesco** is visible, prominently jutting out from Assisi's hillside. Since 2000, the cathedral has been recognized as a UNESCO World Heritage site. Construction of the Basilica began in 1228, only two years after St. Francis' death.

The **Upper Basilica** is the new part of the cathedral, constructed in Gothic style. Various frescoes adorn the cathedral walls, the most famous of which is a series of 28 frescoes by Giotto recounting St. Francis' life. The **Lower Basilica** is the older part of the church complex. After entering the Lower Basilica, a set of steps ahead and to the left of the entrance descends to the **crypt** where St. Francis is buried. The crypt, originally hidden to prevent theft of St. Francis relics, was rediscovered in 1818. The body of St. Francis' is entombed in a coffin in an open space above the altar. The tombs of some of Francis' most faithful followers—Brothers Rufino, Angelo, Masseo, and Leo—occupy the corners of the crypt. At the entrance of the crypt is an urn with the remains of Jacopa dei Settesoli, a dear friend and patroness of St. Francis, whom he lovingly called "Brother Jacopa."

Inside the Upper Basilica di San Francesco

The **Santa Maria sopra Minerva** ("Santa Mary above Minerva") Church is located in the Piazza del Comune in the town center. The church's odd name comes from the fact that the current church was built over an existing temple to the Roman Goddess of Wisdom, Minerva. It was at the altar in this church that St. Francis and his brothers opened the Bible three times, each time to a verse calling the brothers to give up their possessions and follow God (upper church ☉8:30am-7pm, lower church ☉6am-7pm, no cameras).

WAY OF ST. FRANCIS

The **Chiesa Nuova** is built on one presumed location of St. Francis' family home, though other locations for the Bernardone home have been suggested. At the back of the church, visitors can view the cell where St. Francis is said to have been locked by his father and visit the shop where his father sold his cloth.

Up the hill from the Piazza del Comune are the **Cattedrale di San Rufino di Assisi** and the **Home of St. Clare**. This Romanesque Church is the third to be built on this site, all of which contained the remains of St. Rufino, who brought Christianity to Assisi in the 3rd century and was then martyred. The cathedral would have been a major church in Assisi during St. Francis' life. St. Clare (one of Francis' first followers and the founder of the Order of Poor Ladies, a monastic Franciscan order for women) and many other of the original Franciscans were baptized here, and it was here in 1209 that Clare was inspired to join the Franciscan Order, much to her father's dismay, after hearing St. Francis preach. A structure on the side of the church bell tower is said to St. Clare's family home.

Views of Assisi from the Rocca Maggiore

VALFABBRICA TO ASSISI

A few blocks below, on the main road leading to Porta Nuova is the **Basilica di Santa Chiara**, a church dedicated to St. Clare. Her remains are located in the church, though, like the remains of St. Francis, her tomb had been hidden and was only rediscovered in 1850. The church was built on the site where the San Giorgio hospital, church, and school (possibly the one where St. Francis was educated) were located.

Another important site associated with St. Clare is the church/monastery at **San Damiano**. Located in a peaceful location, past Porta Nuova and down a well marked path, San Damiano was the location of the first monastery of the Poor Ladies of St. Clare. This church also played an important role in Francis' conversion. One day in 1205, St. Francis found himself by the near-ruined Church of San Damiano, which he entered to pray. While praying, he heard a voice from the crucifix telling him to "go and repair my church which, as you see, is all in ruins!" Literally heeding the words, Francis sold much of his father's clothes in an ill-fated attempt to fund repairs on the church, starting a series of events that led to Francis' rejection of his family inheritance and commitment to a life of religious service and poverty. The crucifix from St. Francis' vision currently hangs in the Basilica di Santa Chiara. At the end of his life, Francis spent time in a hut at San Damiano, finishing his "Canticle of the Creatures."

In the valley below the old city of Assisi are two more major sites central to the birth of the Franciscan movement: **Rivo Torto** and the **Basilica di Santa Maria degli Angeli**. The latter contains the tiny Porziuncola chapel within. Though populated today, the valley was poorly drained in Francis' time and malaria was common. Few people lived there, with the exception of peasants who pastured their flocks in the valley, lepers, and other poor folk.

Still, Francis and his fellow misfit followers made their first home there, initially living in the ruins of a hut at a place called Rivo Torto ("Crooked Brook"). Each day, Francis and his companions would set out from the hut to care for lepers and the sick and poor in the city, returning at the end of the day to share food that they had begged.

Their life in the hut at Rivo Torto was short lived, however, as they were evicted by a local peasant who wanted to use the hut to shelter his donkey. Today a 19th-century church sits on the location of the original animal shelter.

Francis and his followers later moved to the **Porziuncola**, then a dilapidated church, which was gifted to them by the Benedictines. From this point onward, the Porziuncola was the headquarters of the Friars Minor. Francis returned here often and eventually died at the chapel in 1226. While still alive, Francis had a vision in which Jesus granted forgiveness of sins to all those who prayed in the Porziuncola. Francis petitioned Pope Honorius III, who granted the plenary indulgence (complete pardon of sin) for one day a year, on August 2. As crowds made their way to the Porziuncola annually, the small chapel proved inadequate in size, and in the 16th century, the **Basilica di Santa Maria degli Angeli** was constructed around the Porziuncola.

The church at Rivo Torto is located 2.5km south of San Damiano, in the valley bottom. A 2.7km tile walkway connects the hillside town of Assisi to Santa Maria degli Angeli. Alternatively, a frequent bus travels from a bus stop below the Basilica di San Francesco to a stop directly outside Santa Maria degli Angeli.

VALFABBRICA TO ASSISI

The **Rocca Maggiore** stands on the hilltop above Assisi looking out over Assisi and the Spoleto Valley, which was an important imperial fortification in the region. Records referring to the current castle date back to 1174, when it was rebuilt by Christian of Mainz. In 1198, however, the newly wealthy merchant middle class, of which St. Francis' family would have been a part, rose up and overthrew the soldiers stationed at the Rocca. In the process, they expelled the noble classes from Assisi, confiscating their property and precipitating the war with Perugia (where the Assisi nobility found refuge) in which St. Francis was taken prisoner. Impressive views make the hike up to the castle worth the effort. Tickets to enter the Rocca cost €6.

A final site, visited less frequently, is the **Santa Maria Maggiore Church**. In St. Francis' day, the bishop's residence would have been in the square where the church is located. Either in the church or in the bishop's residence, Francis dramatically threw off his cloak, rejecting his biological father and accepting his heavenly one.

Rocca Maggiore

16-22 ASSISTANT TO RIETI

ASSISI TO RIETI

Farmland and villages in the Nera Valley

Hike the rim of the Spoleto Valley, follow the beautiful Nera River Valley, traverse the holy Rieti Valley.

From Assisi, the Way of St. Francis winds along the foothills of the Central Apennine Mountains on the edge of the Spoleto Valley, passing through beautiful hilltop towns like Spello and Trevi before arriving in Spoleto, a lovely city nestled at the base of the Apennines that hosts a three-week music festival every summer.

The route ascends from Spoleto to the peaceful Franciscan hermitage at Monteluco, then follows rugged hiking trails across the Apennines and into the Valnerina (Nera River Valley), which you follow downstream to the Marmore Falls, a wonder of Roman engineering. From the falls, the route climbs, passing through the sleepy lakeside town of Piediluco and continues to Italy's sacred Rieti Valley, visiting Franciscan sanctuaries at Poggio Bustone and La Foresta on the way to Rieti.

The way is steeped in remembrances of St. Francis, passing various mountainside hermitages where Francis retreated for time of quiet prayer and solitude as his popularity grew. In the market in Foligno, Francis sold his father's wares, hoping to pay for church renovations. A vision in Spoleto turned Francis from aspirations of knighthood toward a life of religious service and poverty. An ancient beech tree—the Faggio di San Francesco—in the mountains between Piediluco and Poggio Bustone once sheltered Francis in a storm, earning the Saint's blessing. And the Rieti Valley, now known as the Holy or Sacred Valley, was one of Francis' favorite destinations. Today the four Franciscan sanctuaries at the corners of the valley attest to his presence here.

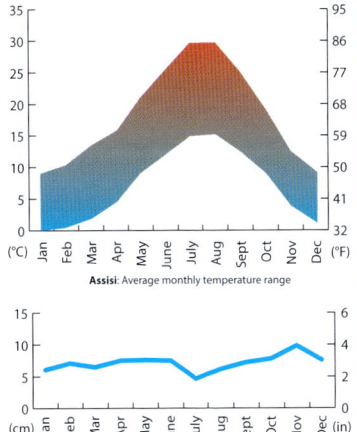

Assisi: Average monthly temperature range

Assisi: Average monthly rainfall

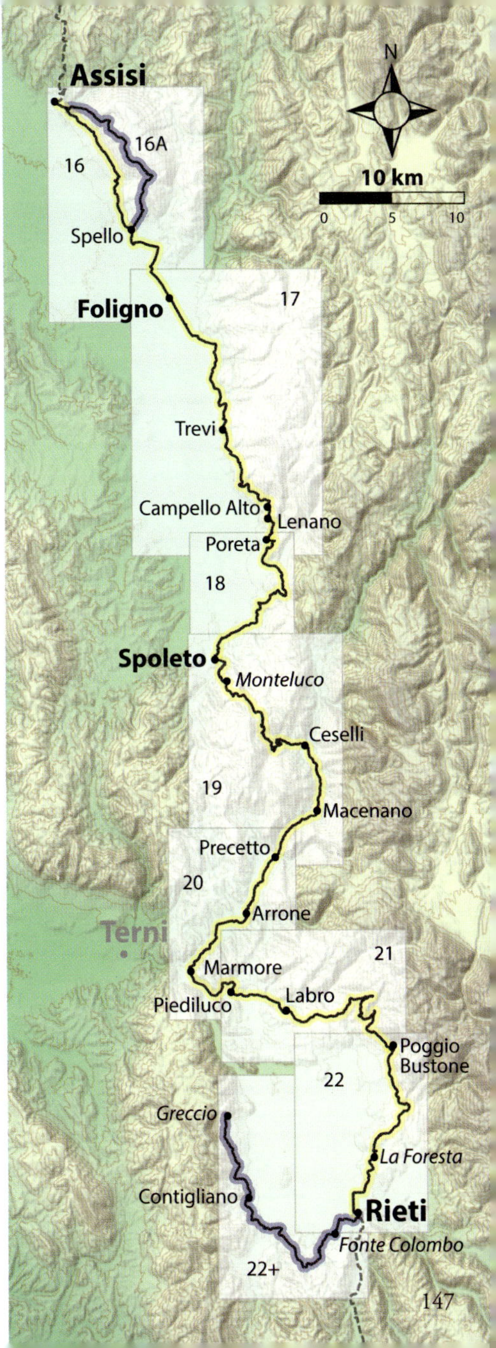

16 ASSISI TO FOLIGNO

19.4km (12.1mi)
▲ 420m / ▼ 540m

⏱ **5.5-7 Hours**
Difficulty: ■ ■ ☐

🅿 77%, 15.0km
Ⓤ 23%, 4.4km

Ⓓ Ⓗ **Lodging:**
Spello 12.8km
Foligno 19.4 km
Trevi 31.8km

✝ **Waymarking:**
Blue/yellow stripes, yellow taus, CAI 350(50)/360(60) (see map, note confusing intersection after Eremo delle Carceri)

Expansive views from Monte Subasio

Cross Monte Subasio, descend through a picturesque medieval village, explore the city where Francis surreptitiously funded his church restoration efforts.

☀ From Assisi, the route leads to Spello, a lovely hilltop town with medieval flare, following either the low or high route from Assisi. Both are wonderful options, with the lower route sacrificing some stunning views from the heights of Monte Subasio in return for easier walking on non-technical trail surfaces with much less climbing. From Spello, the route continues along flat paved roads through the Spoleto Valley to Foligno, a bustling city and transit hub.

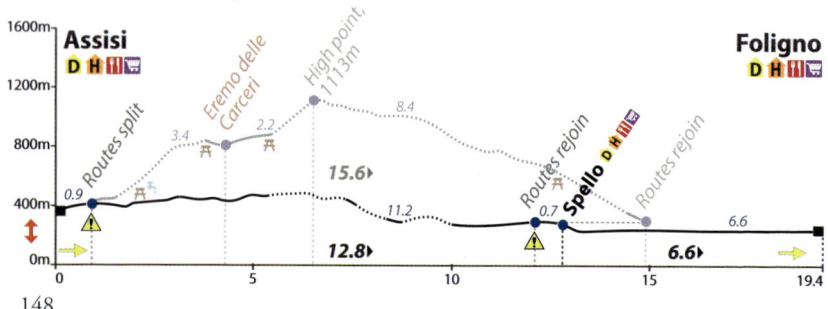

WAY OF ST. FRANCIS

Two Route Options from Assisi to Spello:

❶ ⭐ 16: Low Route to Spello 🟩⬜⬜

This first option follows paved and dirt roads along the side of Mt. Subasio to Spello. The route stays roughly at the same elevation as Assisi, passing through hillside olive groves with pleasant views of the Spoleto Valley. This route is far easier than the second option, as it follows paved and dirt roads, with no rocky hiking trails, and has far less climbing.

From the Piazza del Comune, descend past the Basilica di Santa Chiara and exit Assisi via Porta Nuova. Just after exiting Porta Nuova, continue onto a busier road, angling right and going slightly downhill. Ahead pass a supermarket to the left. From here, the route is well marked with blue/yellow stripes following paved and gravel roads to Spello.

❷ 16A: High Route from Assisi to Spello 🟥🟥⬜

If you're up for the challenge, the second option, the high route from Assisi, is well worth the effort. Not only does this route pass the Eremo delle Carceri, but the challenging climb up Mt. Subasio yields simply stunning views. Portions of this route are quite steep, however, and some sections follow trails with loose, rocky surfaces. We do not recommend taking this route in bad weather, no matter how fit you are.

From the Piazza del Commune, ascend past the Basilica di San Rufino (passing the church to the right). Continue on Via del Torrione to a T intersection with a larger paved road. Turn left; pass a bus station on your right; continue past the Roman Amphitheater on the right; and exit the city via a gate/stone archway. Immediately after the archway, turn right onto a small paved drive (which soon becomes a gravel hiking path), following signs for "Eremo delle Carceri," "Spello," and "Greccio." 250m ahead, after passing the Rocca Minore on the right, reach a T intersection at a gravel road. Turn left, going uphill, passing a picnic area with water fountain on the left. From here follow CAI routes 350 (to just past the Eremo delle Carceri), 360, and 350 to Spello. (Note that 360 is also occasionally marked as route 60 and 350 is occasionally marked as route 50, so 360=60 and 350=50.) Note the following trail junctions:

Rocky trail on the descent from Monte Subasio

ASSISI TO FOLIGNO

- At 4.7km, just after passing the Eremo delle Carceri, route 350 leaves the paved road, climbing left. You stay on the paved road following 360.
- ⚠ At 4.9km, an old "Via di Francesco/Via di Roma" signboard indicates a right turn down a hiking path, but further waymarking has been scratched out below.
  ⚠ Ignore the signboard and continue straight on the paved road.
- At 5.4km, at a sign that says "Rinboschimento, 868m," CAI 354 descends to the right, while you turn left, ascending a rocky hiking path, following CAI 360 and signs for "Sasso Piano," "Madonna della Spella," and "Pontecentesimo."
- At 6.5km, reach the stage high point and continue to follow the now lightly-marked CAI 360 along a hiking path along the side of the mountain face.
- At 9.3km, pass "Fonte Bregno, 1,028m" to the left as CAI 354 descends to the right. Just ahead, turn right down a hiking path following CAI 350 toward "Spello," while CAI 360 continues straight on the gravel double track toward "Madonna della Spella," Madonna di Colpernieri," and "Pontecentesimo."

Alternate 4-day itinerary from Assisi to Spoleto

To stretch the 60km to Spoleto from 3 days into 4:
- **Assisi-Spello:** 12.8km, ▲ +344m (low route) or 15.6km, ▲ +892m (high route)
- **Spello-Trevi:** 19.1km, ▲ +460m
- **Trevi-Poreta:** 12.1km, ▲ +514m
- **Poreta-Spoleto:** 15.4km, ▲ +642m

This itinerary allows you to spend nights in Spello and Trevi, both of which are beautifully-preserved hilltop towns, removed from the hustle and bustle of the more populous Foligno.

To stay in Spello and Trevi and still arrive in Spoleto in three days, walk a long day from Trevi to Spoleto (27.5km, ▲ +1,156m), and consider a rest day in Spoleto to see the city's sites.

Other routes not included in this guide

Several other guides suggest unofficial detours that shorten the final day to Spoleto by traveling directly through the Spoleto Valley from Trevi. These options are poorly marked, and contend with major roads and traffic. Similarly, one of the Franziskusweg itineraries detours from the Via di Francesco in Spello, heads south from Spello and arrives in to Spoleto in two days via Montefalco. This route is not officially waymarked and follows paved roads.

WAY OF ST. FRANCIS

The final few hundred meters before rejoining the low route at Spello follow alongside the remains of a Roman aqueduct.

Monte Subasio rises prominently from the Spoleto Valley, a landmark visible for miles in every direction. Assisi occupies a position on the low northwestern slope of the mountain, while the ancient town of Spello sits on a small spur on the southern slope. Between Assisi and Spello, the mountain ascends to 1,290m above sea level. Stone from the mountain was used to construct many buildings in Assisi, which owe their pinkish-red hue to the distinctive color of the rock.

Eremo delle Carceri

For many centuries, Monte Subasio has been the home to Benedictine monks. The **Abbey of St. Benedict** (located on SP-251 between the low/high routes from Assisi) dates back centuries, and was first officially documented in 1051, along with the Benedictine abbey at Farfa (See Stage 25A for more details, p. 202) A Romanesque church at the site was consecrated by Pope Innocent IV in 1254, along with the Cathedral of San Rufino and Basilica of St. Francis. During St. Francis' time, the Benedictine community was quite important, as the abbots controlled more than 30 churches in the Spoleto Valley in the 12th/13th centuries. In fact, it was the Abbot of St. Benedict of Monte Subasio who granted the Porziuncola and the Eremo delle Carceri to St. Francis.

Approaching Spello on the final descent from Monte Subasio

Eremo delle Carceri (literally, "hermitage of the prison") was once a prison on Monte Subasio before becoming a religious hermitage. St. Francis and his followers regularly retreated to the hermitage, positioned in an isolated location 800m above sea level, for periods of solitary prayer. Most buildings at the hermitage date to the 15th century and St. Bernadine of Sienna, though the inner 12th-century Capella della Madonna was likely there during St. Francis' life. Also at the site is a grotto where St. Francis is said to have slept and prayed. Near the grotto is a dry stream bed that, according to legend, dried up on

ASSISI TO FOLIGNO

St. Francis' command to allow the Franciscan brothers to pray in peaceful silence. Also nearby is the "Devil's hole," a small crevice where St. Francis is said to have cast a demon who tempted Brother Rufino. According to stories about St. Francis, birds gathered in the trees that surround the hermitage to receive a blessing from St. Francis.

There is a very small, touristy café by the Eremo delle Carceri, but don't count on it being open.

12.8 / 15.6 Spello

1. **D Convento Piccolo S. Damiano, Suore Francescane** (par, 50, don), Fonte Vecchia 16, 0742651182, all year, pilgrim hostel at convent of Franciscan nuns, possible to join meals, garden, +570m
2. **D Convento Santa Maria Maddalena** (par, €20): Carvour 1, 0742302259/3396356811, agostinianespello@alice.it, central
3. **H In Urbe Apartments** (€30+/person), Giulia 97, 0742301145/3393434019, vacation apartments
4. **H BB Fratello Sole** (€60), Monterione 6, 3409735174, bebfratellosole@libero.it, apartment with double and twin bed (up to 3 people)
5. **H Residenza dei Cappuccini** (€65+), Cappuccini 5, 3314358591, apartments for 2+ from €65
6. **H Hotel La Bastiglia** (€85/95), Piazza Vallegloria 7, 0742651277

Spello is an ancient town on a hilltop on the lower edge of Monte Subasio's southern slope. Populated by the Umbrian people, the town was known as Hispellum in Roman times. Roman-era gates (Porta Consolare and Porta de Veneri) and the remains of a Roman amphitheater attest to the town's Roman history. Recently-discovered Roman mosaics are housed in the **Villa dei Mosaici** (€6, Apr-Sept Mon-Sun 10:30am-1pm and 3-6:30pm, Oct-Mar 10:30am-1pm and 3-6:30pm).

Every year the Infiorate di Spello, an impressive festival of flowers, brightens the town. For over a hundred years, citizens of the town have designed and created intricate flower carpets with elaborate designs that then line the city's narrow streets for the Corpus Domini Sunday procession (ninth Sunday after Easter). A museum at the central Piazza della Repubblica documents the history of the Infiorate (infiorataspello.it, Fri-Sun, 10am-1pm, 3:30-6:30pm).

Narrow Spello streets

The town is split into a beautifully-preserved old town on the hilltop and a more modern section in the valley bottom. A collection of lovely medieval churches are located within the Old City walls, including the churches of **Sant'Andrea** (11th century) and **San Lorenzo** (12th century). Most notable is the 12th-century **Church of Santa Maria Maggiore**, which contains simply stunning frescoes by Pinturricchio (€3 entry).

19.4 / 22.2 Foligno

1. **Ostello di Foligno** (€20/30/48), Pierantoni 21, 3386318114/0742353776, 9:30am-12pm, 3-10pm
2. **St. Francis Apartment** (€10, €20): Antonio Rutili 15, stfrancisapartaments@gmail.com, price per person in apartment, across from Chiesa di San Francesco (good site-seeing location)
3. **Hotel Le Mura** (€48/56): Augusto Bolletta 29, 0742357344
4. **BB In Centro** (€39/69): Franco Ciri 1, 3315321032
5. **Residenza Galligari** (€45/65): Piazza XX Settembre 7, 3662006420
6. **Hotel Italia** (€54/69): Piazza Giacomo Matteotti 12, 0742350412
7. **Affittacamere Arco Polinori** (€50/60): Cesare Agostini 12, 3663578000
8. **Casa Roncalli** (€42/60): Roncalli 19, 3484050150
9. **Welcome BB** (€36/60): Umberto I 64, 3356614679
10. **Affittacamere Umberto I** (€35/60): Umberto I 92, 3499619839/3473805554
11. **BB La Villetta** (€30/55): IV Novembre 8, 3287057107

Foligno was founded by Umbrians in pre-Roman times, likely around the 8th century BCE. An important rail center, Foligno suffered intense Allied bombing during World War II, and much of the town was destroyed, though some medieval monuments were preserved. On the northern edge of the Piazza della Repubblica is the **Cattedrale di San Feliciano**. The cathedral dates to the 12th century, and though the interior was reworked in the 18th century, the original facade is still largely intact.

ASSISI TO FOLIGNO 16

The **Piazza della Repubblica** also played an important role in St. Francis' conversion. Committed to restoring the San Damiano Church in Assisi, St. Francis came to Foligno with his father's merchandise, selling it and his horse in an attempt to fund the church renovations.

A few blocks southeast of the piazza, the **Chiesa di San Francesco** was built on the site of the first Franciscan pilgrim hostel in Foligno. The church also contains the tomb of Blessed Angela of Foligno, a 13th-century mystic and member of the Secular Franciscan Order (because she was married). Her writings on mystical spiritualism has been translated into Spanish, French, German, and English and distributed widely.

⚠ The final 2.3km into Foligno follow a busy road, but there is either a sidewalk or pedestrian/bike path the whole way into the city.

🛒 A Decathlon gear store is located in the Foligno industrial park on the far south side of the city, 5km past the city center. (See Stage 17 map, p.157)

Cattedrale di San Feliciano in Foligno

17 FOLIGNO TO PORETA

24.6km (15.4mi)
▲ 900m / ▼ 810m

🕒 **7.5-9.5 Hours**
Difficulty: ▅▅▅

🅿 56%, 13.8km
🆄 44%, 10.8km

D H Lodging:
Trevi 12.4km
Alvanischio 14.8km
Compello 21.5km
Lenano 22.3km
Poreta 24.6km

⛨ Waymarking:
Blue/yellow stripes, yellow taus until Trevi

Views of Trevi

Ascend to a stunning hilltop village, trek along a mountainside, descend to a tiny hamlet on the edge of the Spoleto Valley.

☀ Today's walk leaves the populated Spoleto Valley around Foligno and ascends back into the Apennine foothills. The route passes first through Trevi, a beautifully-preserved medieval town perched on the low spur jutting from Monte Serano, then continues through a number of more remote hillside villages before descending to the tiny village of Poreta. Throughout the day, olive groves dot the hillside, while expansive views of the Spoleto Valley are a constant companion.

⚠ The route follows busy roads leaving Foligno. Exercise caution and stick to sidewalks where possible.

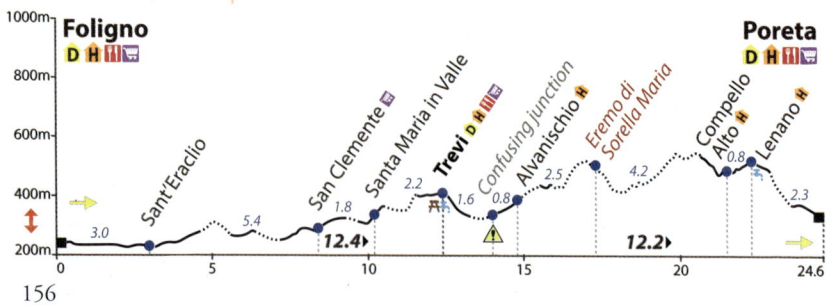

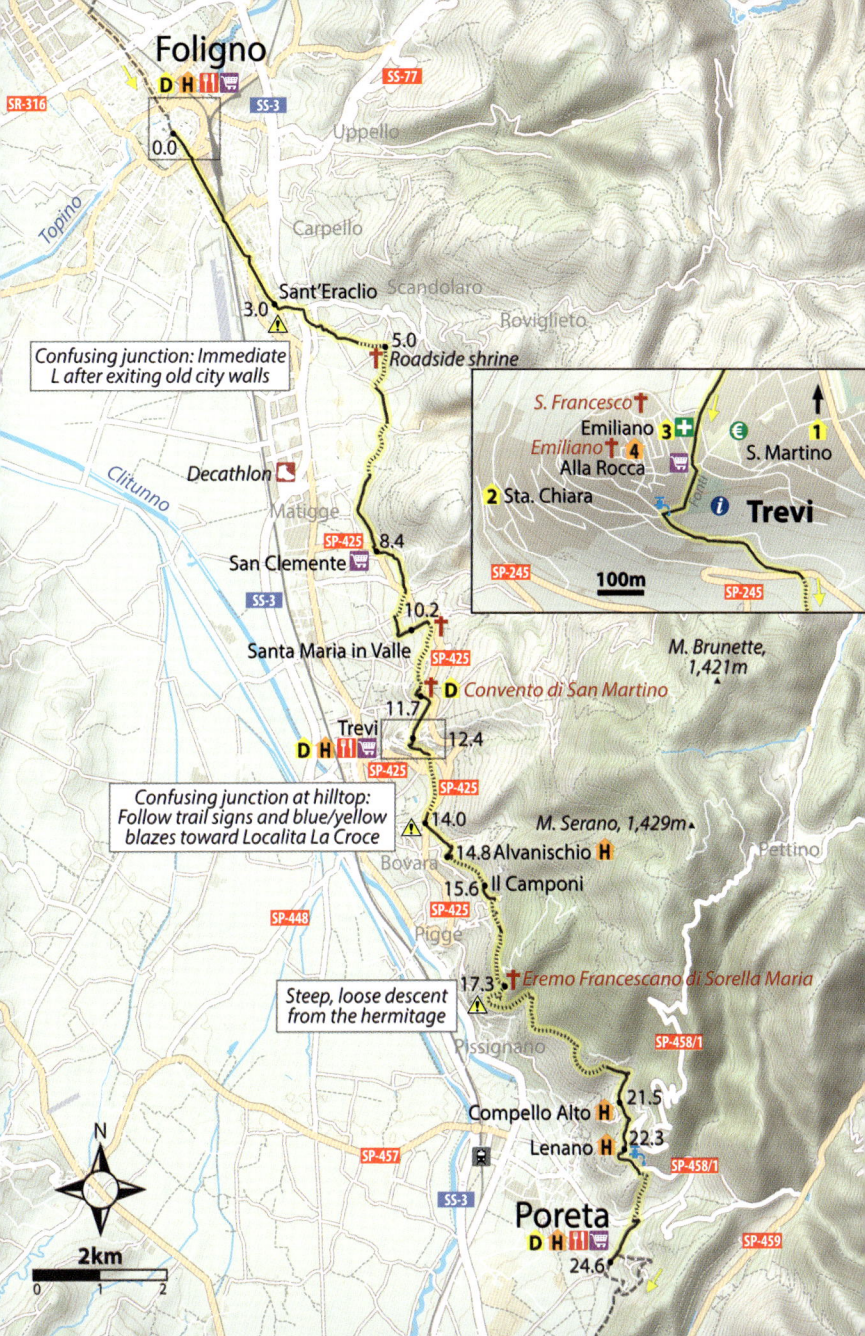

WAY OF ST. FRANCIS

🚆 The train station is in the valley in the more modern part of Trevi.

⚠️🛒 Stock up on food and water in Trevi.

Though a water fountain in Lenano is only 10km from Trevi, the route feels more remote after Trevi, with lots of up and down and a short section of somewhat rocky, technical walking after the Eremo Francescano. What's more, the grocery/café in Poreta is very small, so it's wise to carry lunch for the following day.

Overgrown wall on the approach to Trevi

⚠️ Immediately after exiting the Old City walls of Sant'eraclio, <u>turn left</u>, ignoring a yellow arrow that points straight. Blue/yellow stripe markers begin again shortly. Continue through a highway underpass, then take the next right onto Via Londra.

12.4 Trevi D H 🍴🛒€ℹ️🚆

1. **D** **Convento di San Martino** (par, 🛏5, don 💰): Augusto Ciufelli 14, ☎074278216
2. **D** **Santa Chiara** (par, 🛏17, don): ☎074278613, santachiara.ccn@gmail.com
3. **D H** **Sant'Emiliano** (🛏10, €20/30/45): 📶🌐, Piazza del Municipio, ☎3482285443, claudiomenik@libero.it, 🕐all year, practical, central
4. **H** **Antica Dimora alla Rocca** (€70/85+ 💰): 🍴📶, Piazza della Rocca 1, ☎074238541

Trevi is another beautiful hilltop town with a lovely preserved medieval center. Like Spello, the older part of Trevi sits on the hill top, while the more modern part of town sits in the valley floor.

Trevi's history dates back centuries to the Umbrian civilization. The Old City is enclosed by two circuits of medieval walls, the innermost dating to Roman origins, and contains some 20 churches. The Romanesque Duomo of Sant'Emiliano sits atop the hill. Not far away is the Church of San Francesco. Attached to the Church of San Francesco, the Museo di San Francesco houses a collection of Umbrian artwork from the Middle Ages to the 17th century (🕐Fri-Sun: 10:30am-1pm, 2:30-5pm).

14.8 Alvanischio H

H **Country House Le Vedute** (€70 💰): 🍴📶, Alvanischio 8, ☎0742381337/3393686103

H **Affittacamere Altavista** (€60): 🌐, Alvanischio 14, ☎3473422459/3396069308

FOLIGNO TO PORETA 17

21.5 Compello Alto
- **Relais Al Convento** (par, €20-35), Via Palazzetto 3, 0743382241, contatti.alconvento@barnabiti.net, all year, dinner €15, legend says St. Francis stayed here on trip to Rome
- **Borgo Campello** (€115+): 3204549321, spa/sauna, in hilltop castle

22.3 Lenano
- **BB Le Torrette** (€40/50), Torrette 85, 3393766035/3346192798, all year, can arrange an evening meal (groceries or meal from restaurant) if needed

24.6 Poreta
- **A Casa di Francesco/La Palombaia** (6, €12/-/55): Poreta 11, 3498309327/3491997232, one apartment for 6 with kitchen or private room, tiny grocery on site (open to public), can prepare meals
- **Borgo della Marmotta** (€120): Poreta 1, 0743274137, Apr-Oct, sauna/massage
- **Castello di Poreta** (€70): 3288639570

In Lenano, look for a water spigot on the south side of a building on the left (east) side of the road 20m after passing BB Le Torrette.

Poreta is a tiny little hamlet with very few services, just a tiny grocery and café at A Casa di Francesco/La Palombaia with basic groceries and sandwiches.

Hilly countryside near Campello Alto

18 PORETA TO SPOLETO

15.4km (9.6mi)
▲ 640m / ▼ 640m

🕐 5-6 Hours
Difficulty: ▨▨▢

P 57%, 8.8km
U 43%, 6.6km

D H Lodging:
Spoleto 15.4km
Monteluco 18.9km
Patrico 21.3km,
+3.9km

⛨ Waymarking:
Blue/yellow stripes

🪑 A picnic table and water fountain in Bazzano Superiore make a nice break spot.

☕ There's a small café in Eggi on the left just past the church that is easy to miss.

Walk through the Apennine foothills and arrive in Spoleto, home to one of the last remaining pieces of St. Francis' writing.

💡 Though a relatively short day, several steep climbs make the walk to Spoleto harder than the distance might otherwise suggest. The route continues up and down through the Apennine foothills, on a combination of paved roads, gravel tracks, and hiking paths, which skirt the more populated and busy valley floor. The pleasant small villages of Bazzano (both Superiore and Inferiore, referring to the respective altitudes of the towns) and Eggi offer pleasant break spots. With an early start, you can arrive in Spoleto with time to explore some of the city's main sites.

Views of the Spoleto Valley from the Castello di Poreta

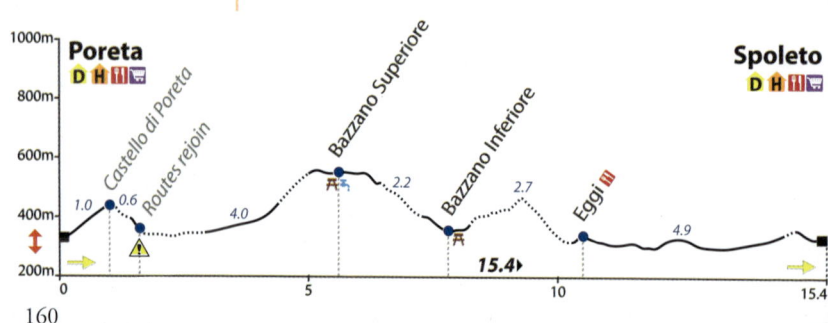

WAY OF ST. FRANCIS

💡 The official route backtracks to the entrance of Poreta village and climbs to the Castello di Poreta. An easier marked alternative route continues south through the village and turns left, rejoining the official route ahead, skipping the climb to the Castello di Poreta. Either is a fine option, but the alternative route misses some views from the castle.

⚠️ Restock in Spoleto. The next reliable grocery store is not for 31.6km in Arrone (though a tiny grocery in Ceselli at 16.3km is theoretically available to pilgrims, but you may have to phone the owner to open it).

15.4 Spoleto

1. **D San Sabino** (par, ⇆25, don): S. Sabino 22, ☎3294485400/0743261177, donboschoimirco@gmail.com, all year, off route, simple but welcoming, **+2.3km**
2. **D Centro Giovanile Giovanni Paolo II** (don): Piazza Garibaldi 35, ☎3313487043/3925887877, pastoralegiovanile@spoletonorcia.it, sleeping bags space on floor
3. **H Ostello Villa Redenta** (€30/60): Villa Redenta 1, ☎0743224936, all year
4. **H BB Villa Massaccesi** (€40/64): XVII Settembre 13-11 ☎3429385405/3394178982, info@villamassaccesi.it, all year, welcoming
5. **H Hotel Clarici** (€60/80): Piazza della Vittoria 32, ☎0743223311
6. **H Casa Religiosa di Ospitalità San Ponziano** (€40/60): S. Salvatore Basilica 2, ☎0743225288, all year
7. **H Hotel Palazzo Dragoni** (€100+): Duomo 13, ☎0743222220
8. **H Hotel Charleston** (€60/75): Piazza Collicola 10, ☎0743220052
9. **H Hotel dei Duchi** (€70/100): Giacomo Matteotti 4, ☎074344541
10. **H Hotel Palazzo Leti Residenza d'Epoca** (€100+): Eremiti 10, ☎0743224930, nice garden with view
11. **H Istituto Suore Bambin Gesù** (par, €35/60): Sant'Angelo 4, ☎366876612/074340232

Spoleto occupies a strategic position at the head of the Spoleto Valley, surrounded by mountains on three sides. The city has a long history dating to the Bronze Age, first as an Umbrian city, then as an important Roman city along the Via Flaminia, the Roman route connecting Rome to Rimini across the Apennines. The first historical reference to Spoletium dates to 241 BCE, and various Roman remains reflect the city's importance in the Roman Empire. The largely-reconstructed open air **Roman amphitheater** is particularly worth a visit (National Archaeological Museum and Roman Theater: €4, Mon-Sun, 8:30am-7:30pm).

WAY OF ST. FRANCIS

Escalators from the lower part of Spoleto ascend to the Duomo and the impressive fortress, the **Rocca Albornoziana**, on the hilltop above town. The Rocca was built from 1359-1370 by architect Matteo Gattapone of Gubbio. It resisted many sieges throughout history and in 1800 was turned into a jail, serving this purpose until the 20th century. Now the fortress serves as a museum. Behind the Rocca, crossing the Tessino River is the Ponte delle Torri, a 13th-century aqueduct and bridge, which today is not in use due to earthquake damage in 2016. Some suggest that the bridge was built on existing Roman foundations, but scholars have not reached agreement on this point.

Near the top of the city, the **Duomo di Spoleto** is an impressive site. Paintings of the Virgin Mary's life by Filippo Lippi adorn the ceiling. His tomb is now housed in the church. The church also holds one of only two original documents known to have been written by Saint Francis, a letter to one of his companions, Brother Leo. Another important church at the entrance to town is the **Basilica di San Salvatore**. (The official Via di Francesco route passes the church on the way into town.) Dating to the 4th century, the church was built on and incorporates the inner chamber of a Roman temple. An important example of early Christian architecture, the church was made a UNESCO World Heritage Site in 2011.

Duomo di Spoleto

If you have the pleasure of visiting Spoleto at the end of June or beginning of July, you'll be treated to the **Festival dei Due Mondi** ("Festival of the Two World"). Founded in 1958, the festival is an important cultural event with three weeks of music, theater, and dance performances, some of which are performed in the Roman amphitheater. A parallel festival takes place annually in Charleston, South Carolina.

Spoleto was also the location of an important event in St. Francis' conversion story. Finding himself ill in Spoleto, Francis was forced to give up on his knightly ambitions. While convalescing, he had a dream in which God told him to reinterpret his visions of knighthood in the Lord's service.

PORETA TO SPOLETO 18

Routes leaving Spoleto:

❶⭐ The preferred way leaves from the lower part of Spoleto, following Via Tiro a Segno east. The route crosses under the SS-3 highway. 100m ahead it turns right, crossing a small bridge, and then makes an immediate left onto a gravel hiking track following CAI 3 in the direction of "Forcella Castelmonte," "Le Cese," and "Ceselli." At 0.9km, the route comes to a nicer hiking path with options right and left. Turn right, following CAI 3 toward "Spoleto Ponte delle Torri" and "Monteluco." Continue on this path to CAI 1, where the routes rejoin and continue in the direction of "Monteluco."

❷ A second option leaves from the south end of Spoleto, crossing busy SS-3 highway on Viale Giacomo Matteotti/SP-462. It then follows SP-462 uphill to a switchback with a small paved drive going to the left toward the Ponte delle Torri, soon joining the other route at CAI 1, in the direction of Monteluco. ⚠ Not advisable; dangerous highway crossing.

❸ ⚠ **Closed!** The traditional Via di Francesco route from Spoleto departed La Rocca and crossed the Ponte delle Torri over the Tessino River. The bridge has been closed since a 2016 earthquake. ℹ Consult the tourist office in Spoleto for current info on Via di Francesco route options leaving Spoleto.

For information on Monteluco and its accommodations see Stage 19, p. 168.

💡 There's lots to see in Spoleto, so if you have time in your schedule, you might consider taking a sightseeing rest day here. Conversely, if you want to stay in a more peaceful, meditative location, consider walking another 3.5km to the Franciscan Hermitage at Monteluco.

Views of Spoleto from Rocca Albornoziana

19

SPOLETO TO PRECETTO/FERENTILLO

26.3km (16.4mi)
▲ 1280m / ▼ 1350m

⏱ **8-10.5 Hours**
Difficulty: ▬ ▬

P 24%, 6.2km
U 76%, 20.1km

D H Lodging:
Monteluco 3.5km
Patrico 5.9km
 +3.9km
Ceselli 16.3km
Macenano 21.5km
Precetto 26.3km
Arrone 31.3km
Casteldilago 32.5km

🚩 Waymarking:
Blue/yellow stripes, occasional yellow taus; CAI routes 3, 1, 4, Greenway del Nera 3 (map notes)

Dirt tracks in the Nera Valley near Precetto

Climb to a tranquil Franciscan sanctuary, follow rugged trails over a mountain pass, enjoy expansive views of the Nera Valley.

💡 The day begins with a long climb to the Franciscan hermitage at Monteluco, high in the Apennine Mountains. From Monteluco, the route follows gravel roads and hiking paths to a pass above 900m. A snaking descent on narrow hiking paths follows. Stunning views of the Nera Valley—some of the most impressive of the entire Way of St. Francis—accompany the journey to the valley floor. Once in Ceselli, the hardest part of the day is done; the day's final 10km are on flat dirt roads, which follow the Nera downstream the entire way to Precetto. See Stage 18 (p. 165) for details of routes leaving Spoleto.

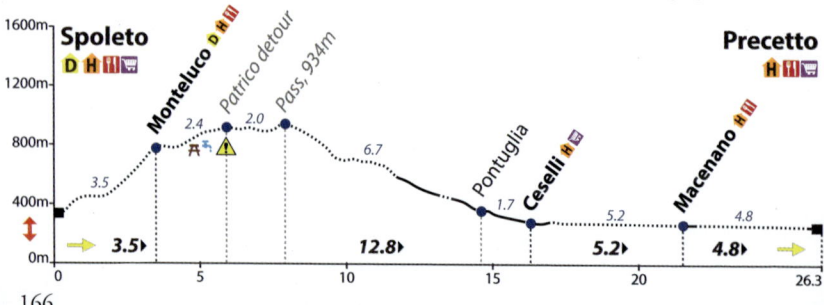

WAY OF ST. FRANCIS

⚠ Between Spoleto and Ceselli, the route could be dangerous in bad weather, particularly on the descent from the pass to Ceselli. Consider staying an extra day in Spoleto if facing inclement weather.

⚠ There are no reliable grocery stores between Spoleto and Precetto. There is a small grocery store in Ceselli. You can call ☎3401454732 and ask the owner to open the store if it's closed when you arrive, but it's not a sure thing.

💡 At 5.9km, a well-signed detour to Patrico (+3.9km) and its lodging leave the main route following the paved road.

3.5 Monteluco, see map p. 163

12. ⚠ **D** Convento San Francesco (par, 🛏9, don): ☎074340711, conventomonteluco@gmail.com, simple, **temporarily closed**
13. **H** Albergo Paradiso (€35-40/50), ☎0743223082, all year
14. **H** Hotel Ferretti (€60): ☎0743222344

Monteluco has been a sacred mountain since ancient times. The name is derived from the Latin *lucus*, which indicates a "grove sacred to a deity." Since the first millennium of Christianity, the mountain has been inhabited by hermits. St. Francis lived with his brothers in the caves here in 1218, and there has been a Franciscan presence ever since. A Franciscan Convent occupies the site today (hours: 9am-12pm, 3-6pm), and St. Anthony of Padova, St. Bonaventure, and St. Bernardino of Siena spent time here over the years. Take some time to explore the peaceful "Sacred Forest" adjacent to the convent, where centuries of hermits found shelter in little grottoes. Views out over the Spoleto Valley are beautiful.

5.9 Patrico, +3.9km

H Agriturismo Bartoli (€35): ☎0743220058, 3355987976, specializes in traditional foods, off-route, easy return without completely backtracking, well reviewed

After crossing a pass at 934m, follow trails descending to the **Valnerina** (the "Nera River Valley"), a tight valley nestled deep in the mountains that feels set back in time. Its secluded nature meant that it was one of the last areas in the region to convert to Christianity, while during WWII it was home to the various resistance movements, including the Garibaldi Brigade. The villages throughout the valley all have distinctive medieval architecture. The economy of the region is based on agriculture, including livestock husbandry, truffle hunting, and trout breeding. The valley's hiking, cycling, and kayaking, as well as sites like the Abbey of San Pietro in Valle and Marmore Falls, are significant tourism draws.

Descending to the Nera Valley

SPOLETO TO PRECETTO/FERENTILLO 19

16.3 Ceselli 🛒

- **H** Casa Vacanze Il Ruscello (€35/50): 🍴🛜⊙, ☎3402296792

21.5 Macenano

- **H** 3 Archi (€30/50): 🍴🛜⊙, SS-209 29, ☎0744780004
- **H** Abbazia San Pietro in Valle (€120+): 🍴W D 🛜⊙, ☎0744780129, spa

The Rocca and Ponte delle Torri while leaving Spoleto

The **Abbazia San Pietro in Valle** ("Abbey of St. Peter in the Valley") sits on the hillside above Macenanon. This Benedictine Abbey was established in the 8th century on the site of an existing Syrian hermitage. For the next 800 years abbots lived here. Now a four-star hotel occupies the restored abbey, and guided tours take visitors through the abbey complex to see the 12th/13th-century frescos, Etruscan and Lombard altars, and the remains of a Roman sarcophagus (sanpietroinvalle.com, call ☎0744780129 for more information/reservations).

26.3 Precetto/Ferentillo

1. **H** Borgo (€35/60): 🛜⊙, ☎0744780186, all year
2. **H** Agriturismo La Pila (€50): 🍴🛜, ☎0744780793, all year, +2.1km
3. **H** Il Gelso Country House (€45/60): 🍴🛜⊙, ☎3331083918, Apr-Sep, +2.1km
4. **H** Agriturismo I Terzieri (€75): 🍴🛜, Macchie, ☎3476292239/3355861015

Precetto is home to one of the stranger sights along the Way of St. Francis—the **Museo delle Mummie** (the "Museum of the Mummies"). The museum, located in the 12th-century Church of Santo Stefano, houses around 20 corpses that were naturally mummified through a combination of minerals and salts in the soil and a particular airflow. Written commentary in multiple languages outlines the tragic backstories of many of the bodies. A unique museum that is not for the squeamish (€3, winter 10am-1pm and 3-5pm, summer 3-7pm, mummiediferentillo.it/info).

ℹ️ +600m off route, across the Nera River, in Ferentillo.

🚌 Buses connect Ferentillo to Terni, which has better transit connections.

20

PRECETTO/FERENTILLO TO PIEDILUCO

17.9km (11.2mi)
▲ 500m / ▼ 380m

⏱ 5.5-7 Hours
Difficulty: ▪▪▫

P 46%, 8.3km
U 54%, 9.6km

D H Lodging:
Arrone 5.0km
Casteldilago 6.2km
Villa Margine, 6.8km
Marmore 12.3km
Piediluco 17.9km
Labro 23.2km

⛟ Waymarking:
Blue/yellow marks,
Nera Greenway
(see map and notes)

Walking along the Velino from Marmore

Stroll through the verdant Nera Valley, visit the impressive Marmore Falls, end the day in a peaceful lakeside town.

💡 With the exception of the tough 150m climb from the Nera Valley to Marmore, today's walk is rather flat and quite manageable. Be sure to time your arrival to the Marmore Falls carefully—scheduled water releases means that the falls are only flowing at certain times of the day. Though the official route approaches the falls from above, an easily-navigable detour allows for arrival at the falls from below, where views are more impressive. From Marmore, pleasant walking along the Velino River leads to the quaint town of Piediluco on the picturesque Lago di Piediluco ("Piediluco Lake").

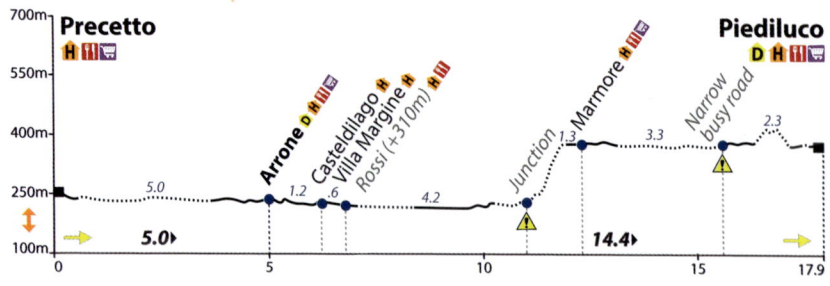

WAY OF ST. FRANCIS

☀ At 11.0km, there's a Y intersection with the Via di Francesco turning left uphill, following signs for the Nera Greenway 15A in the direction of "Piediluco." You'll also see signs for "Sentiero 6." This route climbs steeply to Marmore. From Marmore, a detour from the main route leads to the upper entrance to view the Marmore Falls. ⭐ **If you plan to see the falls, a better option is to go right at the Y before the climb.** This leads to a large parking area and the lower ticket office for the Marmore Falls. From the ticket office, you can enter the Marmore Falls Park from the lower entrance (where the views of the falls are more impressive). "Sentiero 1" then connects to the upper entrance to the falls, where you can reconnect with the main route in Marmore without backtracking. This option adds 1.6km to the day's total distance.

☺ Time your visit to the **Marmore Waterfall** to coincide with the active water period. (Water flow over the falls is controlled by the release of water from a reservoir above the falls.) Times with water flowing vary throughout the year. From Nov-Feb, the falls are inactive during weekdays. From Mar-Oct the falls are active weekdays and weekends, with extended hours on the weekend. Even when water flow is most restricted on weekdays from Mar-Oct, you should be able to count on water flowing from 12-1pm and 3-4pm, though often the water begins flowing before 12pm and continues after 4pm. Contact the Terni Tourism Office (☎0744423047) for current schedules. Tickets to enter the Marmore Falls Park cost €10.

5.0 Arrone
- **Santa Maria** (par, don): Piazza Giuseppe Garibaldi 42, ☎0744389594/3339864664, simple
- **La Loggia sul Nera** (€70+): Mezzocosta 14, ☎3474970188, apartments for 2 or more people, prices vary accordingly, good reviews
- **Casa Vacanza Fiocchi** (€50/75): ☎0744389961, info@residencefiocchi.com, all year

6.2 Casteldilago
- **La Rocchetta** (€72+): ☎3357717129, apartments for 2 or more people, prices vary, off route on hilltop

6.8 Villa Margine
- **Rossi** (€50/65): ☎0744388372, info@rossihotelristorante.it, not far off route across Nera River
- **Casa Mattei** (€45/65): Isola 13A, ☎3389140559, www.casamattei.it

12.3 Marmore
1. **BB Le Marmore** (€25/50): Conti Menotti 24, ☎3276908599, Mar-Oct

The *Cascata delle Marmore* ("Marmore Falls") is a nearly 1,300-year-old human-made waterfall. At 165m, it is the tallest of its kind in the world. The waterfall was built by the Romans in 271 BCE in order to drain the marshy Rieti Valley wetland in an attempt to combat malaria. Though successful

PRECETTO/FERENTILLO TO PIEDILUCO

in draining the Rieti Valley, the Marmore Falls created another problem: now that the Velino River drained directly into the Nera River, the population of Terni (downstream of the falls) was threatened when the Velino was in flood stage. Tensions between Terni and Rieti were so problematic that representatives of the two cities brought the case before the Roman Senate, which, in the end, did nothing to resolve the issue. In the 16th century, additional canals above the falls were constructed to regulate flow, and in the 18th century steps were added to the falls, which resolved many of the flooding problems in the Nera Valley. Today canals above the falls direct the river into hydroelectric plants, greatly reducing the water flow to the falls; water is only released over the falls on a set schedule for a few hours a day.

Marmore Falls

💡 At the T intersection with SR-79, the official Via di Francesco route turns left. Several town services are to the right from this junction.

17.9 Piediluco D H 🍴🛒➕🅴ℹ️

1. **D** **Casa del Pellegrino** (par, 🛏29, don): 🅿️🅾️,
   📞0744368118/3398324942, parrocchia-piediluco@tiscali.it,
   🕐all year, very pleasant, simple pilgrim dorm run by local parish, check in at parochia door to left of Chiese di San Francesco
2. **H** **Hotel Miralago** (€50/70 🍴): 🍴W📶🅾️🛏,
   Vincenzo Noceta 2, 📞0744360022

Piediluco is a charming little town on the Piediluco Lake. The Church of San Francesco in the town center dates to the 14th century and commemorates St. Francis' visit to Piediluco in 1208. Thomas of Celano, in biographies of St. Francis, recalls the saint's interactions with a fish in Piediluco. In the story, a local fisherman gave a fish to St. Francis, who promptly returned the fish to the water. The fish did not swim away immediately, however, and instead waited to hear St. Francis' preaching and receive his blessing before swimming off.

Piediluco retains much of its medieval character and is a tourist destination due to its proximity to the Piediluco Lake. The lake is home to the Italian Rowing Federation, serving as the main location for the national rowing team's training.

💡 **Other routes not covered in this guide**: An alternative Via di Francesco route travels from the lower Marmore Falls to Terni, then back to Rieti, via Stroncone and Greccio, on the west side of the Rieti valley. Between Marmore and Terni, the route is not waymarked, so we do not cover it in this guide, though we do include the leg between Greccio and Rieti as a day detour that allows you to visit Franciscan sanctuaries in Fonte Colombo and Greccio.

21 PIEDILUCO TO POGGIO BUSTONE

20.9km (13.1mi)
▲1100m / ▼650m

🕐 **7-9 Hours**
Difficulty: ▬ ■ ■

🅿 49%, 10.2km
Ⓤ 51%, 10.7km

D H Lodging:
Labro 5.3km
Poggio Bustone
20.9km
La Foresta 32.9km

🕆 **Waymarking:**
Blue/yellow stripes, from Faggio di San Francesco, Cammino di Francesco sign boards also direct to Poggio Bustone

Poggio Bustone, nestled on the mountainside

Visit the beech tree that famously sheltered St. Francis during a storm, descend to Poggio Bustone's Franciscan sanctuary.

💡 Today's route climbs through the mountains north of the Rieti Valley. The way passes through several mountain villages before continuing on more remote tracks to the Faggio di San Francesco, an ancient beech tree that sheltered St. Francis in the midst of a storm. The final few kilometers to Poggio Bustone are largely downhill and pass quickly. Though the day's walk has significant climbs, most are relatively gradual on good surfaces, making it a manageable, if challenging day.

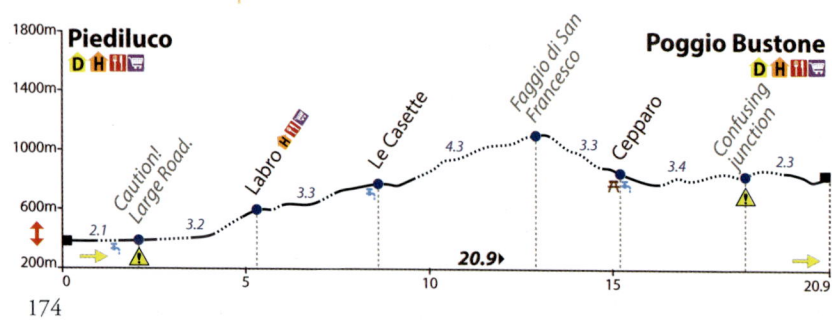

WAY OF ST. FRANCIS

5.3 Labro 🏠🍴🛒➕
H Albergo Diffuso Crispolti (€70/85 🛏️): 🍴📶◉,
📞3355391560/0746636070 ✉️, 🕐Apr-Nov

> 💡 Stock up on food in Piediluco. Outside of a very small grocery/café in Labro, there are no places to buy food before Poggio Bustone.

💡 On the upper end of town outside the city walls, there's a small cafe, grocery, and pharmacy (very limited hours) all housed in the same small building.

The **Faggio di San Francesco** ("St. Francis' Beech") is an old beech tree on the mountain slopes above Poggio Bustone. According to legend, St. Francis was caught in a thunderstorm while wandering through the mountains between Poggio Bustone and Piediluco. He took refuge under a beech tree that wrapped its branches around the saint like an umbrella. Though tradition holds that the beech at this location is the same that protected St. Francis, it's likely only around 250 years old (though this still makes it one of the oldest beech trees in the world).

💡 Descending from the Faggio di San Francesco, the marked route follows a hiking trail that cuts the corners of the paved road. This is more direct than following the road but also steeper and rougher. Walking on the paved road is an option if needed (map p. 175)

The **Rieti Valley**, also known as the Holy or Sacred Valley due to frequent visits from St. Francis, is a large circular valley enclosed on all sides by mountains. Known for its fertile soil, the valley has been nicknamed the "granary of Rome." During St. Francis' life, the valley was economically prosperous, and Rieti was often a papal seat. St. Francis came regularly to the Rieti Valley, first arriving in 1209 then staying for long periods in 1223 and again from fall 1225 to spring 1226.

St. Francis established four important Franciscan sanctuaries at the four corners of the Rieti Valley—Poggio Bustone (Stage 21), La Foresta (Stage 22, p. 180), Fontecolombo (Stage 22+, p. 184), and Greccio (Stage 22+, p. 185), which are important pilgrimage sites today. In these sanctuaries on the borders of the Rieti Valley, St. Francis composed much of the final version of the Franciscan Rule and likely also much of the Canticle of the Sun.

PIEDILUCO TO POGGIO BUSTONE

20.9 Poggio Bustone D H ¶ 🛒 ✚ 🛜 🏠

1. ⭐ **D** Convento di San Giacomo (par, ⌂48, don): 🐕⊙, ✆0746688916, convpbustone@libero.it, ⏲May-Nov, very simple but wonderful pilgrim atmosphere.
2. **H** Locanda Francescana (€30/50 🛍): ¶ W 🛜 ⊙, Francescana 13, ✆3474150455/0746 688688, ⏲all year
3. **H** San Francesco Suite (€55/70-80 🛍): ¶ 🛜 ⊙, Vittorio Emanuele 11, ✆3356199169/3662741665, ⏲all year
4. **H** Buona Gente (€30/50 🛍): 🐕 🛜 ⊙, Mezzo 15, ✆3711285998

💡 There are a number of other accommodation options (small rooms in home via online booking sites).

Poggio Bustone is a lovely little town balanced high on the hillside above the northeast corner of the Rieti valley. Traveling from Piediluco, St. Francis and his followers would have first entered the Rieti Valley in this general area in 1209. Biographers note that Francis retired to a secluded cave near Poggio Bustone to pray. There he had two important visions.

In the first, he received assurance from God that all his sins had been forgiven. In the second, he saw the prodigious growth of the Franciscan movement, starting from Poggio Bustone. Inspired, he left the cave and descended to Poggio Bustone, happily exclaiming to the townsfolk: *"Buon giorno, buona gente!"* ("Good morning, good people!). To this day, the people of Poggio Bustone fondly remember the greeting. In another story, Poggio Bustone was the site of a public confession of St. Francis: while preaching to a crowd gathered at the Poggio Bustone hermitage, Francis amazed the onlookers by confessing that he had eaten lard during lent. The **Convent of San Giacomo** is located at the Franciscan hermitage at Poggio Bustone and contains several chapels and hermit cells. There's also a lovely, simple pilgrim hostel at the site.

Views of the Rieti Valley from Poggio Bustone's narrow streets

22 POGGIO BUSTONE TO RIETI

17.7km (11.1mi)
▲ 470m / ▼ 890m

⏱ 5-6.5 Hours
Difficulty: 🟧🟨⬜

📍 71%, 12.5km
🅤 29%, 5.2km

D H Lodging:
San Felice 9.6km
La Foresta 12.0km
Rieti 17.7km
Contigliano 34.3km
 (22+)

✝ **Waymarking:**
Blue/yellow stripes, Cam. di Francesco signboards for "La Foresta" and "Rieti." Cammino di San Benedetto overlaps with Via di Francesco from Poggio Bustone to a point south of Rieti and is well waymarked.

La Foresta Sanctuary

Visit La Foresta, site of a vineyard miracle, descend to Rieti, an ancient Sabine town on the southern rim of the Rieti Valley.

💡 Mostly downhill, today's journey is easier on the legs. Small pleasant paths and roads with views of the Rieti Valley lead through Cantalice and on to the Franciscan Sanctuary of La Foresta, the site where St. Francis miraculously restored a poor monk's trampled vineyard. From La Foresta, the walking is more monotonous, following a larger paved road. Still, you quickly arrive to Rieti, marking the southern edge of the Rieti Valley.

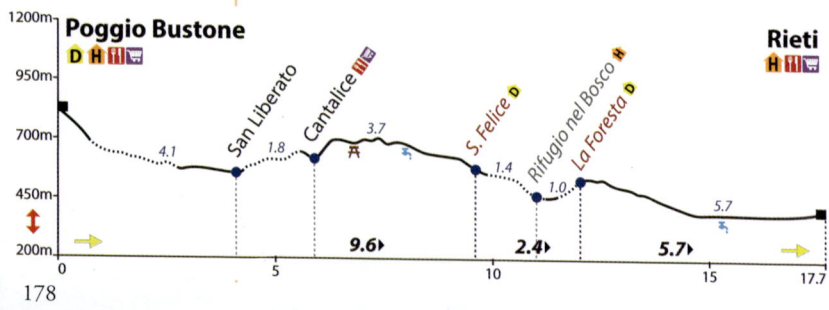

WAY OF ST. FRANCIS

9.6 San Felice D
- **D Ostello San Felice All'acqua** (7, don): Via del Santuario, 3387782930/3470869032, prolococantalice@libero.it

12.0 La Foresta D H
- **D H Rifugio nel Bosco** (€25/50): 3284860867, all year
- ⭐ **D Le Querce di Tara** (16, don): Forest 37, 3484273023, mauro.rinaldi@lequerceditara.it, a bit off route up the hill after La Foresta, very good reviews—a true pilgrim accommodation, pilgrims can either cook or eat a shared dinner

In 1225, Francis set off for Rieti at the request of Cardinal Ugolino (who later became Pope Gregory IX in 1227). Pope Honorius II was in Rieti with his doctors, and Ugolino hoped these doctors could treat an eye disease that was afflicting Francis. As Francis approached Rieti, he learned about festivities that were being prepared in his honor, so to escape the crowds he retreated to the Church of San Fabiano (now the location of the **La Foresta Sanctuary**), where he stayed in a house near the poor officiating priest's vineyard. Upon hearing that Francis was staying at San Fabiano, crowds flocked to the location, trampling the San Fabiano priest's vineyard, which was his only source of income. Taking pity on the priest, Francis promised an abundant harvest, and when the few untrampled grapes were collected, they produced an incredible quantity of wine. Many believe that St. Francis composed his Canticle of the Sun during this stay at La Foresta, though others tie this to his final days in San Damiano.

⚠ From La Foresta, exercise caution on the paved road into Rieti. There are relatively few cars, but there is no sidewalk or road shoulder.

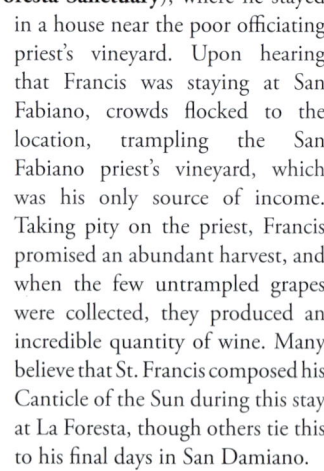

Ascending through Cantalice

POGGIO BUSTONE TO RIETI

17.7 Rieti

1. **H Madre Cabrini** (par, €63/100): S. Francesca Cabrini 5, 0746200727, convent north of town, price includes
2. **H BB Casa Simonetti** (€20/40): 0746483396/3400759816, Apr-Oct
3. **H Convento Divino Amore** (par, €25/50): Gerani 4, 0746200278, all year
4. **H BB La Bifora del Medioevo** (€40/60): S. Agnese 40, 3332944771/0746200288
5. **H Grande Albergo Quattro Stagioni** (€55/75): Piazza Cesare Battisti 14, 0746271071, all year
6. **H BB La Camelia** (€60): Sant'Anna 21, 3498467496
7. **H Terrazza Fiorita** (€25/person): Pellicceria 3, 0746296949/3477279591, very accommodating, good reviews
8. **H Hotel Europa** (€45/65): S. Rufo 49, 0746495149, all year
9. **H BB Acque del Velino** (€50/70): S. Francesco 36, 3803860384
10. **H L'Angelo Pellegrino** (€55/70): Vicolo Barilotto 22, 3515452758, langelopellegrino@gmail.com, all year
11. **H Hotel Cavour** (€45/78): Piazza Cavour 10, 0746485252
12. **H BB da Diletta** (€60): Borgo Sant'Antonio 62/c, 3248851592

Rieti dates to the Iron Age (9th-8th century BCE) and was a major population center of the Sabine nation before the foundation of Rome. According to legend, when Romulus founded Rome, he invited the Sabines to a feast and had his soldiers kidnap the local women. The "Abduction of the Sabine Women" became a frequent subject of Renaissance and post-Renaissance art. After the final Roman conquest (3rd century BCE), Rieti became a strategic point in the early Italian road network, particularly the *Via Salaria* ("Salt Way") which connected Rome to the Adriatic Sea via the Apennine Mountains. After the Roman empire fell into decline, Rieti was sacked by the Saracens in the 9th and 10th centuries, and by the Norman king of Sicily in the 12th century. In WWII, the city suffered Allied bombing, but much of the medieval city remains. On a hill on the southern edge of the Rieti Valley, the city is centered around the **Piazza di Vittorio Emanuelle II**, with its **Fontana dei Delfini** ("Fountain of Dolphins"). Near the piazza is the 12th-century **Duomo di Rieti**, reconstructed several times. Nearby is the bell tower and Palazzo Vescovile.

The Velino River runs through the city, and pedestrian paths along the river offer a nice evening stroll venue.

Under the city, Rieti's underground holds the remains of a Roman viaduct. Check the *i* tourist office for tour details.

22+ RIETI TO GRECCIO

23.8km (14.9mi)
▲ 1000m / ▼ 770m

⏲ 7.5-9.5 Hours
Difficulty: ▬ ▰

P 65%, 15.5km
U 35%, 8.3km

D H Lodging:
Contigliano 16.6km
Greccio 21.6-23.8km

⚑ Waymarking:
Blue/yellow stripes, Cammino di Francesco sign boards for "Fontecolombo" and "Greccio"

Contigliano's hilltop old town

Take a side detour to Fontecolombo, where St. Francis received treatment for an eye disease; continue to Greccio, home to the first nativity scene.

💡 This side route goes in the opposite direction of Rome and adds a day to your journey, but it's a worthwhile detour that allows for a visit to Franciscan sanctuaries at Fontecolombo and Greccio. The latter is the site of the first live nativity scene and likely the most important of the four Franciscan sanctuaries in the Holy Valley. A 3.6km descent to the Greccio train station or 2.2km return to Greccio for a bus allow you to easily return to Rieti via public transportation on the same day.

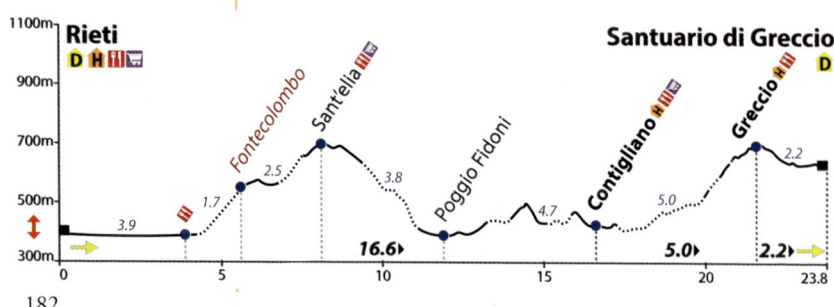

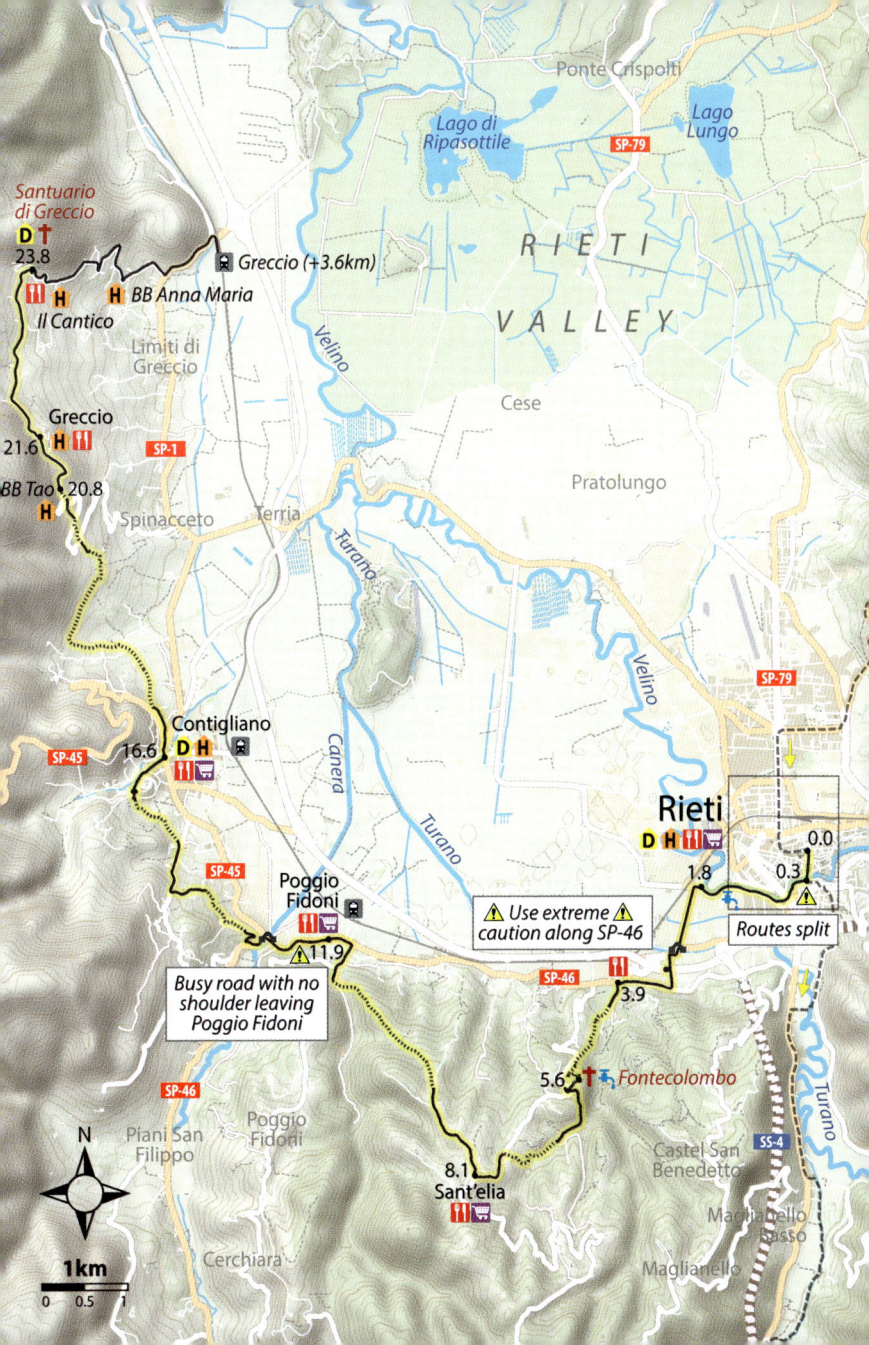

22+ WAY OF ST. FRANCIS

Other routes not covered in this guide
From Greccio, Franziskusweg routes continue northwest, crossing the mountains to Stronconne. From Stroncone, the Franziskusweg options follow unofficial routes west, then south to Farfa before connecting with the main Via di Francesco route in Montelibretti. This option adds considerable distance and a number of days to the overall journey, however, so we do not include it in this guide. Instead, we recommend returning to Rieti from Greccio by train and walking the official Via di Francesco/Via di Roma route from Rieti to Rome.

⚠ Waymarking for the initial part of the day can be confusing, but navigation is relatively simple: Cross the Ponte Romano over the Velino. On the other side, make an immediate right and follow walking paths along the south side of the Velino. At 1.8km, just after a set of pull-up bars, follow white arrows onto paved roads; now follow the day's waymarking. Use extreme caution when walking along SP-46.

⚠ On the way to the Greccio train station from the Greccio Sanctuary, blue and yellow stripes diverge left about halfway down the descent. Disregard these marks and continue on the paved road to the valley bottom.

Fontecolombo is the third of the four Franciscan sanctuaries in the Holy Valley. In 1223, Francis spent the spring and summer in Fontecolombo in a small cave near where the Chapel of San Michele stands today, drafting the final rule that would govern the life of his Franciscan brothers and sisters. In 1224 at Fontecolombo, doctors cauterized St. Francis' eyes in an attempt to treat an eye disease. Though his brothers fled the room, unable to watch the painful procedure, Francis claimed, miraculously, that he felt no pain.

16.6 Contigliano D H 🍴 ➕ € 🚌 🚉

D H Ostello Villa Franceschini (€20 per person): 📶,
Ettore Franceschini 7, ☎746706123/3392274096 📧,
rooms of six people

H BB Girasole (€30/60 🔑): W D 📶 ⊙,
Fontecerro Sud 18/e, ☎0746706043/3384314327 📧,
geared toward pilgrims

H Albergo Le Vigne (€60/75 🔑): W D 📶,
Repubblica 14/b, ☎0746707077 📧

Relief of St. Francis at the Greccio chapel entrance

RIETI TO GRECCIO 22+

21.6 - 23.8 Greccio D H ⏏ 🛏 🚻

D Greccio Sanctuary (par, 🛏4 don): 📞0746750127, 0746750124 ✉, ofm.greccio@tiscali.it, simple, few services in vicinity, though bar at bottom of sanctuary sells basic food

H BB Il Tau (€40/80 🛏): 🛜, Spinaccetto 147, 📞3395860561 ✉

H Hotel della Fonte (€89 🛏): 🍽🛜, Piazza Roma 5, 📞0746753110 ✉

H Agriturismo Antico Borgo de' Ferrari: 🐾🍽🛜, S. Francesco 8, 📞0746753151/3355206816 ✉, apartments with various prices

H BB Il Cantico (€70 🛏): 🛜⊙🍳, Via dei Frati 102, 📞3289642274 ✉, 2 rooms with 2 beds each, €120 for all 4 beds

Greccio village

The picturesque hilltop town of **Greccio** hangs over the western edge of the Rieti Valley. The town was founded by Greeks who had fled their home country as a result of war, hence the name Greccio. Earliest records of the town date to the 10th century. The Franciscan **Sanctuary of Greccio** is 2.2km past the village. Francis came to the hermitage several times between 1209 and 1224. (You can visit the hermit cells where he stayed in the sanctuary.) In December 1223, inspired by his time in the Holy Land and a visit to Bethlehem, Francis organized a live nativity scene, complete with an ox, donkey, manger, and villagers. Considered by many to be the world's first live nativity scene, the tradition continues to this day, and during the Christmas season some 100,000 people visit Greccio for several reenactments of the nativity scene. Fittingly, Greccio's twin city is Bethlehem.

Greccio Sanctuary

💡 The Greccio train station is in the valley, +3.6km from the Greccio Sanctuary. The hilltop town of Greccio is 2.2km before the Greccio Sanctuary.

23-27 RIETI TO ROME

Pleasant pathways leaving Rieti

Walk through rustic Sabine vineyards and olive groves, follow in the footsteps of countless pilgrims' journeys to Rome.

From Rieti, the Way of St. Francis ambles away from the higher Apennine Mountains, winding through the hills of Sabina (home of the pre-Roman Sabine people) and gradually descending to Rome and Italy's coastal plain, roughly following the ancient Via Salaria. The first legs of the journey from Rieti pass through rural countryside. Famous for its olive oil and wine, Sabina's hills are dotted with olive groves and vineyards, and its olive oil even has a protected European designation.

As the route approaches Rome, towns become decidedly more populated, giving way to residential suburbs of Rome. A scenic part of the route south of Monterotondo crosses the fields of the Riserva Naturale della Marcigliana ("Marcigliana Nature Reserve"), but after this, the final 20km to Rome are less than idyllic, braving the hustle and bustle of modern Rome on the way to St. Peter's Basilica in Vatican City.

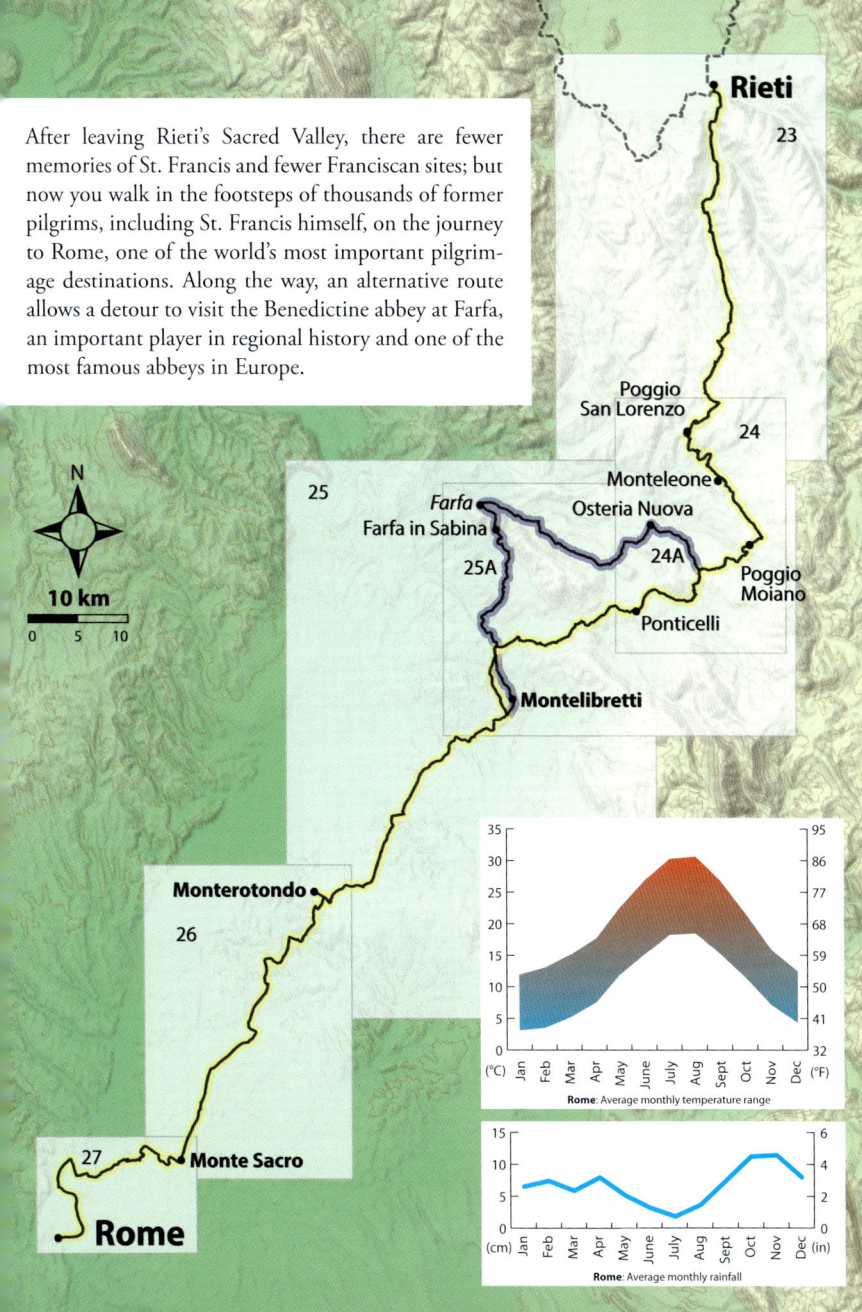

23

RIETI TO POGGIO SAN LORENZO

21.4km (13.4mi)
▲ 540m / ▼ 460m

⏲ **6.5-8 Hours**
Difficulty: ▭▭▭

P 43%, 9.2km
U 57%, 12.2km

D H **Lodging:**
Poggio S. L. 21.4km
Monteleone 27.1km
Poggio M. 31.0km

✝ **Waymarking:**
Blue/yellow stripes, Via di Roma signboards. Leaving Rieti, there are marks for the Cammino di San Benedetto, which overlaps with the Via di Roma/Via di Francesco for the first few kilometers out of Rieti.

Views of Sabine olive groves from Poggio San Lorenzo

Leave the Rieti valley along the Via Salaria, arrive in the peaceful San Lorenzo village after a enjoyable day of walking.

💡 Today's route is another relatively easy day of walking. The first half of the route to Poggio San Lorenzo follows a mix of paved roads and unpaved pathways through a delightful flat valley. Though parts of this section parallel a valley highway, the way sticks to roads and paths that largely keep away from car traffic.

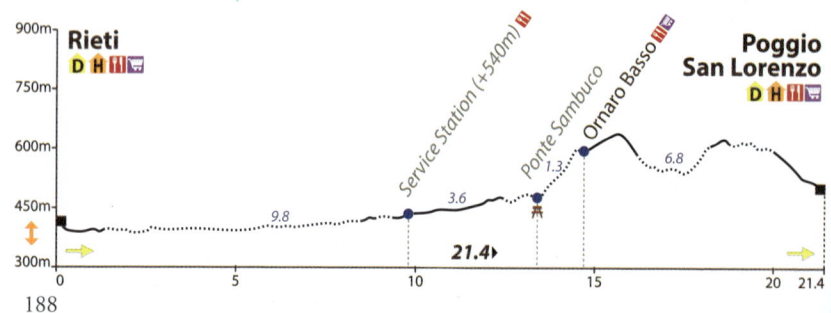

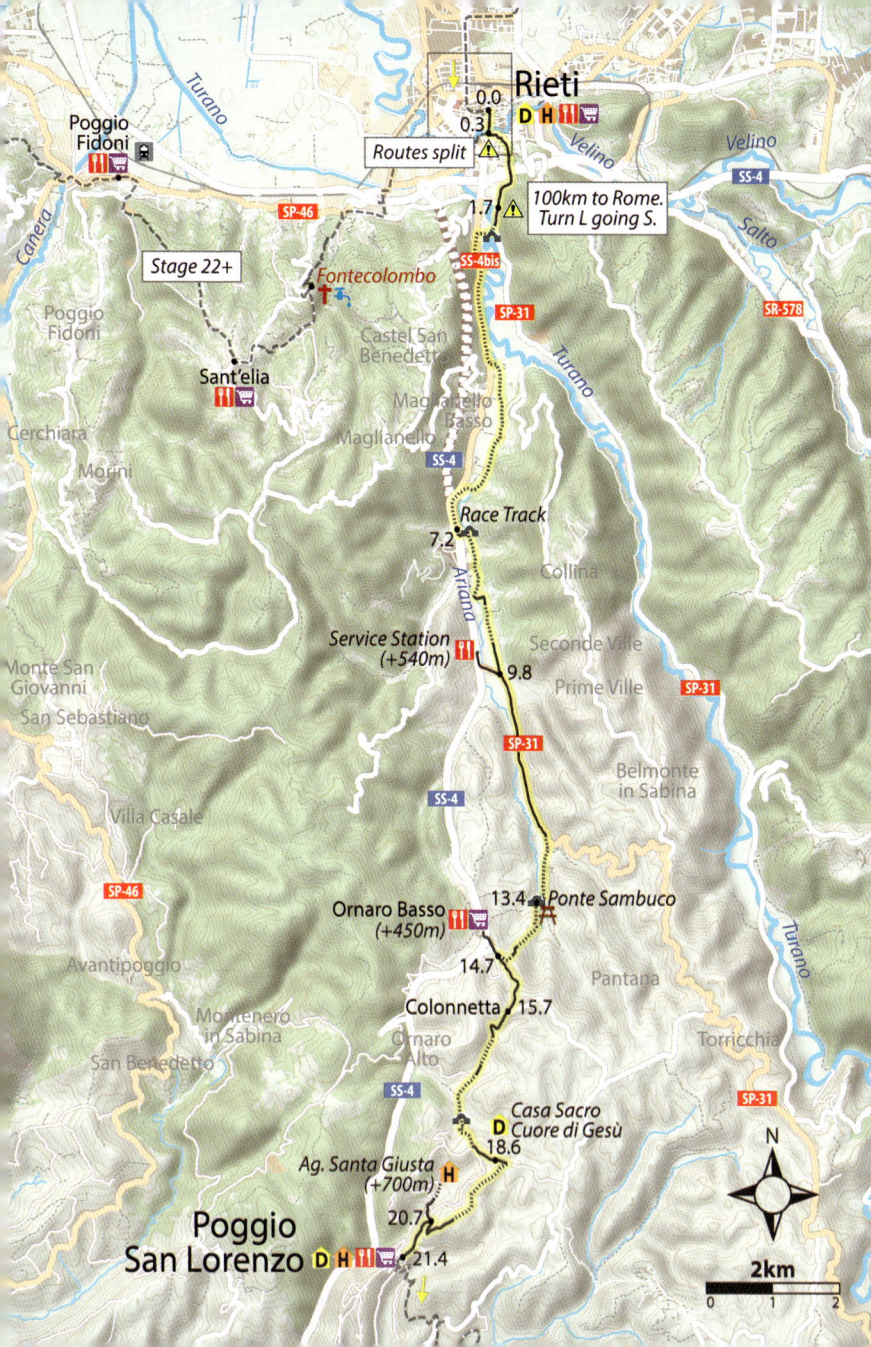

WAY OF ST. FRANCIS

⚠ The Cammino di San Benedetto diverges from the Via di Roma/Via di Francesco 12.3km south of Rieti, so be sure to only use the Cammino di San Benedetto marks for the initial exit from Rieti.

🏕 A picnic area at Ponte Sambuco provides a nice spot for a lunch break halfway through the day. (Stores 1.3km ahead and +450m off route in Onaro Basso offer another possible break point.) From Ponte Sambuco, the path climbs through rural hills on the way to the pleasant hilltop town of Poggio San Lorenzo.

💡 Waymarking is poor leaving Rieti, but navigation is relatively easy. From the Piazza Vittorio Emanuelle II, descend on Via Roma to the Velino and cross the Ponte Romano. Immediately on the other side of the bridge, turn left, passing through Piazza Cavour. Continue past several bus terminals/stops and east on the main street, passing the Chiesa di San Michele Arcangelo to the left. 50m past the church, turn right onto a smaller street (Via Borgo Sant'Antonio) at a memorial to victims of WWII bombings in 1944. Continue straight on this road (which eventually becomes Via Fonte Cottorella). Pass under the highway and reach a larger paved road at 1.7km, where there is a "100km to Rome" sign. Continue straight heading south on this larger paved road (ignore marks indicating a right turn) before turning right onto a walking path leaving the main road 250m ahead. Waymarking is much better from here.

Via di Roma and Cammino di San Benedetto waymarking on the path from Rieti

The **Via Salaria** ("Salt Way") was one of the ancient Roman roads that crossed present-day Italy. As the name indicates, the route was used to transport salt. Prior to the Roman-era, the Sabines traveled this route to bring salt from the marshes at the mouth of the Tiber to Reate (Rieti). Later in the Roman period, the road was connected across the Apennines to salt production sites on the Adriatic coast. Various remnants of the Roman road exist today. The Ponte Sambuco Roman bridge would have been part of the route, and, today, the highway that connects Rome to Rieti (SS-4) bears the same name, "Via Salaria."

RIETI TO POGGIO SAN LORENZO

18.6 **D** *Casa Sacro Cuore di Gesù* (par, 🛏3, don 💡): 🍴📶, Faioni 1, ☎0766735017, 🕐all year, primarily long-term religious retreat guesthouse, but can accommodate a few pilgrims if space is available, contact in advance

21.4 Poggio San Lorenzo D H 🍴🛒📦

D *Casa del Pellegrino* (muni, 🛏10, €15): 🛏🌐📶🍽, ☎3921445940/3336359291, 🕐all year, simple but welcoming pilgrim dorm, in the central piazza

H *Agriturismo Santa Giusta* (€35/70 💡): 🍴📶📀🍽, ☎3394984008, 🕐all year, dinner €18, turn-off 700m before Poggio San Lorenzo, +700m off route

Olive oil ice cream in the Poggio San Lorenzo fair

Poggio San Lorenzo is a small hilltop town that was officially founded in the 17th century as a fief of the Farfa Abbey until the 18th century, though Roman archeological remains suggest a long history of habitation on this hilltop. (Exiting the town, you can see the remains of an old Roman wall at the base of the city.) The town is named after its hilltop location ("poggio," roughly translated, means "hill") and its patron saint, San Lorenzo. A local shop and restaurant (Capo Farfa) with a 400-year history of selling olive products is located at the entrance to town. In the town center, the parish church of San Lorenzo dates to the 16th century, but was completely rebuilt in the 18th century.

Festa in Poggio San Lorenzo

24

POGGIO SAN LORENZO TO PONTICELLI

20.2km (12.6mi)
▲ 750m / ▼ 920m

⏱ **6-8 Hours**
Difficulty: ▭▭▭

🅿 34%, 6.8km
Ⓤ 66%, 13.4km

D H Lodging:
Monteleone 5.7km
Poggio 9.6km
Ponticelli 20.2km
Nerola 24.5km,
Montelibretti 33.2km
On alternative route:
Osteria 18.3km
Toffia 26.3km
Farfa 29.8km
Fara 31.9km

✝ **Waymarking:**
Blue/yellow stripes,
Via di Roma
signboards

Santa Vittoria chapel

Traverse olive groves, visit a chapel commemorating a Christian martyr who famously confronted a dragon.

💡 Today's route winds past little towns and through olive groves and vineyards, while descending into and ascending from various small valleys that cut through the rural landscape. Poggio Moiano splits the day roughly in half, and the town's little center offers a nice location for a lunch break. A steep descent and climb from town are demanding but short. Several lovely kilometers along gravel roads through lightly forested countryside follow.

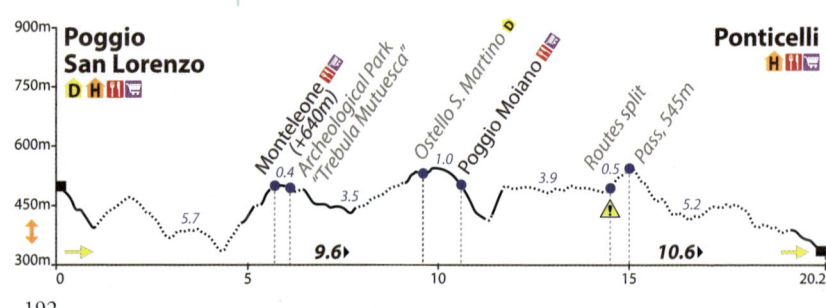

WAY OF ST. FRANCIS

Near the end of the day, an alternative route branches from the main route. One must decide to either follow the main route to Rome via Ponticelli or detour to the Benedictine abbey in Farfa. Over the final few kilometers to Ponticelli, be sure to pause and enjoy stunning views of hilltop towns in the distance.

⚠️**Farfa Route Junction**: 3.9km after leaving Poggio Moiano's main square, the route splits at a T intersection at the base of a hill. The main route goes left, climbing to a low pass, then continuing on gravel roads to Ponticelli. The Farfa alternative route turns right and detours to the Benedictine abbey in Farfa before rejoining the main route just before Montelibretti.

Farfa Alternate - 24A ▭▭▫ / 25A ▭▭▪
See chapter 25A for details of the route from Osteria Nuova to Monterotondo.

As you decide whether or not to walk to Farfa, consider the following factors:
1) The Farfa alternative adds roughly 16km and an extra day to your journey, but also some wonderfully beautiful views from Mt. Buzio.
2) The Farfa Abbey is charming, but you can only visit the interior with a guide who may or may not speak English.

The Farfa alternative is less trafficked and much more poorly marked than the main route. Much of the walking is quite nice, but we don't recommend taking it without GPS navigation. There are a variety of different itinerary options for the Farfa detour, though we'd suggest two primary options to walk from Poggio San Lorenzo to Monterotondo in three days:
- Poggio San Lorenzo-Osteria Nuova (24A, 18.3km, ▲ +630m)
- Osteria Nuova-Montelibretti (25A, 24.8km, ▲ +832m)
- Montelibretti-Monterotondo (second half of stage 25, 17.5km, ▲ +365m)

If you prefer an itinerary to sleep in Farfa or Fara in Sabina, you could walk the following itinerary. This leaves a long day to Monterotondo, but both Poggio Moiano and Fara in Sabina have accommodations with more of a pilgrim feel than Osteria Nuova.
- Poggio San Lorenzo-Poggio Moiano (9.6km, ▲ +433m)
- Poggio Moiano-Fara in Sabina (22.2km, ▲ +702m)
- Fara in Sabina-Monterotondo (28.6km, ▲ +692m).

18.3 Osteria Nuova
💡 A relatively uninspiring town along the highway that connects Rome to Rieti with sufficient services.
1. 🛏️ **BB Il Gelsomino** (€32): 📶, ☏3286905734, good reviews

POGGIO SAN LORENZO TO PONTICELLI

5.7 Monteleone Sabino, +640m

H Santa Vittoria (€45/50), Trebula Mutuesca, ©3475988875

Trebula Mutusca was an ancient Sabine city situated across three hilltops in the area of what is today Monteleone Sabino. At an archeological site (fenced off) half a kilometer past the turnoff to Monteleone Sabino, there are the remains of an amphitheater, thermal baths, and ancient roads.

Not far down the road is the **Church of Santa Vittoria**. The current building dates to the 12th century but was built on the location of an existing chapel and shrine said to contain the sarcophagus of the 3rd-century martyr Vittoria. According to legend, Vittoria refused to marry a non-Christian lord, and in return was exiled to Sabina.

At the time, a dragon threatened Trebula Mutusca. In exchange for the townspeople's conversion, she chased the dragon away. However, some citizens later informed Roman authorities that she was a Christian, and she was martyred when she refused to renounce her religion.

Views of olive groves on the approach to Ponticelli.

9.6 Poggio Moiano

D Ostello San Martino (muni, 11, don): ☏3400807262, ostellosanmartino1@gmail.com, all year, simple, but very pleasant pilgrim lodging in old church, good intermediate lodging option

20.2 Ponticelli

H Casale Il Viandante (€35/50): (€5), XX Settembre 13, ☏3490914666, cristina.stempel@gmail.com, Apr-Nov, may open for groups in winter, good reviews

H Agriturismo La Ripa (€70+): ☏3384677159, not far from Santa Maria delle Grazie

Ponticelli is a small, peaceful hamlet, with lovely views of the surrounding hilltop towns, including Nerola and Scandriglia. The first documentation of the town dates to the 11th century, but people likely inhabited the area prior to that date.

Ponticelli on the hilltop

POGGIO SAN LORENZO TO PONTICELLI

The Santa Maria del Colle church on the town's hilltop has a Romanesque facade and contains 14th- and 15th-century frescoes. Across the valley south of town is the **Sanctuary of Santa Maria delle Grazie**, which was built by the wealthy Orsini family and donated to a reformed branch of the Franciscan order in 1662. Inside is a famous restored icon of the Virgin Mary (santuariodisantamariadellegrazie.org).

On the official route 1.6km past Ponticelli are the remains of another Roman bridge that was part of the Via Salaria. Called the Ponte del Diavolo ("Bridge of the Devil"), the bridge was likely so named because of the frequent robberies that occurred in its vicinity.

💡 The owners of Bar Mariani in Ponticelli happily welcome pilgrims. They might be able to help find accommodation in a local home in a pinch (📞076589249). The bar is just before the town center.

Country roads after Poggio Moiano

25

PONTICELLI TO MONTEROTONDO

29.7km (18.6mi)
▲ 760m / ▼ 940m

⏲ **8-10.5 Hours**
Difficulty: ▭▭▯

🅿 70%, 20.8km
Ⓤ 30%, 8.9km

D H Lodging:
Nerola 4.3km
Montelibretti 13km
Monterotondo 30km

✝ **Waymarking:**
Blue/yellow stripes,
Via di Roma
signboards

Statue of walkers in the fields outside of Monterotondo

Amble through rural landscapes, watch for remnants of the Via Salaria, end the day in a suburb of Rome.

💡 A long day, but outside of a few short climbs the way is comparatively flat, while all walking surfaces (largely paved and gravel roads) are manageable. Throughout the day, the route continues to pass through enjoyable countryside, full of olive groves. As you approach the day's end, the surroundings become more populated and several busy roads and intersections require caution and care. Finishing in Monterotondo, a residential suburb of Rome, you're only 30-some kilometers from your final destination!

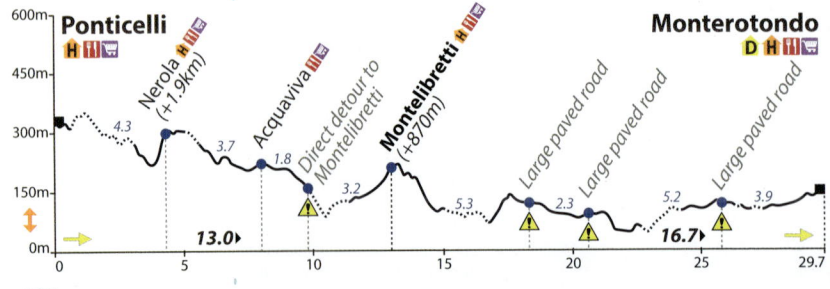

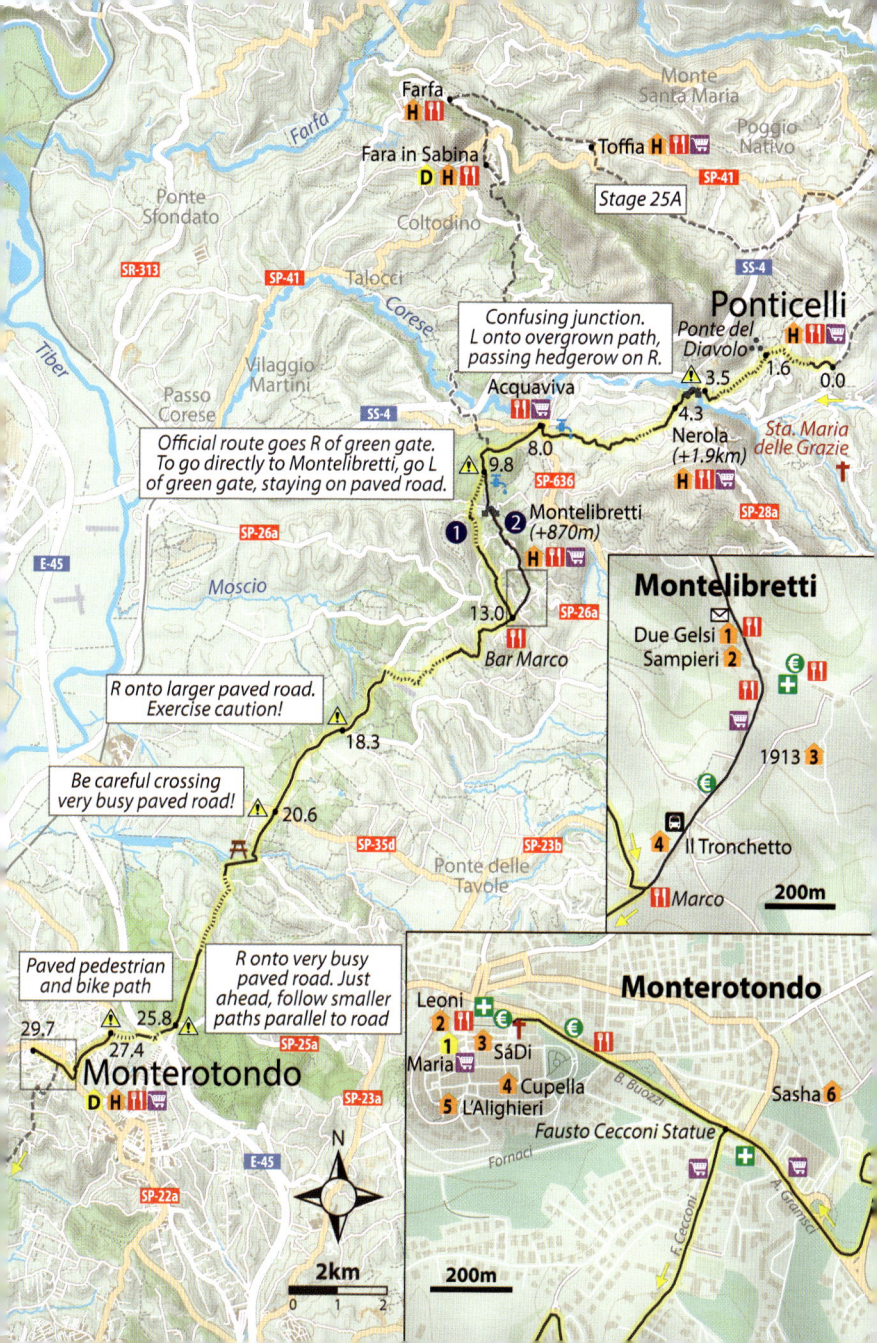

WAY OF ST. FRANCIS

4.3 Nerola, +1.9km

Castello Orsini (€85+), Aldo Bigelli, 0774683272, hotel in historic, renovated castle, shuttle

This hilltop town has a imposing castle, which once belonged to the powerful Orsini family and now serves as a hotel.

💡 If planning to go to Montelibretti, there are several options for entering town. ❶ ⭐ The first, and easiest navigationally, is to simply walk on the official Via di Roma route to Bar Marco on the edge of Montelibretti. From there, turn left, leaving the official route and ascending to the center of town. ❷ A second option allows you to walk directly into Montelibretti without backtracking. At 9.8km, you reach a point where you are facing a green gate held up the two brick columns. The clearly-marked Via di Roma descends to the right of the gate on a gravel double track. You can, however, continue straight on the paved road, passing the gate on the right. Then descend into the valley, turn left at a T intersection and soon cross a bridge. Ascend and pass a cemetery on your left. Then, immediately reach a T intersection with a larger paved road. Turn right on the larger paved road; then make an immediate left onto a narrow paved lane, which ascends into Montelibretti.

Alternative Itinerary:
💡 As this stage is long and has a number of steep (if short) climbs, you may want to split it in half by staying in Montelibretti—a pretty hilltop town with very pleasant lodging.

⚠ Between Montelibretti and Monterotondo, the path crosses several busy roads. Exercise extreme caution when crossing and remain vigilant.

Walking through vineyards and olive groves to Montelibretti

PONTICELLI TO MONTEROTONDO

13.0 Montelibretti +870m
1. ⭐ BB I Due Gelsi (€30-35/50-60/75), Garibaldi 23, ☎3476412908/3461881485, bbiduegelsi@gmail.com, all year, central, accommodating, prices vary based on private/shared bathroom
2. Apartamento Sampieri/Casa Lory (€60), S. Rocco 12/A, ☎3497926286
3. BB 1913 (€35/55): (€35/55), ☎3318538445, Valle dei Prati 60, all year
4. B&B Il Tronchetto (€35/60), Via Roma 160, ☎3349599935/0774609830, tancredinovella@gmail.com

Montelibretti is an old hilltop Sabine town, named from a Roman villa owned by Commodus' father-in-law. The town occupies a strategic position at the crossroads of major routes running north-south and east-west. The town later passed to the Orsini family, followed by the Barberini, then the Sciarra.

29.7 Monterotondo
1. Santa Maria Maddalena (par, 30, don), Ricciotti Garibaldi 22, ☎3496062789/3403502589, all year, true pilgrim dorm, dinner €15, washer €5
2. Albergo dei Leoni (€55/65), Vincenzo Federici 23, ☎0690627534, all year
3. BB SáDi (€40/50), Guglielmo Oberdan 17, ☎3518578371, extra cost for use of kitchen/washer
4. BB La Cupella (€50/60), Vincenzo Bellini 36, ☎3384224137
5. L'Alighieri (€65/80), Via dante Alighieri 27, ☎3334146459, well reviewed
6. BB La Casa di Sasha (€25/45), Massimo Pelosi 15, ☎3283760262, all year except Aug

Some historians connect **Monterotondo** to the ancient Sabine city of Eretum. The town was a historic strategic point to defend Rome. Now a commuter city, its residents travel regularly to Italy's capital. Once owned by the powerful Orsini family, the impressive **Palazzo Orsini** rises up above the Parco del Cigno and houses the town hall. Also of note is the Baroque **Santa Maria Maddalena** church.

⚠ There's a particularly tricky junction just before Monterotondo. At 25.8km, turn right onto the quite busy SP-25a. Ahead you'll see a large, limited-access highway. Walk along SP-25a for 180m, then follow marks right, leaving the main road and continuing onto a smaller paved lane. This lane soon becomes a walking path that then descends back to the main paved road, where you follow a sidewalk on the side of the road through a tunnel under the limited-access highway. On the other side of the road, follow well-marked walking paths that run parallel to but removed from the paved road. At 27.4km, join a paved bike/pedestrian path the rest of the way into Monterotondo.

Chiesa di Santa Maria Maddalena

25A

PONTICELLI TO MONTEROTONDO (VIA FARFA)

24.8km (15.5mi)
▲ 830m / ▼ 1000m

⏱ **7.5-10 Hours**
Difficulty: ■ ■ ■

🅿 71%, 17.5km
Ⓤ 29%, 7.3km

Ⓓ Ⓗ **Lodging:**
Toffia 8.0km
Farfa 11.5km
Fara Sabina 13.6km
Montelibretti 25km

✝ **Waymarking:**
Blue/yellow stripes, CAI 351 between Farfa and Fara in Sabina. ⚠ Overall, the alternative route to Farfa is more poorly waymarked than the official route to Rome via Ponticelli. If walking this route, use GPS tracks to navigate, in addition to this book's maps.

Visit a famous Benedictine Farfa Abbey, climb to the "Terrace over Rome," stroll through olive groves to Montelibretti.

☀ From Osteria Nuova the routes descends a long valley following paved roads and dirt tracks before ascending to the Farfa Abbey, a famous Benedictine Abbey with a long history. From the abbey, the route ascends to Fara in Sabina, a small town perched atop Monte Buzio. Stunning views from the mountaintop accompany the descent to small towns and rural valleys on the way to Montelibretti, a picturesque hilltop town with views of the surrounding countryside.

Views from Fara in Sabina, the "Terrace over Rome"

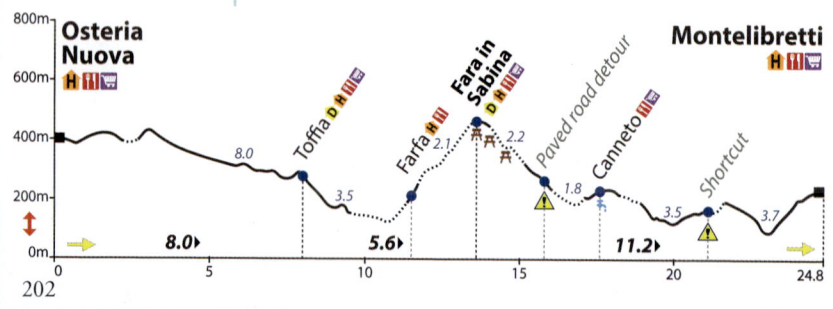

25A WAY OF ST. FRANCIS

Follow paved roads from Osteria Nuova, roughly parallel to the limited access highway. Cross under the highway (2.3km) on an unpaved road and turn R at a T. Climb and descend to another highway underpass (3.4km), down the valley to Toffia.

8.0 Toffia D H 🍴🛒➕🚌

D Col di Melo (⇌6, don): 📷🛜, Col di Melo, ✆3342181305/3343388900, foster home with organic farm, +1.7km, shuttle service on request

H BB Monte degli Elci (€40/60 🛏): 🍴🛜⊙, Farense 33, ✆3474747012

H Il Gelsomino (€40/80 🛏): 📷 W 🛜, Collitrone 66B

H La Vecchia Pietra (€70 🛏): 📷, Collitrone

H BB Toffia (€35): 📷🛜, Vocabolo Marignano, ✆3385210157

💡 After Toffia, navigation can be confusing on gravel roads descending the valley. At an unmarked 3-way junction, take the middle, best-maintained, gravel road. Not far ahead is a stream crossing (no bridge); take a rough gravel road to Farfa.

11.5 Farfa H 🍴

H Suore dell'Ordine del SS. Salvatore di Santa Brigida (par, €35/70 🛏): 🍴🛜⊙, Piaz. Schuster 1, ✆0765277013

Located on the northern flank of Monte Acuziano is the Benedictine **Farfa Abbey**, named after the nearby river of the same name. According to legend, St. Laurence of Syria, then Bishop of Spoleto, founded the abbey in the 6th century when he became enamored with secluded monastic life. The abbey was likely built on the remains of an existing Roman temple. Over the centuries, the abbey was at times destroyed or abandoned, but by the Middle Ages the abbey had accrued a considerable amount of wealth and power in the region, owning many churches, towns, and other properties. To this day, the abbey is home to Benedictine monks who live a simple, spiritual way of life. Entry into the abbey is possible with a guided tour (€5, ⊙hourly Tue-Sun, 10am-1pm, 3:30-6:30pm).

💡 Visits to the Farfa Abbey must be accompanied by a guide, some of whom do not speak English.

13.6 Fara in Sabina D H 🍴ℹ️🚌

D H Monastero delle Clarisse Eremite (par, €25/person): 🍴⊙, Santa Maria in Castello, 3341732880/3296061580, panicristina@hotmail.it, rooms for 1-4, €35 with 🍴 & 🛏

H La Casa di Donatella (€30-85): W 🛜⊙, Filippo Mercuri 16, ✆3200823279

OSTERIA NUOVA TO MONTELIBRETTI 25A

Perched atop Monte Buzio (482m), **Fara in Sabina** commands expansive views, earning the nickname *Terrazza su Roma* ("Terrace over Rome"). On a clear day, the seven hills of Rome are visible. Historically an important administrative center and home to many wealthy families of Sabina, the town boasts an uncommonly-high number of aristocratic homes with unique, skilled architecture.

A popular tourist destination because of its panoramic views, the town is decidedly busier on weekends. The **Museo Civico Archeologico** is located in the Palazzo Brancaleoni, a 15th-century mansion that belonged to the Brancaleoni family. Exhibits in the museum contain archeological remnants of the cities of Cures and Eretum (two ancient Sabine towns) and other artifacts of the Sabine culture. (€3, ☉Sep-May Fri-Sun 10am-6pm, Jun-Aug Fri-Sun 10am-8pm, weekdays by appointment, ☏0765277321/3468187972).

Farfa Abbey

The **Clarisse Eremite Monastery** is housed in a medieval castle. In the 17th century, Cardinal Francesco Barberini donated the castle for use as a monastery for the Poor Clares, who took strict vows to live in silence and separation from the outside world. Those rules remained in force until 1963. In 1944, Allied bombing severely damaged the monastery, putting its future in doubt, but in 1963 the Monastery of Santa Chiara in Rieti joined with the Poor Clares to restore the damaged monastery of Fara in Sabina.

After leaving Fara in Sabina, descend to the small village of Montegrottone. At 15.8km, at the bottom of the village, reach a 4-way intersection with a larger paved road. The marked route crosses the larger paved roads and descends on a smaller paved road (Via Catone). In the valley below, however, the route becomes quite overgrown and brambly. At the 4-way intersection, consider turning left and following the larger paved road, rejoining the marked route in Canneto.

🏛 "Museum of Silence" (by appointment via Museo Civico Archeologico) is attached to the monastery complex is accessed from outside the Clarisse Eremite Monastery in Fara in Sabina. The museum includes a series of projections that evoke themes of daily monastic life. The monastery itself also hosts visitors, including pilgrims. (*clarisseremite.com*, ☏0765277021 from ☉12-1pm or 8-9pm)

24.8 Montelibretti 🛏🍴☕➕€🚻
💡 See Stage 25 for routes to Montelibretti & Monterotondo.

26

MONTEROTONDO TO MONTE SACRO

18.7km (11.7mi)
▲ 380m / ▼ 490m

⏱ **5.5-7 Hours**
Difficulty: ▪️▫️▫️

🅿 82%, 15.4km
🆄 18%, 3.3km

D H Lodging:
Monte Sacro 18.7km
Rome 33.7km

✝ **Waymarking:**
Blue/yellow stripes, Painted keys of St. Peter, Via di Roma sign boards. ⚠ Near Rome, waymarking quality deteriorates. navigation is relatively easy, mind notes at tricky intersections.

Walking through hilly countryside into the Marcigliana Reserve

Cross the peaceful Marcigliana Nature Reserve before arriving in the hustle and bustle of Rome's outskirts.

☀ From Monterotondo, the first half of the day includes pleasant paths through rural countryside, past small towns, and through the Marcigliana Nature Reserve. After this peaceful respite from cars and people, the final half of the day is an urban slog along busy roads (all of which have sidewalks) to Monte Sacro. From there, it's only another 15.0km walking (or a short subway ride) into the center of Rome.

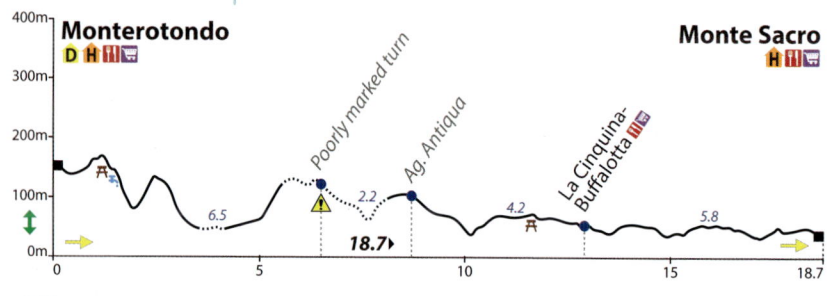

WAY OF ST. FRANCIS

The **Marcigliana Nature Reserve** covers a series of hills bounded by the Tiber, Bufalotta, and Casale Rivers. Much of the land is arable, designated for cultivation or grazing, while the valley sides are covered with scrub vegetation. The reserve, located on the northeastern edge of Rome, is a refuge to animals threatened by urbanization, such as foxes, martens, weasels, badgers, and porcupines. It's also home to a number of traditional agricultural estates.

⚠ Waymarking is largely nonexistent through the Marcigliana Nature Reserve, though few turns are required. Pay particular attention to the following intersection, however:

At the top of a climb at the northern edge of the nature reserve (entrance to the reserve marked by a green metal gate), the trail turns right and follows a gravel road along the hilltop. Continue 900m to a building to the right with a faded sign for "La Tempestosa" at 6.5km. Here, turn left onto a gravel road, descending into the valley. There are no markings at this turn, and it's easy to miss.

💡 After leaving the Marcigliana Nature Reserve, cross Via della Marcigliana and continue straight on Via di Tor S. Giovanni, entering the populated outskirts of Rome. 2.2km ahead, turn left onto Via della Bufalotta (careful, this is a busy intersection) and cross under a limited-access highway. Stay on this road all the way until Monte Sacro.

MONTELIBRETTI TO MONTE SACRO

18.7 Monte Sacro 🏨🍴🛒➕🚊🏧🚻

1. 🏨 **Domus Città Giardino B&B** (€80 🛏): 🍴📶, Adriatico 20, ☎0687195387/3347312707
2. 🏨 **Casa Per Ferie Santa Rita** (par, €20 per person 🛏): 📶, Nomentana 514, ☎0686800016, economical pilgrim option, good reviews
3. 🏨 **City Break Nomentana** (€65/72 🛏): 📶, Piazza Sempione 19/B, ☎3420145360
4. 🏨 **Hotel Ars** (€65 🛏): 📶, Monte Altissimo 20-24, ☎0687180200
5. 🏨 **Hotel Aniene** (€55 🛏): 📶, Tirreno 74, ☎068189779
6. 🏨 **BB Città Giardino** (€65 🛏): 📶, Moncenisio 45, ☎3355637986

💡 Monte Sacro is connected to Rome's metro system. Though we highly recommend walking all the way to St. Peter's Square so that you have the satisfaction of arriving on foot (and so that you qualify for a Testimonium), the rest of Rome is an easy metro ride away from Monte Sacro.

Farmland south of Monterotondo

27

MONTE SACRO TO ROME

15.2km (9.4mi)
▲ 300m / ▼ 370m

⏱ 4-5.5 Hours
Difficulty: 🟩⬜⬜

🅿 100%, 15.2km
🆄 0%, 0km

D H Lodging:
Rome 15.2km

🕆 Waymarking:
Blue/yellow stripes, Via di Roma signboards. ⚠ Marking on the last 15.2km to St. Peter's Basilica is very infrequent. Pay close attention to trail notes.

Crossing the Tiber River

Follow the Tiber River to the satisfying journey's end, explore the Eternal City and claim your Testimonium

💡 The journey's final day is a short and sweet walk to St. Peter's Basilica in Vatican City. Though all urban walking, the route almost exclusively follows dedicated bike/pedestrian paths, making the walk about as pleasant as an urban walk can be. The final few kilometers along the Tiber River are particularly nice approaching Vatican City.

From Monte Sacro, cross the Aniene River on Ponte Tazio. On the far side of the bridge, turn right into a parking lot and join a paved pedestrian/bike path that leads most of the rest of the way to St. Peter's Basilica along the Aniene and Tiber Rivers.

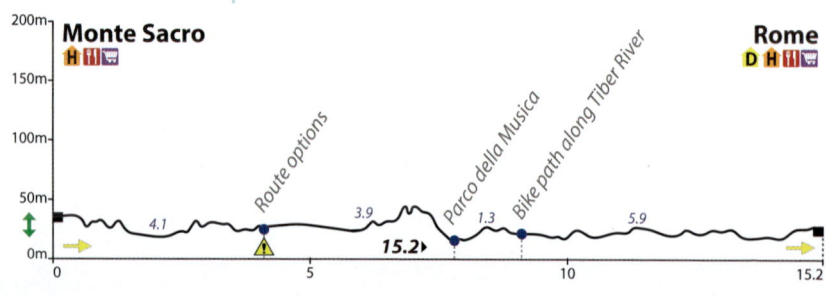

MONTE SACRO TO ROME

At 3.2km, the path winds around a highway interchange. Ahead, at 4.1km, the path crosses a major intersection at a stoplight. ⚠ On the other side of the intersection, marks indicate descending from the bike path to a paved road that passes by Villa Ada Park before reconnecting with the ped/bike path. ⭐ Alternatively, we recommend staying on the bike path, curving around the park and its hill. This adds only 200m, and avoids car traffic.

On the west side of Villa Ada Park and hill, pass a mosque to the right and the Aquaniene Sport Club to the left. Continue on sidewalks, passing the Villa Gloria Park on your right.
At the far side of the park, turn right, then left, soon passing the Parco della Musica to the left. Not far after the Parco della Musica, turn right onto Corso di Francia (the road with the tram line running down the middle).

Continue to the Tiber River, crossing on Ponte Flaminio bridge. On the other side of the river, turn left onto the ped/bike paths (there is a low and a high option). Follow these paths along the Tiber all the way to the final turn to St. Peter's Basilica. (Note that the low path along the river stays further from cars, but the final turn is easier to miss.)

Following a bike and pedestrian path along the Tiber River to Vatican City

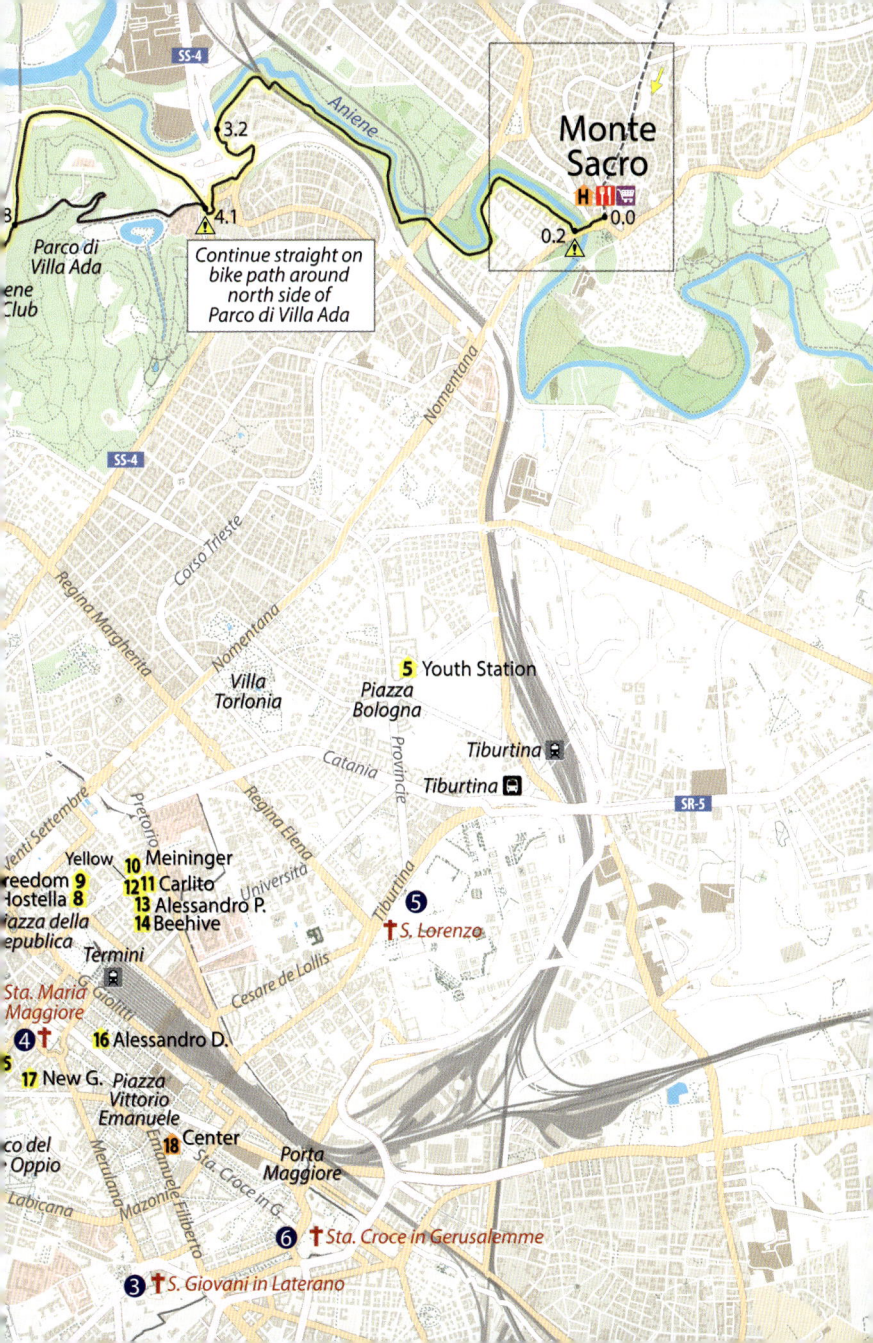

27 WAY OF ST. FRANCIS

15.2 Rome D H 🍴📞🧴⊙➕€ℹ️🚉✈️

As one of the most-visited cities in the world, Rome has thousands of accommodations options. We list just a few convenient options.

1. ⭐ **D Spedale Divina della Provvidenza di San Giacomo** (par, 📞24, don 🛏️): 🍴⊙, Genovesi 11B, 📞064959590, 🕒3-10:30pm, all year, lovely, peaceful pilgrim hostel in the midst of bustling Rome, communal dinner, breakfast, and foot washing ceremony, must have proof of walking last 100km to Rome, maximum 2-night stay
2. **H Istituto Orsoline Maria Immacolata** (par, €35/60): 📶, Dandolo 46, 📞065812150/3315444895, pilgrim-oriented
3. **H Casa per Ferie Santa Maria alle Fornaci** (€50/80 🛏️): 📶, Piazza Santa Maria alle Fornaci 27, 📞0639367632, pilgrim-oriented
4. **D H Comics Guesthouse** (€27/-/64+): 🍳📶, Giulio Cesare 38, 📞0694879873/3405236953
5. **D H Youth Station Hostel** (€25-30/-/70): 🍳Ⓦ🅞📶, Livorno 5, 📞0644292471/3337575596
6. **H Ostello Marello** (par, €54-64/75): 🍳📶⊙, Urbana 50, 📞064882120, 🕒all year, relatively popular pilgrim option, €27 per person in double w/shared bathroom
7. **D H RomeHello Hostel** (€40+/-/120): 🍳🍴Ⓦ🅞📶, Torino 45, 📞0696860070
8. ⚠️ **H Hostella** (€33-35 🛏️): 🍳📶, Gaeta 70, 📞064467553, female guests only, <u>temporarily closed</u>
9. **D H Freedom Traveler** (€27-32/-/70 🛏️): 🍳📶, Gaeta 23, 📞0648913910
10. **D H Meininger Roma Termini** (€28-37/75/90): 📶, S. Martino della Battaglia 16, 📞0694801352
11. **D H Carlito's Budget Rooms** (€18-22/-/70): 📶, Villafranca 18/A, 📞064440384
12. **D H The Yellow** (€30-37/85/100 🛏️): 🍳Ⓦ🅞📶, Palestro 51, 📞064463554
13. **D H Alessandro Palace Hostel & Bar** (€25-29/-/100+): 🍳🍴📶, Vicenza 42, 📞064461958
14. **D H The Beehive** (€40/-/110): 🍴Ⓦ📶, Marghera 8, 📞0644704553
15. **D H Sandy Hostel** (€35/-/80): 📶, Cavour 136, 📞335225945
16. **D H Alessandro Downtown Hostel** (€26-32/-/90+): 🍳📶, Carlo Cattaneo 23, 📞064461958
17. **D H New Generation Hostel** (€35-40/-/90): 🍳📶, Quattro Cantoni 35, 📞0690215141
18. **H In the Center Guesthouse** (€50/90): 🍳📶, Emanuele Filiberto 50, 📞3281015077

Arriving to Rome, a huge metropolitan city that attracts millions of tourists annually, can be jarring after 500+ kilometers walking through more peaceful slices of Italy. Still this ancient city with its rich cultural and religious history spanning 28 centuries makes an impressive endpoint for the journey.

St. Francis in Rome

Rome, the home of the Catholic Church, played an integral role in the story of Saint Francis, and he traveled here at several important junctures in his life. First, in 1205, during the beginning period of his conversion, Francis journeyed to St. Peter's Basilica and, appalled by the miserliness of people there, gave away all of his money and exchanged his clothes with a beggar outside the church.

MONTE SACRO TO ROME

In 1209, Francis returned to Rome to petition the Catholic Church for official approval of his new order. Church leaders were initially sceptical of Francis, but according to legend, Pope Innocent III had a dream: he saw the Church of St. John of Lateran falling in on itself. Miraculously, a man in peasant clothes appeared, holding up the church on his shoulders. Convinced of Francis' importance, the pope approved the new Franciscan Order.

Francis returned regularly to Rome, with documented trips in 1212, 1215, 1220, and 1223. In Rome, St. Francis met Jacqueline de Settesoli, later endearingly called "Brother Jacopa" by St. Francis. Initially married into the wealthy Frangipani family, Jacopa was widowed at an early age. Hearing Francis preach, she sought his spiritual guidance, eventually joining the Third Order of St. Francis (today the Secular Franciscan Order) and dedicating her life to charitable works. She regularly hosted St. Francis on his trips to Rome and donated some of her family's property in Trastevere to the Franciscans for use as a lepers' home.

Vatican City

The Way of St. Francis ends at St. Peter's Square in Vatican City, an independent city-state enclave contained within Rome. With an area of only 110 acres encircled by a 2-mile wall and a population of only around 1,000, Vatican City is technically the smallest country in the world. As the capital of the Catholic Church, Vatican City serves as the religious center for Catholicism's 1.3 billion adherents around the world.

Arriving to St. Peter's Square

WAY OF ST. FRANCIS

From 1656-1667, the sculptor and architect Gian Lorenzo Bernini led the construction of the current St. Peter's Square, designing colonnades surrounding a wide open space, so that the largest number of people possible could witness papal blessings. An ancient Egyptian obelisk sits in the center of the square. The red granite obelisk was originally located in Heliopolis, Egypt and later moved to Alexandria. In 37 CE, Caligula transferred the obelisk to Rome, placing it at the center of the Circus of Nero, where it witnessed the martyrdom of St. Peter. In 1586, the obelisk was moved to its current site. Today the column acts as a sundial: a granite meridian shows when the obelisk's shadow marks noon. As day lengths change throughout the year, marble discs mark winter and summer solstices and when the sun moves into a new sign of the zodiac.

St. Peter's Basilica presides over the square (open 7am-7pm). According to Catholic tradition, the basilica was built over the burial place of St. Peter (St. Peter's tomb is said to be directly below the basilica's altar). Peter was one of Jesus' apostles, and the Catholic Church considers him the first pope. Many later popes have since been buried in the Basilica. Starting in 1506, the current basilica was designed primarily by Michelangelo, Bramante, Maderno, and Bernini and is considered one of the most well-known works of Renaissance architecture.

i Approaching St. Peter's Basilica, the **Pilgrim Office** is located to the left, just after entering St. Peter's Square (Piazza Papa Pio XII 9, open Mon-Sat: 8:30am-4:30pm; Sun and Holidays: 9am-1pm, 0669896379). The office issues Testimonia and provides helpful tourist info.

St Peter's Square

MONTE SACRO TO ROME

The Sistine Chapel is not to be missed, housing some of Michelangelo's most famous works of art. The chapel is located in the Apostolic Palace, the official residence of the pope, and is named after Pope Sixtus IV, who had it restored. Its ceiling was painted by Michelangelo from 1508-1512, and is one of the most important pieces of High Renaissance art and includes the iconic *Creation of Adam*. Michelangelo's *Last Judgment* covers the altar wall. Other Vatican museums contain public art and sculpture from the pope's collection.

💡 Purchase advance tickets for the Sistine Chapel and Vatican Museums to avoid long lines (museivaticani.va). Tickets cost €17 plus a €4 online booking fee. Additional fee for audio guide. The Sistine Chapel and Vatican Museums are open 🕘Mon-Sat, 9am-6pm (last entry at 4pm) and for free on the last Sunday of each month from 9am-2pm (last entry at 12:30pm).

When visiting the Vatican, consider the following:
- The Vatican Museums are closed on Sundays, except for the last Sunday of each month, when the museums are free.
- The pope holds audience at St. Peter's Basilica on Wednesdays (except for in July), so the whole area is crowded and the basilica closed from 12-1pm.
- Saturdays the city is filled with weekend visitors and tends to be very busy.

Crossing the Tiber on Ponte Milvio with a view of the Chiesa Parrochiale Gran Madre di Dio

WAY OF ST. FRANCIS

Pilgrim Churches of Rome

Rome is the home of the Pope and the relics of many Christian saints and martyrs and has long been a pilgrimage destination. Many pilgrims visited the tombs of St. Peter and St. Paul, while some visited others to receive specific indulgences. In the 16th century, Italian priest Philip Nero proposed an itinerary visiting seven churches associated with early saints to create a shared religious pilgrim experience.

The churches, still visited by pilgrims today, include:

❶ Basilica di San Pietro (St. Peter's Basilica)
See p. 216

❷ Basilica San Paolo Fuori Le Mura (Basilica of St. Paul outside the Walls)
Basilica founded by the Roman Emperor Constantine over the burial place of St. Paul. Outside Vatican City but overseen by the Holy See (south, off map).

❸ Basilica di San Giovanni in Laterano (Cathedral of St. John Lateran)
The cathedral church of the Diocese of Rome and the seat of the Roman Pontiff. Also the church held up on the shoulders of St. Francis in a Pope Innocent III vision.

❹ Basilica di Santa Maria Maggiore (Basilica of St. Mary Major)
Basilica that enshrines the "Salus Populi Romani," a Byzantine icon of the Madonna with Christ as a child holding a gospel book.

❺ Basilica di San Lorenzo Fuori Le Mura (St. Lawrence outside the Walls)
The shrine and tomb of St. Lawrence, one of the first seven deacons of Rome.

❻ Basilica di Santa Croce in Gerusalemme (Holy Cross in Jerusalem)
According to tradition, the basilica houses relics of the Passion of Jesus brought to Rome from the Holy Land.

❼ Santuario della Madonna del Divino Amore (Our Lady of Divine Love)
Shrine with two churches dedicated to the Virgin Mary (south, off map).

MONTE SACRO TO ROME

Other sites in Rome
There are countless world-renowned historical and cultural sites to visit in Rome, and many, many guidebooks, which cover them in depth. Visiting the archeological ruins of the **Colosseum**, **Roman Forum**, and **Palatine Hill** can easily take a day. Single-entry tickets are €16 each; buy in advance at coopculture.it/en/colosseo-e-shop.cfm (☉8:30am-4:30/7:15pm depending on season).

A popular walking circuit easily completed in an afternoon starts from **Piazza Navona** and continues to the **Pantheon, Fontana di Trevi, Piazza di Spagna,** and **Piazza del Popolo** before returning to the start along the east bank of the Tiber.

After your long journey, congratulations on arriving to Rome, following in the footsteps of millions of pilgrims who have sought this historic and holy city! Take time to explore all that Rome has to offer, and enjoy well-earned rest and time for reflection.

Trevi Fountain

Colosseum

Italian Phrasebook

Vowels
a - Like "a" in "father"
e - Like "ay" in "say" or "e" in "net" (depending on location in word)
i - Like "ee" in "feet"
o - Like "oa" in "oat"
u - Like "oo" in "boo"

Consonants
c - Before "i" or "e" like "ch" in "cheese"
Before "a," "o," or "u" like "c" in "cat"
g - Before "i" or "e" like "j" in "jungle"
Before "a," "o," or "u" like "g" in "get"
h - Silent
q - Like "k" in "rake"
z - Like "ts" in "rats"

Combinations
Double consonants (*cc*, *zz*, etc.) - Elongated and enunciated with force
ch/gh - An *h* following a *c* or *g* before an *i* or and *e* hardens the "c" or "g":
che is pronounced like "kay"
ghet in "spaghetti" is pronounced "get"
sce/sci - When followed by *i* or *e*, *sc* sounds like "sh" in "she"
gn - Pronounced like the Spanish "ñ" or the "ny" in "canyon"
gli - Pronounced like "lli" in "billion"

Question Words:
What? - *Che cosa?*
When? - *Quando?*
Why? - *Perché?*
How? - *Come?*
How much? - *Quanto?*
Where is? - *Dov'è?*

Greetings and Small Talk
Hello - *Salve/ciao*
Goodbye - *Arrivederci/ciao*
Good morning - *Buongiorno*
Good afternoon/evening - *Buonasera*
Good night - *Buonanotte*
Yes/no - *Sì/no*
Please - *Prego/per favore*
How are you? - *Come stai?* (informal)/ *Come sta?* (formal)
How's it going? - *Come va?*
I'm fine. - *Sto bene.*
Where are you from? - *Di dove sei?* (informal)/*Di dov'è Lei?* (formal)
I'm from _____ - *Sono di* _____
Thank you/Thank you very much - *Grazie/Grazie mille*
What is your name? - *Come ti chiami?* (informal)/*Come si chiama?* (formal)
My name is _____ - *Mi chiamo* _____
(So) Nice to meet you. - *(Tanto) Piacere*
Excuse me/sorry/pardon - *Scusa (informal)/Scusi (formal)*

Common Phrases
Do you speak English? - *Parli inglese?* (informal)/*Parla inglese?* (formal)
I don't speak Italian (very well). - *Non parlo italiano (molto bene).*
I don't understand. - *Non capisco.*
Speak slowly please. - *Parla piano, per favore.* (informal) *Parli piano, per favore.* (formal)
How much does ___ cost? - *Quanto costa ___?*
Left/right/straight - *Sinistra/destra/dritto*
Where is _____? - *Dov'è?*
the bathroom - *Il bagno/la toilette*
the ATM - *Il bancomat*

ITALIAN PHRASEBOOK

the laundromat - *La lavanderia*
the supermarket/grocery store - *Il supermercato/il negozio di alimentari*
Do you have _____? - *Hai* (informal)/*Ha* (formal)/*Avete* (you all) _____?
  Wi-Fi - *wifi* (pronounced like English)
  laundry service - *servizio di lavanderia*
  (pilgrim) stamp - *timbro (del pellegrino)*
Do you serve _____? -
 Servi? (informal)
 Serve? (formal)
 Servite? (second person plural) _____?
    dinner - *la cena*
    lunch - *il pranzo*
Is breakfast included? - *È inclusa la colazione?*
When is _____ open? - *A che ora _____ aperto?*
Can I make a reservation _____? - *Posso fare una prenotazione _____?*
  for one person - *per una persona*
  for a single room - *per una camera singola*
  for a double room (double bed) - *per una camera doppia (con un letto matrimoniale)*
  for tonight - *per stasera*
  for tomorrow night - *per domani sera*
I arrive _____ - *Arrivo _____*
  today/tomorrow - *oggi/domani*
  at 5 - *alle cinque*

Days

Monday - *Lunedì*
Tuesday - *Martedì*
Wednesday - *Mercoledì*
Thursday - *Giovedì*
Friday - *Venerdì*
Saturday - *Sabato*
Sunday - *Domenica*

Numbers

0 - *zero*
1 - *uno*
2 - *due*
3 - *tre*
4 - *quattro*
5 - *cinque*
6 - *sei*
7 - *sette*
8 - *otto*
9 - *nove*
10 - *dieci*
11 - *undici*
12 - *dodici*
13 - *tredici*
14 - *quattordici*
15 - *quindici*
16 - *sedici*
17 - *diciassette*
18 - *diciotto*
19 - *diciannove*
20 - *venti*
21 - *ventuno*
22 - *ventidue*
23 - *ventitré*
24 - *ventiquattro*
25 - *venticinque*
26 - *ventisei*
27 - *ventisette*
28 - *ventotto*
29 - *ventinove*
30 - *trenta*
40 - *quaranta*
50 - *cinquanta*
60 - *sessanta*
70 - *settanta*
80 - *ottanta*
90 - *novanta*
100 - *cento*

Recommended Reading

Biography and Other Scholarship

<u>Traditional modern biographies:</u>
St. Francis of Assisi by Omer Englebert, 1965. A popular biography. Very comprehensive, narratively organized, and easy to follow. A good starting text.

St. Francis of Assisi by G.K. Chesterton, 1923. Brief biography by well-known 19th-20th century academic. A little confusing if you're not already familiar with St. Francis. Public domain, freely available on *archive.org*. Numerous subsequent print/ebook editions by various publishers.

St. Francis of Assisi in The Catholic Encyclopedia by Paschal Robinson, 1913. Quite concise, yet thorough, encyclopedic entry on St. Francis. Public domain, freely available in various online locations.

<u>Recent, modern research for more source-critical audiences:</u>
Francis of Assisi: A New Biography by Augustine Thompson, 2012. A thorough standalone biography with a close examination of historical sources

Francis of Assisi: The Life and Afterlife of a Medieval Saint by Andre Vauchez, 2012. Excellent St. Francis biography followed by detailed examination of the development of Francis' posthumous legacy.

Saint Francis and the Sultan: The Curious History of a Christian-Muslim Encounter by John Tolan, 2009. Detailed account of the Crusade-era encounter between St. Francis and Sultan Malik al-Kamil and the various ways the event has been interpreted in subsequent literature and art.

The Saint and the Sultan: The Crusades, Islam, and Francis of Assisi's Mission of Peace by Paul Moses, 2009. A more narrative account of the same incident.

Writings of St. Francis and His Contemporaries

Though there are many, many different translations/printings of the writings of St. Francis and his contemporaries (the early Franciscan sources), the most exhaustive collections with the most recent and academically rigorous translations are *Francis of Assisi: Early Documents* and *Clare of Assisi: Early Documents* (New City Press). Thanks to the efforts of the Commission for the Franciscan Intellectual Tradition (FCIT) and the books' copyright holders, these volumes are available for free online (after signing up for a free account) at franciscantradition.org/early-sources.

Francis of Assisi: Early Documents: Vol. 1 (The Saint), Vol. 2 (The Founder), Vol. 3 (The Prophet), Vol.4 (Index) by Regis Armstrong, J.A. Wayyne Hellmann, and William J. Short, 2002.

The Lady: Clare of Assisi: Early Documents by Regis J. Armstong, 2006.

Particularly famous among these are early writings are:

The Canticle of Brother Sun (or Canticle of Creatures): St. Francis' famous song of praise for a natural world made in God's image.

The First and Second biographies of St. Francis by Thomas of Celano: Celano, a follower of St. Francis, was the first to write about the early life of the St. Francis' adherents.

The Legend of St. Francis by St. Bonaventure: Bonaventure, another follower of St. Francis, was commissioned by church leaders to write this official, authoritative 1260 biography

The Legend of the Three Companions: 13th-century writings about the St. Francis generally attributed to Brothers Leo, Angelo, and Rufino.

The Deeds of Blessed Francis and His Companions, better known as the *Fioretti di San Francesco or Little Flowers of St. Francis*: by Hugolino and an unknown collaborator in the 14th century, the Fioretti are a collection of "little flowers," or anecdotes and sayings, attributed to Francis and his followers.

Devotional Texts

Eager to Love: The Alternative Way of Francis of Assisi by Richard Rohr, 2014. Well-known Franciscan Richard Rohr examines the religious tradition practiced by St. Francis and how his example can enrich modern spiritual lives.

The Lessons of Saint Francis: How to Bring Simplicity and Spirituality into Your Daily Life by John Michael Talbot and Steve Rabey, 1997. Thoughtful writings on how to apply the example of St. Francis to our to modern lives.

Pilgrimage Travel Guides

Every Pilgrim's Guide to Assisi and Other Franciscan Sites by Judith Dean, 2002. Easy-to-read, concise guide to Assisi and other important Franciscan sites

Traveling with the Saints in Italy: Contemporary Pilgrimages on Ancient Paths by Lucinda Vardey, 2005. Succinct descriptions (with very general travel directions) of pilgrimage sites throughout Italy connected to various saints, including St. Francis.

Roman Pilgrimage: The Station Churches by George Weigel, Elizabeth Lev, and Stephen Weigel, 2013. Well-regarded book focusing on the tradition of Lenten Christian pilgrimage to Rome's station churches. Useful guide with helpful background information, even outside of the season of Lent.

Pilgrim Paths to Assisi: 300 Miles on the Way of St. Francis by Russ Eanes 2023. A contemporary pilgrim's travelogue along the entire length of the Way of St. Francis, from Florence to Rome

About Us

Matthew Harms is a walker and cyclist, at heart a traveler who believes in slower forms of transportation that allow for a closer understanding of people, communities, and landscapes. He spent many years in the Balkans and Middle East, helping to develop hiking routes in both regions. He has traveled thousands of miles on foot and by bike in the Middle East, Europe, and the United States, and he is currently based in Colorado, where he works as a nurse when not traveling or exploring the Rocky Mountains.

David Landis and **Anna Dintaman**, founders of **Village to Village Press**, bring over 15 years of experience working with trails in Europe, the Middle East, Asia, and their home area in the Shenandoah Valley of Virginia. David cofounded the Jesus Trail, a hiking trail in the Galilee, and developed the TransVirginia gravel bikepacking route. The pair are active in supporting and developing hiking and cycling routes and enjoy introducing their children to the joys of the outdoors and learning from other cultures.

Feedback welcome: info@villagetovillagepress.com

facebook.com/caminoguidebooks
instagram.com/caminoguidebook

Village to Village Press specializes in publishing guidebooks and supporting trail development projects worldwide.

CaminoGuidebook.com
Visit for free planning information including easy online booking, digital interactive maps, GPS tracks for navigation and frequently asked questions.

Kindle versions also available

VILLAGE TO VILLAGE PRESS
WWW.VILLAGETOVILLAGEPRESS.COM

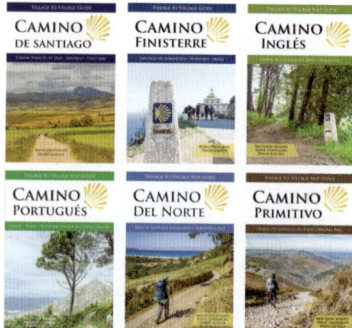